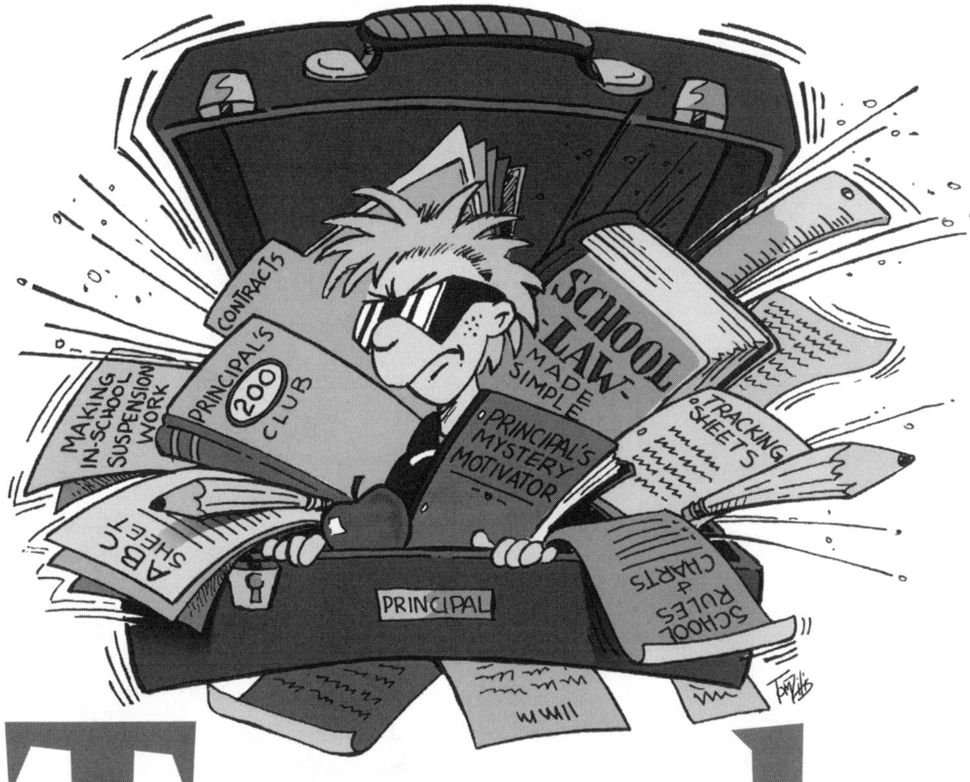

The Tough Kid®

Principal's Briefcase

A Practical Guide to Schoolwide Behavior Management and Legal Issues

BOSTON, MA • NEW YORK, NY • LONGMONT, CO

William R. Jenson, Ph.D. • Ginger Rhode, Ph.D. • Cal Evans, M.Ed. • Daniel P. Morgan, Ph.D.

09 3 4 5 6

ISBN 1-59318-587-1

Illustrations by Thomas Zilis

Printed in the United States of America

Published and Distributed by

SOPRIS
WEST™
EDUCATIONAL SERVICES
A Cambium Learning™ Company

4093 Specialty Place • Longmont, Colorado 80504
(303) 651-2829 • www.sopriswest.com

242/1-06

This book is dedicated to our beloved Seth,
the original Mystery Motivator kid.

Disclaimer

Information in this book that is related to legal issues does not constitute the rendering of an opinion on any particular factual situation. Specific advice should be obtained prior to acting on any of the comments, advice, or recommendations contained in this book.

Contents

Section 1

What This Briefcase Will Do For You and Your School

Does Any of This Sound Familiar to You?

- There are seven students waiting for the principal in the main office. They have been sent by their teachers for insubordination and defiance. This is the third trip to the principal's office in the past week for four of the seven students.
- The number of office referrals has increased dramatically in the school over the past six months, and the principal is not sure why. Out of the 750 students in the school, 304 students had at least one referral, 155 had at least five, and 46 students had more than 20. One student had *96* referrals.
- The number of expulsions and short-term suspensions in the school has increased more than 185% in the past three years.
- The school's drop-out rate is higher than the state average.
- The number of safe school violations involving students and staff has also increased significantly over the past three years.
- The principal is beginning to think that the school's "get tough" zero-tolerance policies are not working.
- Teacher morale is low, and student morale seems even lower. The principal's own morale is not great either.
- A vocal group of parents on the school's community council have written a letter to the Board of Education about school safety concerns and the need for more effective programs and practices.

We hope that *none* of this sounds familiar to you! Poor school practices greatly increase the likelihood that the kinds of outcomes just described will be all too familiar to the school administrator who is ultimately held accountable for what goes on in the school. Such practices are also likely to cause significant harm to the overall academic, behavioral, social, and emotional climate of the school. Our intention with this Briefcase is to provide you with the tools you need to *prevent* many of the problems we have described and to *deal effectively* with the ones that do occur.

How This Briefcase Can Help

If you have read this far, you are probably a school principal or assistant principal looking for some practical and effective solutions to your school's discipline problems. If this description fits you, we think you will find this Briefcase helpful. The main focus of this Briefcase is the challenge faced by all school administrators in our schools today: creating and maintaining a safe, orderly, and positive school environment in which teachers are free to concentrate on teaching and students are able to achieve high academic, behavioral, and social standards.

School principals know that concerns about student misconduct are not new. Poll after poll confirms that student behavioral problems, violence, aggression, and general defiance and disrespect of authority are at the top of the public's concerns about our schools (Evans, 1999; Northwest Regional Educational Laboratory, 2004; Sprague & Nishiolia, 2003). School discipline is truly everybody's problem, but it is only by the principal's leadership that successful solutions to the problem can be achieved.

Research tells us that principals who assume an effective leadership role in improving schoolwide discipline enthusiastically embrace the following responsibilities:

1. Demonstrate a passionate commitment to improving the performance of all students.
2. Challenge all students and their teachers to achieve high academic and behavioral standards.
3. Foster a school culture that is designed to support appropriate student behavior.
4. Establish administrative and instructional strategies and procedures that support appropriate student behavior.
5. Identify, develop, and implement a continuum of interventions for students who are not successful within the school's general discipline program.
6. Insist on the use of research-proven interventions and supports in all schoolwide discipline efforts.
7. Collect and, more importantly, use data for decision-making about a schoolwide discipline program.
8. Put sufficient resources behind all school improvement efforts.

Much has been written about school discipline problems and the principal's role in improving school discipline and climate. This Briefcase provides you with current information about practical, research-based strategies for improving both of these areas in your school. We describe how to both *prevent* many student behavioral problems and *deal*

effectively with the ones that do occur. These strategies and procedures are not panaceas, nor are they magical solutions or the latest fads in school discipline. They are, however, well grounded in research, and are practical and ready to use right out of this Briefcase!

What We Believe Works Best

Before we go any further, we want to share our professional viewpoint with you. In planning this Briefcase and in deciding which strategies and procedures to include, we could have compiled a collection of many different ideas drawn from a variety of sources, with no consistent underlying foundation to them. Some would call this an "eclectic" approach. Although such ideas may be cute, innovative, and politically correct, they might also be seriously lacking in one important way: the missing element is support in scientifically based research.

There is nothing wrong with being eclectic when it has to do with food tastes, clothing styles, movies, music, and so on. When it comes to running a school, however, we believe that being eclectic is risky. Some might define an eclectic person as "one who has his feet planted firmly in mid-air." We are determined that this will not be the outcome for the users of *The Principal's Briefcase.* We want you to have your feet planted firmly on the ground, confident in your knowledge of proven behavior management practices and well on your way to using them proficiently.

A positive outgrowth of the public's serious concerns about school discipline and student misconduct has been a significant increase in finding effective answers to the problems we have described. These efforts have resulted in:

- The development of models of prevention and intervention that are *proactive* rather than reactive
- A focus on the *active teaching* of appropriate or desired student behaviors, providing ample practice opportunities and reinforcement for them
- Efforts to create positive and safe learning environments for *all* students

An effective schoolwide discipline program emphasizes an instructional approach that focuses on what students are expected *to do*, not just on what they are expected *not to do*. Most importantly, an effective schoolwide discipline program actively and consistently teaches and encourages expected, desired behaviors. It also actively, consistently, and effectively discourages undesired behaviors. *Table 1-1* succinctly summarizes our beliefs about what works best in schoolwide discipline.

We also know quite a bit about some school practices that promote or result in serious schoolwide discipline problems. These are described in *Table 1-2*.

These are the types of school practices we mentioned at the beginning of this section—practices that cause significant harm to the overall mission, the school climate, and the desired academic, social, and behavioral outcomes.

Organization of This Briefcase

We have organized this Briefcase manual into six main sections. This introductory section has laid some groundwork and explained what you can expect from the remainder of the Briefcase. Section 2 gives you information about what makes a school successful or unsuccessful. It also lays out the intervention needs of *all* students in a school, including the toughest ones, and discusses the principal's role in the school. Section 3 describes the *Principal's 200 Club*, a unique, innovative, and effective component of a positive discipline program for your school. We describe this program in detail so that you can

Table 1-1

What We Believe Works Best in Schoolwide Discipline

1. Accept the fact that there are no easy answers or "magic bullet" solutions. Sound ideas and proven strategies require time, effort, and commitment.
2. Emphasize what students are expected *to do*, not what they are expected *not to do*.
3. Create a school environment that is committed to supporting appropriate student behavior.
4. Emphasize a *teaching* approach to dealing with problem behavior. Actively teach the desired behavior you expect.
5. Understand that *telling* students how to behave appropriately is not the same as *teaching* them how to behave appropriately.
6. Provide specific, individualized interventions for students who do not respond to the basic schoolwide discipline program.
7. Remember that students have a very difficult time connecting to school if they think that school staff does not like them or want them.
8. Realize that short-term school removals or suspensions produce short-term results. They do not produce permanent or durable changes in student behavior.

Table 1-2

School Practices That Promote Serious Discipline Problems

1. Unclear rules and expectations regarding behavior.
2. Inconsistent and punitive schoolwide, classroom, and individual behavior management practices.
3. Failure to correct rule violations as well as to recognize and reward adherence to rules.
4. Ineffective instruction that results in academic failure.
5. Failure to adapt to individual learner differences and to provide appropriate differentiated instruction options.
6. Ineffective overuse of verbal reprimands, restrictions, suspensions, expulsions, and other aversive consequences to "control" student behavior.

implement it on a schoolwide basis. Section 4 provides specific details for effectively implementing some widely used, but often poorly implemented, undesired consequence systems for limiting inappropriate behavior. These systems are Other Class Time-Out and several kinds of In-School Suspension. Section 5 offers important information concerning school legal issues as well as tips for staying out of legal trouble. Finally, Section 6 summarizes additional schoolwide strategies that may be helpful in dealing with some common but difficult school-related discipline problems. This section also includes other resources to help you with more difficult behavioral problems.

Summary

Best of luck to you as you accept the task to carry out the needed work to create a school where teachers can teach and students can learn! There is no doubt that providing the structure and leadership to create such a school is a challenging task at best. However, we urge you to remember that there is no job more important than yours to influence the future for all of us.

Section 2

What Makes a School Successful?

Introduction

To answer the question "What makes a school successful?" we'll begin by defining what we mean by success. For us, success means having a whole-school approach to discipline that is primarily positive and proactive, or preventive. This is basically what *Positive Behavioral Supports* (PBS)—a term you have probably encountered in recent years—means. In schools with PBS, many of the common behavior problems that plague other schools are prevented or greatly decreased. The success of PBS is reflected in reduced numbers of office referrals for discipline problems and suspensions.

Whole-School Applications and Positive Behavioral Supports

In schools that have a sound PBS foundation, the idea is to keep students in an instructional environment and keep them learning. This may be tough for a student-minded principal to initiate in school systems with long traditions of removing students at a high rate for behavioral problems. The most common response to dealing with significant student behavioral problems in the United States is to use either in-school or out-of-school suspension. The PBS approach stressed in this Briefcase begins with the development of a meaningful Mission Statement for students and staff. It also includes the development of:

- All-school rules that clearly describe behavioral expectations for students
- An all-school positive discipline system that is based on recognizing and rewarding expected student behavior
- A Behavior Management/Discipline Committee that has a meaningful role in the school

Figure 2.1

Student Intervention Needs Triangle

We do recognize that having *only* positive behavioral supports in a school is not enough for *all* students. Our view is that there is a continuum of intervention needs across the whole school that lends itself to depiction in triangular form. This Student Intervention Needs Triangle is more fully described within the extensive, federally funded *Positive Behavioral Interventions and Supports* project developed by the University of Oregon (www.pbis.org). *Figure 2-1* shows our version of this triangle for the student intervention needs in a typical school.

The three levels of the triangle are described below:

Level 1 (All students)—The base, or bottom level, of the triangle represents 100% of the students in a typical school. All students benefit from proactive or preventive strategies that improve social skills, decrease the likelihood of behavioral problems, and help create a positive climate that is conducive to learning. All students in a school are subject to the general schoolwide discipline system to begin with, until behavioral data that have been collected say otherwise. Out of an entire school, 80%–90% of the students typically respond positively to a well-planned and implemented schoolwide system in which there are good school rules and reasonable consequences in place. These students do not have chronic or serious behavioral problems.

Level 2 (Some students)—The middle level of the triangle represents 15%–20% of students who require some type of special individual or group intervention. These students respond well to strategies such as Other Class Time-Out, Behavioral Contracts, and Home Notes. While these students are "at risk," they generally do well in school with appropriate, timely intervention and supports. The longer the school waits to intervene, the bigger the behavioral problems of these students become. This outcome is especially true for student truancy, tardiness, and violation of school rules, with some noncompliance and defiance thrown into the mix. School Behavior Management/Discipline Committees can be very effective at designing interventions for these behavioral problems, especially at the stage before referrals are made for specialized services or special education.

Early identification is the key for managing this middle group. This means that a school must have an effective data-collection system in place. This system must keep track of which students are having the most behavioral problems, which problematic behaviors are occurring most often, and where and when the behaviors are taking place. The data system must also identify which teachers are struggling with the most behavioral problems and referrals. Section 6 provides information about how to use an effective commercial schoolwide data system.

Level 3 (A few students)—The tip of the triangle represents the true Tough Kids who make up about 5%–7% of a school's students. For the sake of clarity, we refer to these students as the "Seven Percent Students"; they are the ones who chronically misbehave and present severe behavioral problems in school. Any whole-school behavior management system must deal effectively with the Seven Percent Students—the Tough Kids—or be prepared to suffer the consequences of not doing so. Understanding these students is one of the critical keys to designing effective behavior management programs for them. To accomplish this, we strongly suggest that principals and schoolwide Behavior Management/Discipline Committees complete Functional Behavior Assessments (FBAs) for the Seven Percent Tough Kids in the school. (Section 6 also provides details of how to do this.) An FBA provides a road map that shows what "sets off," or triggers, specific behavioral problems. It also defines how the behavioral problems are rewarding or "paying off" the student. Once these factors are understood, school staff are in a good position to design individual plans that interrupt nonproductive patterns of behavior and foster and teach substitute behaviors that are more appropriate.

Tough Kids: The Top Seven Percent

The first thing to understand about the Tough Kids who make up 5%–7% of a school's student body is what we mean when we refer to behavior "management" for them. What we mean is that these students typically will not be "cured" by a school's interventions. Research is abundantly clear that the Seven Percent Students generally have ongoing problems throughout their school years (Bowen, Jenson, & Clark, 2004; Lewis & Sugai, 1999; Sprick, Sprick, & Garrison, 1992). Management is the key and, if carried out correctly, the Seven Percent Students can have a successful school experience.

Behavioral Excesses

Seven Percent Students are referred most for help or services for their behavioral excesses of noncompliance, aggression, defiance, and arguing. Other students may occasionally exhibit these behaviors, but Seven Percent Students exhibit them too often or too intensely to be tolerated. These behavioral excesses must be decreased by an effective whole-school management system and individual interventions. Strategies such as Other Class Time-Out, Prime Time In-School Suspension, and Restrictive In-School Suspension can go a long way toward limiting the behavioral excesses of the Seven Percent Students. However, in our view, assigning Out-of-School Suspension or using In-School Suspension as "retributional punishment" ultimately makes the situation worse for the students and the school. We discuss these issues in more detail in Section 4, which is devoted to the topic of effective In-School Suspension techniques.

Behavioral Deficits

It is also important to understand that the Seven Percent Students have massive behavioral deficits, or behaviors that there are "not enough of." Most often, these deficits are evident in a lack of self-management skills, social skills, and academic skills. An effective school program must ultimately provide help to these students in these areas. In working with behavioral deficits, the following factors are relevant:

1. If left unsupervised, Seven Percent Students will usually cause trouble because of their lack of self-management skills and their tendency to be impulsive. We recommend "behavior-tracking" supervision to provide them the support they need. These students should check in with an adult in the morning and check out with the same adult after school with a verbal self-report on how well the day went. We suggest that more problematic students regularly carry a Tracking Sheet across the day (see Section 4 for details). In using a Tracking Sheet, a student is required to have each teacher initial the sheet, indicating how his behavior was in that class. At the end of the day, the student turns in the Tracking Sheet to a designated adult for review. Research shows that this simple supervision technique can significantly reduce behavior problems for Seven Percent Students (Hawken, 2002).
2. Most Seven Percent Students have academic deficits; reading skill deficits are typically Number 1. No behavior management strategy can help a Tough Kid who is inappropriately placed in

a class where he/she is not capable of doing the required academic tasks. The outcome in this situation is predictable: placement is bound to result in failure and humiliation for the student. Tough Kids will revert to their behavioral excesses of noncompliance, aggression, and having tantrums to escape environments in which they are bound to fail. This is why most In-School Suspensions may not work for Seven Percent Students. Tough Kids would rather engage in behavioral problems and be placed in In-School Suspension with their friends than remain in frustrating and punishing academic environments. Behavior Management/ Discipline Committees must assess Tough Kids' academic capabilities in order to effectively manage their behaviors. FBAs are especially useful in determining whether or not a Tough Kid is escaping a certain academic environment in order to be sent to In-School Suspension.

3. Over the years, Seven Percent Students have usually been exposed to massive doses of punishment at home, at school, and from their peers. As a result, they are effectively "immune" to most punishments dished out to them by schools. It is not uncommon to hear from educators, "I gave him a real talking to and he did it (the behavioral problem) even more!" In effect, negative comments, reprimands, and yelling may serve to reward Seven Percent Students because this is often the only attention and recognition they receive from adults. Any program to manage Tough Kids *must* have strong positive supports built into it. Techniques such as recognition and rewards for expected behavior through the Principal's 200 Club, individual contracts that reward good behavior, provision of Mystery Motivators, and serving on the Other Class Time-Out Party Committee can be powerful ways to strengthen desired behavior.

So What Does It All Mean?

The Seven Percent Tough Kids in schools are the most difficult students with whom principals work. Understanding that these students must be identified early and that their behavior will be *managed* only through effective interventions is critical for administrators. Recognizing that these students display both behavioral excesses and deficits is also important for their school success (see definition in *Table 2-1*).

If a school's behavior management program focuses only on stopping behavioral excesses, it will ultimately fail; behavioral deficits must also be addressed. Additionally, no Tough Kid will ever succeed in a school that is basically unsuccessful. Principals need to evaluate whether their schools are successful or not.

Table 2.1

Practical Definition of a Tough Kid

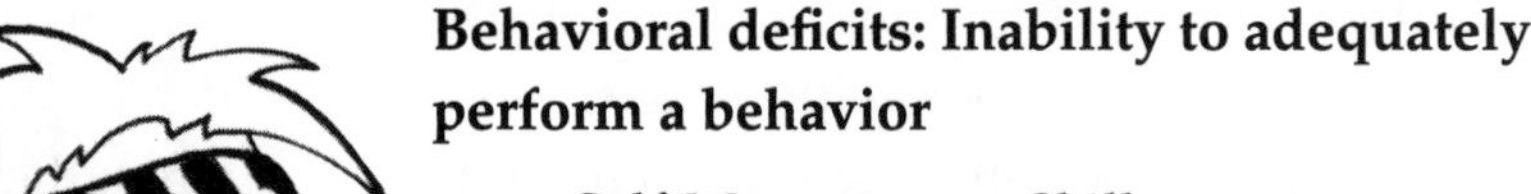

Behavioral excesses: Too much of a behavior

- Noncompliance
  - Does not do what is requested
  - Breaks rules
  - Argues
  - Makes excuses
  - Delays in complying
  - Does the opposite of what is asked
- Aggression
  - Has tantrums
  - Fights
  - Destroys property
  - Vandalizes
  - Sets fires
  - Teases
  - Verbally abuses
  - Is revengeful
  - Is cruel to others

Behavioral deficits: Inability to adequately perform a behavior

- Self-Management Skills
  - Cannot delay rewards
  - Acts before thinking (impulsive)
  - Shows little remorse or guilt
  - Does not follow rules
  - Cannot foresee consequences
- Social Skills
  - Has few friends
  - Goes through friends fast
  - Is uncooperative and bossy
  - Does not know how to reward others
  - Does not display affection
  - Has few problem-solving skills
  - Constantly seeks attention
- Academic Skills
  - Is usually behind in academics (especially reading)
  - Is off-task
  - Fails to finish work
  - Is frequently truant or tardy
  - Forgets acquired information easily

Characteristics of Successful and Unsuccessful Schools

The research literature is clear regarding the characteristics of successful schools. Successful schools have two things in common: (1) a certain level of behavior expectation by school staff for their students; and (2) a strong principal who is a leader (Jenson, Sloane, & Young, 1988). Dropping the expectation level for an individual student because he/she comes from a difficult home or a poor environment is a bad idea. Likewise, dropping expectations because a student has been assigned a label such as attention deficit hyperactivity disorder (ADHD) or oppositional defiant disorder (ODD) or is learning disabled (LD) or behavior disordered (BD) is a disservice to all students. Examples of statements that inappropriately lower expectations include:

"What can we do with him? He comes from such a dysfunctional, uncooperative family"; "You know she has been abused; we need to cut her some slack"; or "We can't possibly expect him to follow the rules; he's ADHD." The Seven Percent Tough Kids at the top of the triangle come with a multitude of labels as well as special and unfortunate circumstances. The moment that behavior expectations are lowered for these students, their performance drops to meet the lowered expectation. *Box 2-1* depicts the relationship between expectations and performance.

The expectation should be that school is a safe, positive place where learning is fostered. Student or staff behaviors that interfere or violate these expectations cannot be permitted. Everyone has circumstances or experiences that could conceivably justify making an exception for them, so stick with one behavior standard for everyone: **All students will follow the school rules.** *Table 2-2* summarizes the characteristics of successful schools (Jenson, Sloane, & Young, 1988).

There are also characteristics of unsuccessful schools. Malcolm Gladwell (2000) wrote in his book *The Tipping Point* that "little things count." What he indicates is that if the little things slip and are permitted to go wrong, then the whole social system—including schools—can go over the tipping point into inefficiency and chaos. Gladwell gives an example of the "broken window" phenomenon to explain this. He says that if an abandoned building has all its windows intact, then little vandalism will occur. However, if just one small window is broken, it is only a matter of time before many or all of the windows are broken by vandals. In essence, seeing one small broken window gives others permission to break more windows and vandalize.

Box 2.1

The Relationship Between Expectations and Behavior

High Expectations

Low Tolerance for Problematic Behavior

Higher Student Achievement

Fewer Behavioral Problems

Table 2-2

Characteristics of Successful Schools

1. Principal as instructional leader for the school.
2. High behavioral and academic expectations for all students.
3. Adoption of school rules that reflect these expectations.
4. *Much* more positive than negative in nature (behavior specified in school rules recognized and rewarded at a *high* rate and undesirable limit-setting consequences for problematic behavior).
5. Data-collection systems in place for problematic behavior to support decision-making.
6. Staff working collaboratively and consistently in implementing behavior interventions.
7. Adults modeling the behaviors they expect from students.
8. Academic "downtime" is low; academic "engagement time" is high (e.g., 70%).
9. Teachers prepared and organized before school starts each day.
10. Emphasis on basic academic skills such as reading and math.
11. Dynamic feedback systems in place to track student progress.
12. High rate of parent and community involvement.
13. Adequate student supervision during class time, school transitions, and before and after school.
14. Teachers staying "on the move" in classrooms and spending little time at their desks.
15. Early staff identification of problematic behavior and stopping it early in a low-key manner.

Similar events happen in schools when little things are left unattended, thus giving students permission to vandalize and behave badly. If a school is dirty and in disrepair, with many broken fixtures or items, then students are given de facto permission to damage the building even more. Letting little things slip concerning the behavior of teachers and students is even worse. If teachers model inappropriate behavior (e.g., not following the school rules, using bad language, making humiliating comments, engaging in horseplay in the halls, being disrespectful, yelling), then the whole student body slips. It takes only one or two teachers displaying these little behaviors to influence others to go over the tipping point. Similarly, not being consistent with even a small number of students, looking away when inappropriate behavior occurs because there is not enough time to deal with it, not enforcing school rules, or not following through with a promised positive consequence for appropriate behavior allows the whole system to slip.

Little things *do* count—in both successful and unsuccessful schools! The characteristics of unsuccessful schools are described in *Table 2-3*.

Not every school is perfect or totally efficient. However, no schoolwide behavior management system will work in a school with poor leadership and low expectations, and where the small things have slipped. In these schools, expect the percentage of Tough Kids to be higher than seven percent, Out-of-School Suspensions to increase, parents to be dissatisfied, academic achievement to drop, and legal issues to increase.

Strong Leadership: The Principal's Role in the School

Much has been written about strong school leadership that includes concepts such as having a vision, being decisive, giving a school direction, and more. However, what is needed is a nuts-and-bolts description of what strong principals specifically do in schools. Following are two characteristics we feel to be essential for strong leadership in principals.

First, effective principals know how to delegate responsibilities to competent staff for whole-school behavior management applications. They can set up and delegate responsibility to Behavior Management/ Discipline Committees to design All-School Rules, set up a whole-school behavior management system, and manage difficult

Table 2-3
Characteristics of Unsuccessful Schools

1. A weak, leaderless principal.
2. "Old guard" staff who are not willing to change and who put down any new ideas for change.
3. Low academic and behavioral standards.
4. Staff who constantly blame others (e.g., students and parents) for the problems in the school.
5. Punitive discipline strategies that frequently remove students from the instructional environment.
6. No whole-school behavior management systems or consistency. Each classroom and school setting is a separate and segregated unit with its own way of handling discipline.
7. No effective professional development programs or ways to introduce new ideas into the school.
8. No feedback systems to students to let them know how well or poorly they are performing behaviorally. If there is feedback, it is random or very delayed.
9. The small things—upkeep of building plant, behavior of staff and students—have begun to slip and go over the "tipping point."

Tough Kid cases. Note, too, that effective principals do not micromanage.

Second, effective principals get out of their offices and roam the school, show up in classrooms, and interact with the student body. They give overwhelming positive feedback to staff for good practices and highlight their efforts in front of other staff and students. They are decisive in giving corrective feedback to both staff and students when they observe the "little things" slipping in school—they do not wait or make excuses. A strong principal understands the words "The buck stops with the principal." They see themselves as not only the instructional leader but also the person directly responsible for student behavior, including discipline in the school. For whole-school applications, the principal should convey her vision and leadership through these specific actions:

1. Defining the school's *Mission Statement* expectations.
2. Formulating specific *All-School Rules* that are based on observable and measurable behaviors, and seeing that students know ahead of time *exactly* what the behavior expectations are.
3. Working with a *Behavior Management Committee* to assist with the planning for and management of a schoolwide behavior management system. The committee should also work with and provide support to teachers having difficulty with problematic students. Most such committees are made up of seasoned teachers, support staff, and a school administrator. (See Section 6 for specific information on setting up a Behavior Management Committee.)
4. Putting in place the *supports* for rule-following behavior and the undesired consequences for problematic behavior.
5. Ensuring that *effective classroom management* systems are in place before implementing a schoolwide behavior management program, and making certain that classrooms are primarily positive places in which to learn.
6. Setting up an effective *data-gathering system* to stay continually informed about the status of office referrals per day, per month, by problem behavior, by location, by time of day, by student, and by number of referrals per student. (See Section 6 for specific information.)
7. Knowing enough about classroom management to provide leadership and support to teachers and other school staff.

Without a principal's total support and knowledge of her role, no schoolwide behavior management system—including the Principal's 200 Club—will work. One of the first steps in setting up the schoolwide behavior management system is to develop a meaningful school Mission Statement.

School "Mission Possible" Statement

Most school Mission Statements are virtually worthless because they are meaningless to most students, are complex, and do not specifically relate to the school's rules. They can read like a legal document, a solution to the world's problems, or a preamble to a constitution. This type of complex, ineffective Mission Statement is written for adults, not for students. It cannot be used for effective behavior management because students do not understand its meaning. The acid test for any school Mission Statement is to randomly stop any student in the school and ask, "What does our school Mission Statement mean?" If you get a blank stare or the student responds, "I don't know," then the Mission Statement has failed.

We believe that a Mission Statement should incorporate both behavioral and academic expectations to form a firm foundation on which All-School Rules are derived. The All-School Rules should flow from key words embedded in a simple Mission Statement. The All-School Rules, in turn, form the basis for the Principal's 200 Club. A school may not have a Mission Statement, or one may exist but be in need of updating and refining to make it effective. Section 6 details the steps to formulate a new Mission Statement or to "kick the tires" on an existing one. This step should be completed before adopting All-School Rules and implementing the Principal's 200 Club.

Rules Rule!

Rules that serve the whole school—All-School Rules—should define expectations for all students in the school. As such, they form the *foundation* for a school's positive behavior management system. Typically, the rules will be formulated by the school's Behavior Management/Discipline Committee, which is described in detail in Section 6. There are several considerations in selecting All-School Rules:

1. Select rules that are *logical* and *necessary* in order to have a safe, positive environment in which learning is fostered.
2. Make *as few* rules as possible—usually no more than four—that still clearly convey school expectations. Keep the wording *simple*.
3. Keep the rules worded *positively* whenever possible. For example, you might use the statement, "Follow staff directions immediately" rather than "Do not disobey school staff."
4. Make the rules as *specific* as possible so that they are not open to interpretation. For example, you might state, "Be on time to class with all needed materials" instead of "Be a good citizen."
5. Make the rules describe behavior that is *observable* so that you can make an unequivocal decision as to whether or not they have been followed. Your rule might state, "Keep hands, feet, and objects to yourself," rather than, "Be respectful."
6. Have the rules describe behavior that is *measurable*. That is, you must be able to count or quantify the behavior in some way for monitoring purposes. You might say, "Raise your hand to speak," instead of "Don't disrupt."

7. Tie the rules directly to both positive and undesired consequences. Spell out the positive consequences of following the rules as well as the undesired consequences that will be earned by not following them.
8. Always include a *compliance rule* such as, "Do what school staff ask immediately." Student noncompliance is commonly one of the most problematic behaviors in schools and often escalates into much more serious or violent behaviors.

All-School Rules are in effect over an entire school campus, including transition environments, the lunchroom, the playground or yard, and the halls. The rules add consistency throughout a school so that everyone (i.e., teachers, administrators, students, lunch staff, bus drivers, custodians, etc.) is operating from the same base. In addition to general All-School Rules that apply to the entire school campus, there should be subsets of school rules that support the All-School Rules for the specific locations just mentioned. Rule subsets, typically consisting of only two or three rules, should be prominently displayed along with the All-School Rules in the location to which they apply. For example, lunchroom rules should be prominently posted in the lunchroom and hall rules in the hallways. All-School Rules should be prominently and publicly posted in every school setting, including where location-specific rules are posted. *Table 2-4* lists examples of possible All-School Rules for elementary schools, and *Table 2-5* lists examples for secondary schools.

Educators sometimes wonder whether students should help in deciding the rules, believing students may "buy in" to the rules

Table 2-4
Sample Elementary All-School Rules

General Rules

1. Follow staff directions immediately.
2. Keep hands, feet, and objects to yourself.
3. Do not use bad language.
4. Take care of other students' and the school's property.
5. Keep toys and nonschool items at home.

Halls

1. Use a hall pass.
2. Walk quietly.
3. Do not push or shove.

Lunchroom

1. Talk quietly.
2. Stay in your seat until you are ready to leave.
3. Put trays and trash where they belong.
4. Walk when entering and leaving.

Recess

1. Once outside, stay outside.
2. Use play equipment properly.
3. Do not throw snowballs.
4. Line up to come in as soon as the bell rings.

Assemblies

1. Stay in your assigned seat.
2. Clap to show appreciation.
3. Do not talk during the assembly.

Table 2-5
Sample Secondary All-School Rules

General Rules

1. Follow staff directions immediately.
2. Keep hands, feet, and objects to yourself.
3. Do not use vulgar language or gestures.
4. Use recreational equipment outside only in designated areas.
5. Do not use illegal substances.

Halls

1. Use a hall pass during class time.
2. Do not deface lockers.
3. Walk quietly in the halls.

Lunchroom

1. Eat in designated areas.
2. Put trays and trash where they belong.
3. Walk in the lunchroom.
4. Leave as soon as you are finished eating.

Assemblies and Special Activities

1. Sit in assigned seats.
2. Keep paper and other items to yourself.
3. Avoid disruptive talking or noises.

more if they have a say in making them. Actually, there is no indication in the research literature that this democratic approach is more effective. In our experience, it is better if only the adults set the rules, based on the expectations that are needed to support the school's mission. Students will buy in to the rules if there is an effective, exciting motivation system like the Principal's 200 Club in place to back them up.

Summary

In this section, we discussed what makes a school successful or positive and proactive (i.e., preventive) in its approach to discipline. Such an approach to discipline meets the student intervention needs of *all* students in a school, including the Seven Percent of Tough Kids who chronically misbehave and present severe behavioral problems. Meeting these needs requires that a school not only stop students' behavioral excesses but also address their behavioral deficits. We also described the characteristics of unsuccessful schools, the strong leadership role principals must play in their schools, and the specifics to which principals must attend in order to be successful.

Section 3

The Principal's 200 Club

Introduction

The Principal's 200 Club is one of the powerful positive behavior support systems for the whole school. Designed to serve as a major component of the school's comprehensive positive behavior support system, it is just one component of a more extensive school behavior management system. Used successfully in dozens of elementary, middle, and junior high schools, the 200 Club effectively increases positive behavior and rule-following in schools.

The 200 Club also provides an element of positive variability to keep students motivated. It includes a dynamic feedback system, continually informing students and staff about who is following the school rules. The term *dynamic feedback* means the contents of the information system are constantly changing, and students are never quite sure when they might be "caught" and recognized for good behavior. The backbone of the 200 Club consists of a system of All-School Rules or expectations with additional positive behavior management systems.

Box 3-1

The Principal's 200 Club focuses on positive behavioral change and increases positive interactions between students and staff across the whole-school environment.

The program cannot be mandated from the school district's central office, implemented by a Behavior Management Committee operating independently, or started solely by motivated teachers. Our experience with the 200 Club is that without the full support and involvement of the school principal, this program—or *any* behavior management system that does not have a principal's commitment—will fail. Lose the principal, and you lose the 200 Club.

Box 3.2

The Principal's 200 Club results in students' associating the principal's office with positive consequences rather than negative consequences.

Purpose

The purpose of the 200 Club is to "catch" students following the All-School Rules and behaving appropriately. It is designed to be easy to use and to involve a school's staff, students, and parents. When implemented correctly, the 200 Club effectively increases positive behavior and rule-following in a school. This, in turn, reduces office referrals, especially for the Seven Percent Students with chronic discipline problems. In practice, the principal's office serves as the hub of the 200 Club for the entire school.

Box 3-3

OK, we have a dilemma that we need to discuss here. Across the country, many of you are already familiar with what we have called the "Principal's 200 Club." The 200 Club Chart has had 200 boxes on it.

The downside of a 200-box chart is that 200 is not a prime number; thus, a 200-box chart cannot be square in shape. It is impossible to have a total of 200 boxes with the same number of individual boxes in each vertical, horizontal, or diagonal row. Having some rows shorter gives students whose names are on those rows an unfair advantage because their rows have a better chance of filling up more quickly than the longer rows. Thus, those students are more likely to win than students whose names are on the longer rows.

We attempted to correct this problem by selecting a prime number of boxes—225—for the chart, with 15 boxes per row for all rows. We then called the system the "Principal's 225 Club." As we adopted this new terminology, we encountered an unexpected outcry. Friends and colleagues claimed that the new name did not have a good ring to it. They indicated they were too familiar with the name the "Principal's 200 Club" to change. Even our publishers protested. In spite of this, everyone seemed to like 225 boxes on the chart better than 200.

Our solution was to create a new chart with 225 boxes on it (15 in every direction) and maintain the familiar "Principal's 200 Club" as the name. Incongruent, we admit; but, there you are. So, no letters, please, pointing out that the Principal's 200 Club actually operates on a 225-box system. We know. We did it on purpose.

Setting Up the Principal's 200 Club

All but one of the necessary materials to implement the Principal's 200 Club are included in *The Principal's Briefcase*. The following list specifies the necessary materials, which are described in more detail later in this section:

- The 200 Club Chart (a 225-square matrix, laminated)
- All-School Rules Chart
- 225 plastic disks, numbered 1–225
- 200 Club Celebrity Book
- Water-based marking pen
- A master sheet of 200 Club tickets (for you to copy)
- The Principal's Mystery Motivator (the only item not provided in the kit; provided by the principal)

Getting Started

1. Post the All-School Rules and the school's Mission Statement somewhere near the main office where all students will see them. High-traffic areas are best!
2. Post the 200 Club Chart right next to the All-School Rules and the Mission Statement. (*Figure 3-1* provides an illustration of the Principal's 200 Club Chart.)
3. Copy a supply of 200 Club tickets on colored paper, usually about 30 sheets to start with. Cut the sheets into individual 200 Club tickets. You will notice that each ticket has spaces for the name of the staff member who awarded the ticket, the name of the student who received it, the behavior for which the ticket was awarded, and the date. (At the end of this section, you will find a sheet of 200 Club tickets to copy.)

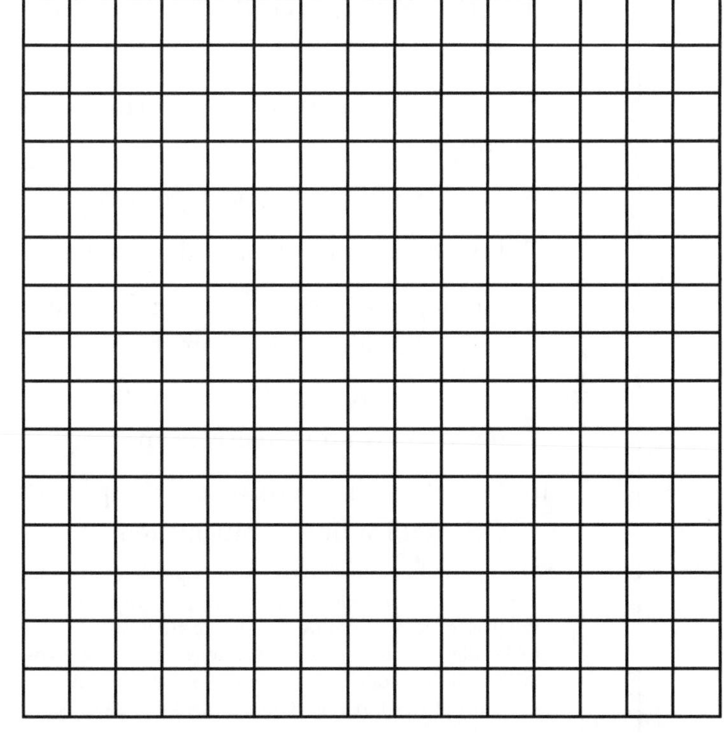

Figure 3.1
200 Club Chart

4. Each morning, *distribute* 15 of the 200 Club tickets among teachers' mailboxes, one ticket per mailbox. You may distribute the tickets randomly or rotate their assignment to teachers so that all teachers receive tickets over time. As the program becomes established, teachers often request the tickets!
5. Place the Principal's Mystery Motivator near the posted 200 Club Chart or on the door to the principal's office. To make the Mystery Motivator, use a manila envelope (usually 6" x 9") and draw several large question marks on the envelope with a marker. (*Figure 3-2* shows what a Mystery Motivator envelope looks like.) Write a reward you are willing to give on a slip of paper, fold it several times, place it in the envelope, and seal the envelope. *Table 3-1* gives examples of rewards principals have given out, but let your own preferences and creativity guide you.
6. Place the 200 Club Celebrity Book in the principal's office. In some schools, it has

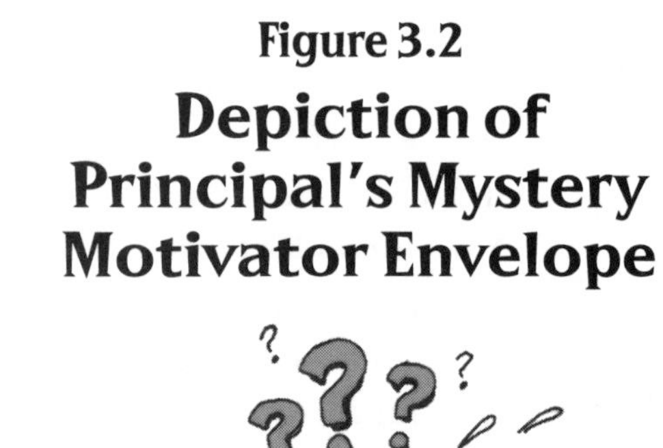

Figure 3.2

Depiction of Principal's Mystery Motivator Envelope

Table 3-1

Examples of Principal's Mystery Motivator Rewards

1. Movie passes donated by local theaters.
2. Fast-food coupons donated by local businesses.
3. A choice of snack/treat food from the principal's supply.
4. A treat for each student's homeroom class.
5. A book to keep from the principal's supply.
6. An item with the school logo on it.
7. Lunch with teacher of student's choice.
8. Homework passes excusing the bearer from a homework assignment.
9. Opportunity to be first in line for lunch (excused 5 minutes early from class).
10. One choice from principal's supply of Oriental Trading Company items.*

* The Oriental Trading Company is a great resource for inexpensive, high-interest items (e.g., sticky, glow-in-the-dark eyeballs; gummy vampire teeth; unusual hacky sacks; disguise items). Request a catalog online at www.orientaltrading.com, call 1-800-875-8480, or write the company at P.O. Box 2308, Omaha, NE 68103-2308.

been placed on a dictionary stand just outside the door of the principal's office, where parents can easily find it when they visit the school.

Putting the 200 Club Into Action

The ideal time to start the 200 Club is at the beginning of the school year; however, it can be started at any time during the year. Assuming you have followed all of the "Getting Started" steps just described, you are ready to put the 200 Club into action. *Table 3-2* gives suggestions for what to do first.

Table 3-2

Start-Up Suggestions for the 200 Club

1. After posting the 200 Club Chart in a very public location in the school, wait several days before giving any explanation. This allows students a good chance to see the chart and wonder what it is.
2. After several days, refer to the 200 Club Chart when you make the morning announcements. You might say something like, "You may have noticed the big chart with all of the squares on the wall by the office."
3. Make a game of it by inviting several students or entire classrooms to guess what the chart is for and how it works. Announce that you will reveal what the chart is all about at a special assembly in a few days.
4. Take the 200 Club Chart, the All-School Rules chart, and the Mission Statement to the assembly.
5. At the assembly, ask for additional guesses from students about the 200 Club Chart and how it works. Make sure you call only on students with raised hands. After ten or so guesses, explain the 200 Club to the entire assembly.

Setting Up an Assembly

Schedule a school assembly to introduce the Principal's 200 Club. At the assembly, review and explain the following information:

- **The Teachers' Role**
  Approximately 15 teachers, their identities unknown to students, will be given a certain number of 200 Club tickets to distribute each school day.
- **Caught You!: Type 1**
  Teachers with tickets will be on the lookout for students who are following the All-School Rules. Each of these teachers will stop a student who is following the rules sometime during the day, ask his name, write it on the ticket, specify the behavior that earned the ticket, write the date, and sign his name to the ticket. With this strategy, we think it is best if the student is not one of that teacher's students. This way, students will know that tickets are likely to come from any teacher, not just their own. The teacher will ask the student to take the 200 Club ticket to the principal's office. Some schools have special times during the day—before school, at lunchtime, during recess—when the tickets can be

taken to the principal's office; be sure to explain to the selected students when those times are. At some schools, the principal announces that it is 200 Club time over the intercom at the end of the school day or at the beginning of the next day. He or she will then invite the students who have earned 200 Club tickets to bring them to the office to trade in. One benefit to this method is that it provides additional "public posting" of the students who have earned 200 Club tickets that day, recognizing them on another level for their rule-following behavior.

- **Caught You!: Type 2**
  Some of the teachers, especially during the first few weeks of school, will stop students and ask them what the All-School Rules are or what the school Mission Statement and its core words are. Students who can answer correctly will earn a 200 Club ticket.

- **The 200 Club Celebrity Book**
  When a student turns in her 200 Club ticket to the principal's office, she will be asked to write her name in the Principal's 200 Club Celebrity Book, the date, and the behavior that earned her the ticket. As an alternative to writing in the book, some schools have students tape their 200 Club tickets in the book. Generally, one member of the office staff is assigned to oversee this part of the program.

- **The Parent**
  After a student signs the 200 Club Celebrity Book, the assigned office staff member will attempt to call the student's parent at home or at work in the student's presence. When the parent answers the phone, the staff member will say, "Congratulations! I have only a minute, but I'm calling from Evergreen Elementary School where we have a program that lets parents know when their child is doing a good job of following the rules at school." The staff member will describe specifically what the student was doing right and will then invite the parent to stop by the office to look at the 200 Club Celebrity Book for the child's name during their next school visit. Then the staff member will hand the telephone to the student so that she can speak to the parent for a moment. *Table 3-3* provides a few pointers about contacting parents.

- **The Chance**
  After the student has signed the 200 Club Celebrity Book and the parent has been called, the student will select a disk from an opaque container. (The plastic disks, numbered from 1 to 225, are provided with the Briefcase.) The student will look away, reach into the container, and select a disk. Once the disk has been picked, the staff member will look at the number on it with the student. The student will write her name with a water-based marking pen in the numbered square on the 200 Club Chart that corresponds

Table 3-3
Pointers for Contacting Parents

- Most parents expect to hear negative information about their children when the school calls. This is why it is important to immediately say, "Congratulations!" when a parent answers the phone. This procedure turns a contact that the parents expect to be negative into a positive one.
- Some staff may say they do not have time to make the parental call. Explain to them how important it is to make the time. It takes only a few minutes and provides huge returns! Our experience with this aspect of the program shows that it has a dramatic impact on parent-school relations over time. Imagine the effects on parents if ten positive calls are made every day throughout the school year. Parents think school staff who positively recognize their children are more capable staff members.
- More than 50% of the time, parents will not be available (e.g., they may be running errands or away from their desks at work) when you call. If they have voicemail, leave a message. If no one answers or there is no voicemail option, use a prestamped postcard to notify them. To save time, you might consider having "What I Was Doing Right Today" printed on the cards; have the student fill one out with the behavior for which she was recognized, her name, and the date. Add your signature, and mail the postcard. Many PTAs are willing to fund postcards for such a positive program.
- It is extremely important to recognize the office staff member who runs this program at the introductory school assembly and on an ongoing basis as the program is being carried out. As the principal, you should not only encourage her to keep doing such a great job but also reward her socially with praise for her efforts. Otherwise, this assignment is only one more thing for her to do. There is nothing worse than a positive behavior management program being run by indifferent or grumpy staff!

to the number on the disk she selected. *The staff member does not put the selected disk back in the container!* The selected numbers are kept separate in a manila envelope or another receptacle away from the container from which students select their disks. That way, no other student will select the same number while the program is in progress.

- **The Payoff**
  As teachers distribute the 200 Club tickets each day, the numbered squares of the 200 Club Chart will be randomly filled in by students. The first 15 students whose names appear in a row, column, or diagonal are the winners. When the 15th square in any of these configurations is signed on the chart, the 15 names on the winning row, column, or diagonal are announced over the school intercom. All 15 students will receive the Mystery Motivator that was secretly written on a piece of paper in the Principal's Mystery Motivator envelope. The principal can announce that there is a winning row the moment it happens, at the end of the day, at the beginning of the next day, or on a specific day each week (e.g., Friday, during morning announcements). This is the principal's choice. All the names on the 200 Club laminated chart are then erased, the numbered disks that were selected by students in this round of the 200 Club are returned to the container, and the entire process starts over.

Other Helpful Information

This program sounds simple, and it is. Our experience shows that if fifteen 200 Club tickets are awarded each day, it takes about two weeks to get a winning row, column, or diagonal of fifteen winning names. As the 200 Club progresses, students will congregate at the 200 Club Chart, especially as it fills up. Just as with any other game, the closer students get to winning, the higher the interest in the game. At this point, what the chart does is advertise or show off names of students who are following the All-School Rules to the entire student body. Students will be particularly interested if their names or the names of their friends are on the chart. Students whose names are on the chart but not in the winning row, column, or diagonal are still rewarded by having their parents notified and their names written in the 200 Club Celebrity Book and publicly displayed on the 200 Club Chart.

Troubleshooting the 200 Club

Problem: *You have complaints from several parents about how you are operating the 200 Club.*

Solution: Stop trouble before it starts. Explain the Principal's 200 Club ahead of time to parents in a letter, the school handbook, or the discipline disclosure material that is sent home to parents. Also, explain it to the PTA, and ask for its support in acquiring prestamped postcards to send home for "I've Been Following the Rules" as well as program rewards for both students and teachers.

Problem: *You have one or more teachers who think that students should just do what they are supposed to do without rewards and recognition.*

Solution: Be prepared for the arguments. Some teachers will object that the Principal's 200 Club is a bribe for something that students should be doing anyway. Explain that a bribe is "an inducement for an illegal or illicit behavior." Following the All-School Rules as well as knowing and reciting the Mission Statement are not illegal or illicit. Point out that businesses commonly use incentive systems to motivate their employees and recognize them for good performance. Recognizing good performance is always appropriate. Even adults respond and perform better when there is positive recognition for the good things they do.

Problem: *You suspect you have one or more teachers who refuse to give out 200 Club tickets.*

Solution: To determine this, keep a record of the teachers you give tickets to each day to. If a teacher misses handing out tickets more than two or three times, call the teacher in and ask why he is not participating. Among common excuses are "I lost the ticket"; "I don't have time"; or "I have my own system for discipline." Indicate that the 200 Club is a program that all faculty members wanted and chose. Explain how important it is for him to participate, and give him a ticket to award the next day. While you should initially meet with this teacher alone, if the problem continues, spend some time observing in his classroom. It may be that he needs some help with behavior management. At the very least, his classroom responses should be primarily positive (a minimum of 2:1 positive to negative teacher comments or actions), and the classroom should be operating smoothly.

Problem: ***You have teachers who want to change the system so that if a student is caught breaking an All-School Rule, her name will be taken off the 200 Club Chart.***

Solution: Resist this suggestion. In our experience, this will render your system ineffective in the long run. Use other undesired consequences for those students who break the rules. The Principal's 200 Club is *only* for recognizing positive behaviors.

Problem: ***Students may lose their 200 Club tickets or report that they have been stolen.***

Solution: Give students a chance, and check with the teachers who awarded the tickets. If the teachers can confirm that they awarded the tickets, believe the students the first time and replace their tickets. Let the students know that this is a one-time replacement. If the situation happens again, not even the awarding teachers can help. You will find that chronic losses of tickets are rare.

Making the 200 Club Even Better

1. The school intercom can be a very effective tool to enhance the effectiveness of the 200 Club. When you are making general announcements, use the opportunity to give students hints about what the Principal's Mystery Motivator might be. You might say something like, "It's brown, and I've noticed that a lot of students like it." You can also check the 200 Club Chart and announce the names of students who are getting very close to a possible win.
2. Instead of calling your program the Principal's 200 Club, you may want to substitute the name of your school's mascot. For example, you might call your program the Principal's Tiger Club or the Principal's Eagle Club.
3. Select a relatively big reward about one in every five times to maximize the power of the rewards. Some of the most powerful Mystery Motivators include special recognition and attention. In some schools, sharing a pizza with the principal at the principal's table is the most powerful reward of all.
4. You can also reward teachers and staff for handing out 200 Club tickets to students who are following the All-School Rules. As students turn in their tickets to the principal's office, collect them in a grab bag or other container. At the end of each month, randomly draw one or more tickets and provide rewards to the teachers who issued them. One principal of a middle school was able to provide a cash prize and a certain amount of money for teachers to spend on school supplies. Another principal took the winning teacher's class for an hour while the teacher used the time for planning or grading papers. PTAs and local businesses are often generous in contributing teacher prizes for the Principal's 200 Club.
5. Along with the lucky teacher who wins each month, provide something special

for the student who earned the winning ticket as well. This serves as a bonus for both the student and the teacher.

6. Ask teachers to give a 200 Club ticket to a student they don't know at least every third time they award a ticket. Students soon realize that staff they do not know may catch them following the All-School Rules. You may want to write "Unknown" on two of the 15 tickets you place in teacher mailboxes each day. This signals those teachers to give their tickets to an unknown student that day.
7. Ask teachers to make an effort to catch some of the school's Tough Kids who are following the All-School Rules and award them tickets. Once their names are posted on the 200 Club Chart, go out of your way to stop those students as you see them around the school. Tell them how much you appreciate their following the rules.
8. Consider using the Principal's 200 Club to augment other programs you want to start in your school such as schoolwide social skills or bully-proofing programs. Instead of rewarding rule-following with tickets, use them to reward the "social skill of the week" or other specific behaviors you want to promote throughout the school.
9. Initiate a "Mission Possible" program. At the beginning of the school year, announce to students that you are going on a Mission Possible quest. The quest is to stop every student during the first week and ask him/her to recite the core words in the school's Mission Statement as well as the All-School Rules. Have 15 teachers award 200 Club tickets for this accomplishment each day. The catch is that students won't know which teachers have tickets to pass out and which ones do not.

Summary

Refer to this section often to remind yourself about the needed day-to-day details in keeping the Principal's 200 Club working effectively. It is human nature for details to slip away when they are not reviewed regularly! Also, fine-tuning over time will accommodate the needed adjustments you have identified. This will keep your school a mostly positive place—the way you want it to be. Once your positive system is planned and implemented to increase the amount of good behavior from your students, you are then ready to take a closer look at behavior problems. Even in a well-run school, there will be some students—your Seven Percent Tough Kids—who will continue to exhibit chronic behavior problems. What should you do about chronic, really difficult behavior? Stay tuned. Section 4 will help you with this!

I FOLLOW THE RULES! 200 Club Name ______ Behavior ______ Issued by ______ Date ______	I FOLLOW THE RULES! 200 Club Name ______ Behavior ______ Issued by ______ Date ______
I FOLLOW THE RULES! 200 Club Name ______ Behavior ______ Issued by ______ Date ______	I FOLLOW THE RULES! 200 Club Name ______ Behavior ______ Issued by ______ Date ______
I FOLLOW THE RULES! 200 Club Name ______ Behavior ______ Issued by ______ Date ______	I FOLLOW THE RULES! 200 Club Name ______ Behavior ______ Issued by ______ Date ______
I FOLLOW THE RULES! 200 Club Name ______ Behavior ______ Issued by ______ Date ______	I FOLLOW THE RULES! 200 Club Name ______ Behavior ______ Issued by ______ Date ______
I FOLLOW THE RULES! 200 Club Name ______ Behavior ______ Issued by ______ Date ______	I FOLLOW THE RULES! 200 Club Name ______ Behavior ______ Issued by ______ Date ______

Section 4

What About Really Difficult Behavior?

Introduction

Okay, you now have your positive system, the Principal's 200 Club, set up and running to encourage and reward appropriate student behavior. While the 200 Club system will maximize good behavior, some problematic behaviors will still inevitably occur. Sometimes, students without much of a history of problem behavior will just have bad days. They may break school rules, get into minor altercations with other students, or simply lose their tempers because of temporary stress. After all, kids are kids, and it is in the nature of kids to test limits!

A system should be in place to manage these inevitable behavior problems. However, a system is also needed to handle the 5%–7% of students mentioned in Section 2 of this Briefcase, who chronically cause problems and push the school's behavior management system to its limits. These Tough Kids engage in fighting, bullying other students, severe noncompliance, destruction of property, using illegal substances, and defiance toward teachers and other staff. In fact, defiant behavior by students is the leading cause of expulsion and suspension in secondary schools! In essence, there are two broad types of ongoing, serious school behavior problems:

1. Acute, occasional behavior problems
2. Chronic, severe behavior problems

We have effective strategies for you to use to reduce the occurrence of both types of problematic behaviors. In many cases, these strategies can all but replace Out-of-School Suspension (OSS) as a consequence. In this Briefcase, the main purpose of the strategies we suggest is *not* retribution! Instead, our strategies operate on a gradient, from mild forms of In-School Suspension (ISS) to more restrictive forms of suspension, depending on the severity and nature of the behavior. Again, these techniques are designed as tools for behavior change, *not* for retribution. Whenever possible, it is our goal to keep students where we think they belong—in school and learning. In this section, we first walk you through the preliminary things to consider in setting up and implementing an effective Other Class Time-Out (OCT) program. We also cover a range of other forms of ISS. OSS is discussed only briefly.

Preliminary Facts and Issues

Many Other Class Time-Out and In-School Suspension programs are set up ineffectively in schools because educators do not understand the principles of behavior upon which they are based. Then, overreliance on OSS is frequently the result. If OCT and ISS are to be set up correctly to ensure that they will work, a number of facts and issues must be understood about them.

Facts

1. ISS and OSS are the strategies used most often at the secondary level to manage intense, disruptive behaviors. However, in spite of their wide use, many educators seldom consult empirical research regarding how to use them effectively. This includes a general lack of information regarding the conditions that must be present in order for these strategies to work.
2. Many who are charged with designing and setting up OCT, ISS, and OSS programs have little or no training or background in their use as effective behavior management strategies.
3. Of almost any student intervention strategy implemented in schools, ISS and OSS have some of the highest potential for educational abuse. This is because they often take students out of their learning environments for long periods of time and frequently place them in unsupervised or undersupervised settings. This is especially true for OSS.
4. ISS and OSS are often used as strategies of retribution rather than as strategies to help students change their unacceptable behavior. What we mean by retribution is that students are expected to endure some type of punishing experience as a form of "payback" for having engaged in inappropriate behavior. The emphasis is on "doing your time for your behavior."
5. When ISS or OSS is used for retribution, little, if any effort is typically expended on collecting data. Data collection is essential to determine the effectiveness of undesired consequences in actually *changing* the problematic behavior or *reducing* the likelihood that it will occur again. Generally, the students who are most often assigned suspensions that remove them from their classrooms and school are the students who can *least* afford to miss the instruction!

Box 4-1

"Rule-Following" as a Life Skill

In addition to creating an environment in which teachers can teach and students can learn, it is critical for students to learn rule-following to be successful in life. There is virtually no station in our society where there are no rules or expectations. Your students will be expected to follow rules on the job, in a movie theater, while driving, in the community swimming pool, on the beach, during a hospital stay, and at a friend's home. Think about it. ***Teaching your school rules and expectations*** to students—and providing the support they need to follow them—***helps to prepare students for life itself!*** Setting aside school rules or excusing students from following them does students no favors! Punishing students for *not* following the rules and expectations for the sake of punishment alone does not help them, either.

6. When suspensions are used as retributional strategies, there is a general tendency to add more time cumulatively for each recurring instance of misbehavior. For example, the first rule infraction may result in a one-day suspension (in or out of school), the second infraction in two days' suspension, a third infraction in three days' suspension, and so on. The end result of suspension may *not* help students change their problematic behaviors, but it does serve to keep them out of the learning environment for ever-increasing amounts of time—time they can ill afford.
7. When suspensions are used for retribution, there may be little effort to separate the severe, chronic offenders from the acute, occasional offenders. There is good evidence to suggest that chronic offenders will actually use ISS or OSS times to *escape* educational settings in which they are incapable of performing well, both academically and socially. Also, some chronic offenders manipulate their ISS and OSS times to be with their friends.

Issues

1. Suspension programs such as OCT, ISS, and OSS are basically *time-out* procedures. We define time-out as taking a student from a rewarding environment and placing him in a less rewarding environment for a period of time because of his inappropriate behavior. *It is not possible to time-out a student from a negative environment to a more positive environment!* To do so, by definition, is not time-out. If the school or classroom is punishing, frustrating, and associated with repeated failure, then suspension or removal to another environment may actually be viewed positively by the student. In this case, suspension serves to reward the student for the inappropriate behavior. The net effect, then, is to increase the problem behavior and actually make it worse! The educational setting must be primarily positive for any type of suspension strategy—or time-out—to work.

2. Students who are chronic offenders frequently try to escape punishing environments by getting themselves assigned to a suspension environment. They may prefer to be sent home, to another classroom, or to an ISS room where their friends have already been sent. Reasons for this include:

    - In some ISS settings, students are allowed to socialize or even sleep. (Observe any ISS program; if students are talking, socializing, not working, sleeping, or in any way having a good time, the program is ineffective.)
    - With OSS, students often run unchecked through the community with their friends.
    - With OSS, students may enjoy sleeping in, watching TV, and having a great time—unsupervised—at home.

   Effective suspension programs that actually change student behavior will *identify* chronic student offenders, *assess* why they are repeaters, and then *implement* interventions to reduce recurrences. Remember, students who continue to earn what appear to you to be undesired consequences are always getting some type of reward or payoff for continuing to behave badly. Your job is to figure out what that payoff is.

3. A guiding rule for a good suspension program designed to bring about behavior change is to keep the student in the learning environment as much as possible. If she must be removed from it, get her back into it as quickly as possible. Most of the time spent in suspension programs translates into lost instructional time.

Box 4-2

Use the least amount of suspension time needed to bring about behavior change, and return the student to the learning environment as soon as possible.

4. Collecting data is critical when using any form of suspension. These data should include:

    - *Who* is being sent to the suspension programs
    - *What behaviors* are causing the student to be sent to these programs
    - *What time(s)* during the school day is the student being sent
    - *How long* the student is in these programs
    - *Which staff or teachers* are sending the student

   Typically, chronic student offenders are avoiding certain times of the day, certain people, and certain environments. High-frequency, problematic behaviors that often result in suspensions mean there is a problem somewhere. Teachers who frequently send students to suspension programs are often those with weak classroom management systems who do not know what else to do. In some cases, these teachers may simply want to "get rid" of certain students rather than find solutions to work with them. Functional behavior assessment (FBA) techniques and the software program described in Section 6 of this Briefcase are valuable assessment tools to help in gathering these data.

5. When problematic behaviors do occur, suspension techniques should be implemented *immediately*, if possible. The longer the wait for students to experience suspension after they have earned it, *the less effective it will be.*
6. Even though these tactics are used frequently, ample evidence clearly indicates that simply talking to students about their bad behavior, issuing repeated warnings, negotiating, or pleading with them actually makes the situation worse over time.
7. Educators sometimes look the other way, hoping the situation will go away if it is ignored. This hardly ever happens. It is essential to train staff to identify behavior infractions and to respond to them swiftly in a preplanned, effective way.

Box 4-3

Behavior problems are like weeds. Ignore them, and they just get worse!

—Unknown

8. Suspension programs should be used on a gradient from *less restrictive* to *more restrictive*. Always use the least restrictive suspension program that will stop the problematic behavior and decrease the likelihood that it will happen again. This suspension gradient has two dimensions: location and time. This means that keeping students *as close* to their instructional environments as possible, and using the *shortest* amount of suspension time that is likely to bring about the desired results.

We have presented some of the facts and issues in using suspension techniques as a means of reducing chronic and acute behavior problems. Now let's look more closely at the specifics of how to use them effectively in your school.

Part I of the Suspension Gradient: Other Class Time-Out (OCT)

We will introduce you to three basic ISS techniques in this Briefcase, all along a gradient of location and time. The first technique is Other Class Time-Out. The other two are Prime Time Suspension (PTS) and Restrictive In-School Suspension (RISS). The basic difference between OCT and the PTS and RISS suspension programs is that OCT is a decentralized strategy that is implemented at the classroom level. With OCT, the student is sent from his own classroom to a different prearranged one for a brief period of time. Both PTS and RISS are done on an all-school level in a centralized location. However, it is important to realize that all of these techniques are basically a form of time-out behavior management strategies.

We do not discuss Out-of-School Suspension further here because, as we have mentioned, it is our goal to keep students within the school environment when we can. When we do recommend OSS, it is for the safety of the school or when less restrictive techniques have completely failed. OSS is viewed as the extreme end of the time-out gradient, when students may be taken out of school for long periods of time and placed in unsupervised or undersupervised settings. OSS, in our view, is a last-resort technique and will be discussed at the end of this section under "Special Cases and Techniques."

When to Use OCT

OCT is a well-researched strategy that has been shown to effectively manage many of the problematic behaviors that occur daily in classrooms. This type of strategy has also been referred to as "Think Time" (Nelson & Carr, 1996) and "Inter-class Time-out" (Reavis, Kukic, Jenson, Morgan, Andrews, & Fister, 1996). OCT is a preferred suspension strategy because it is the least restrictive of all of the types of suspensions, and it requires only two cooperating teachers and relatively little training.

OCT is very effective for the less severe problematic behaviors that occur in classrooms. We recommend combining the OCT procedure as part of an undesired consequence hierarchy for classroom rule-breaking. Violating classroom rules might encompass behaviors such as not following the teacher's directions, coming to school unprepared, talking out, talking with a neighbor, talking back to the teacher, and being in the wrong place at the wrong time. As part of the undesired consequence hierarchy, OCT is used *immediately* when a student breaks a classroom rule for the third time in one day.

> **Box 4-4**
>
> **Technique Hint**
>
> You can learn more about combining the OCT procedure with an undesired consequence hierarchy by referring to the "What If?" rules system described in *The Tough Kid Book* (Rhode, Jenson, & Reavis, 1992) and *The Tough Kid New Teacher Kit* (Rhode, Jenson, & Morgan, 2003).

A common mistake involving OCT is waiting too long to use it. If the student is out of control, arguing vehemently, or throwing a fit (temper tantrum), it is usually too late to use OCT. Other mistakes include issuing repeated warnings, talking to the student about the problematic behavior, asking why she can't behave, and threatening to send a student to OCT rather than doing it once a student has earned it. Use OCT early and follow the steps for implementing it.

Steps for Implementing OCT

Step 1: Ask each teacher to arrange with one or more teachers in the building to receive students who earn OCTs. Each teacher can then send students to the receiving teacher's classroom for OCT. It is helpful if teachers can find cooperating teachers located near their own classrooms, when possible.

Step 2: Ask each participating teacher to set up an extra student desk and chair, designated specifically for OCT, in her classroom. The desk and chair should be placed away from other students and be in as unobtrusive a location as possible. The desk and chair should not be placed where there are interesting things going on. It is also important that the receiving teacher be able to clearly see and supervise the student at the desk at all times.

Step 3: Provide teachers with a supply of OCT hall passes. (*Figure 4-1* depicts a sample pass. A sheet of these passes from which you can make copies is provided at the end of this section.) When a sending teacher hands a student an OCT pass, this is the student's signal that she must immediately go to the OCT receiving classroom.

Figure 4-2

Sample OCT Return Contract

Other Class Time-Out

RETURN CONTRACT

My Name ______________ Time ______ Date ______
Teacher Who Sent Me ______________
Teacher Who Received Me ______________
Problem behavior that earned my OTC ______________
____
What I will do next time instead ______________
____
____

❑ Yes, I am ready to go back to my own classroom.
(check)

❑ I would like to talk to my teacher.
(check)

____
Student's Signature

Step 4: Make copies of the OCT Return Contract (also at the end of this section) for all teachers. (*Figure 4-2* depicts a sample contract.)

Step 5: Instruct teachers that, as soon as a student earns OCT, the teacher must verbally identify the behavior that has resulted in the OCT. For example, the teacher might say, "Dan, that is talking back. You have earned OCT." The student is then given an OCT hall pass and is told to go to the receiving teacher. When OCT classrooms are within sight of each other, the sending teacher can step to her classroom doorway and observe the student making the transition to the receiving classroom. When the classrooms are farther apart, an escort is sometimes needed for a student

Figure 4-1

Sample OCT Hall Pass

Other Class Time-Out Hall Pass

____
Student's Name

____
Sending Teacher

____
Receiving Teacher

______________ ______
Time Sent Date

who is unlikely to arrive on his own. The escort selection *must* be prearranged.

When the student who earned the OCT arrives at the receiving classroom, he should wait by the door until the receiving teacher acknowledges him and escorts him to the OCT desk.

Box 4-5

Possible escorts include a school counselor, an office worker, an aide, or other school personnel you are comfortable designating. In this case, the escort must be called, typically over the classroom intercom system, or by a note sent with another student to the designated adult with whom the OCT student will make the trip.

Step 6: Ensure that the receiving teacher has the student who earned OCT sit at the assigned desk for 15 minutes. After the time is up, and as soon as the receiving teacher can find time, she should quietly ask the student, "Are you ready to go back to your classroom?" If the answer is "Yes," the student will fill out the return contract, which asks for the following information:

- The student's name
- The sending teacher's name
- The receiving teacher's name
- The problem behavior that earned OCT
- What the student will do instead of the problem behavior in the future
- A reaffirmation that the student is ready to return to his classroom
- Whether the student would like to talk to his teacher about the incident

Step 7: Advise the receiving teacher to make certain that the student has both her OCT hall pass and Return Contract before sending her back to her classroom. The receiving teacher should step to the classroom door to supervise the return.

Step 8: If the student says she is not ready to return to her classroom, instruct the receiving teacher to simply ignore her, leave her at the OCT desk without further conversation, and return in another ten minutes to ask again if she is ready to return. The receiving teacher should repeat this step, as needed, up to three times. When the student is ready to go back to her classroom, the receiving teacher carries out Step 7.

Step 9: Inform the sending teacher that when the student returns to her classroom she should wait by the door until acknowledged by her teacher and invited back in. It is important that the teacher handle this reentry in a positive, matter-of-fact manner. The teacher should not extract verbal assurances for good behavior nor draw any attention to the fact that the student has just completed OCT time. A simple statement is appropriate, such as, "We're on page 47 in our English book. Please take out your book." As soon as possible, without interrupting the flow of ongoing instruction, the teacher should stop by the student's desk to help her orient to the task at hand. The student should be encouraged and praised for her efforts to get back to work. Upon the student's reentry, the teacher should collect the OCT hall pass and Return Contract from the student, noting the time the student returned to the classroom on the contract. If the student checked the box on the contract that she would like to talk to her teacher about the incident, the teacher should arrange a time for this to take place. For an elementary student, recess may be a good time. For a secondary student, the time could be during lunch or after school.

Step 10: Advise the sending teacher to keep the Return Contract on file for documentation and future reference. If a student has recurring behavior problems, the teacher should refer to previous Return Contracts to identify needed adjustments or intervention changes to make in the classroom. They may include strategies such as setting up a self-monitoring/self-management program, moving the student away from other problem students, or restating and clarifying the classroom rules and consequences. Or, they may involve setting up a Home Note system or a Behavioral Contract, both of which are explained in detail in Section 6. Refer to "Making OCT Even Better" at the end of this section for additional suggestions about evaluating recurring problems.

Plan Ahead of Time

There are several things you will need to take care of before your teachers begin to use Other Class Time-Out.

1. **All teachers must introduce OCT procedures by thoroughly explaining and preteaching them to their students before implementing the program.** It is also helpful for teachers to assist students in role-playing the procedures from beginning to end. The procedures include:
   - Telling a student that she has earned OCT and giving her an OCT hall pass.
   - Leaving the classroom appropriately.
   - Taking her seat at the OCT desk in the receiving classroom as instructed.
   - Filling out the Return Contract.
   - Returning to her own classroom once the OCT time has been completed.
2. **Teachers must inform their students ahead of time of the behavior expectations while in OCT.** Teachers must review the expectations, explain them, and make certain their students understand them. Teachers must post the rules beside each student desk provided for OCT recipients, where the students can clearly see them. Typical rules for OCT are simple:
   - Sit quietly.
   - No sleeping.
   - Stay in your seat.
3. **Teachers must inform their students ahead of time what will happen if they break OCT rules.** Generally, it is appropriate to add ten minutes of time for each OCT rule violation. If a student continues to break OCT rules (up to three times), the teacher should immediately request help from the office. The student is then assigned to one of the other ISS programs (discussed later in this section), or she can spend her OCT time at a desk in the main office under supervision. If the student is removed to the main office, make sure the desk is placed in a secluded location where no interesting activity is taking place. It is also important to call the student's parents immediately and inform them of the problem.

Troubleshooting OCT

Problems will sometimes occur and are to be expected with any behavior-management strategy. Educators who use OCT should be prepared to respond to problems.

Problem: ***A student who has earned OCT has been given her OCT hall pass and has been directed to go to the receiving classroom. However, she refuses to leave her own classroom.***

Solution: The vast majority of students will go to the receiving OCT classroom when they are asked to do so. However, there may be an occasional time when a student refuses to go. Do not get into a power struggle with the student. Arrange ahead of time for another adult to come to the classroom immediately. This adult may be an aide, school psychologist, counselor, assistant principal, or someone else who has been trained in this role. The designated adult should enter the classroom, stand next to the student, and *calmly* and *quietly* say, "When you're ready to go, I'll walk with you to the OCT classroom. Are you ready to go?" If the student still does not leave, the adult should take a seat next to the student. Talking to the student should be held to a minimum; in other words, no pleading, warnings, threats, lectures, or negotiations. Every ten minutes, the adult should again ask the student if she is ready to go (up to three times). Until the student actually does leave, the extra adult serves to kick up "proximity control" a notch. The majority of students will agree to leave in a relatively short period of time with an adult waiting next to them. After the third request and the passage of 30 minutes, however, further action is called for. Refer to the second and third bullets under "Explosive Crises" in this section for additional suggestions.

Problem: ***Once the student has been asked to go to the receiving classroom, she procrastinates or wastes time before doing so.***

Solution: In this case, you have several options:

- Add extra time (ten minutes) to the assigned OCT.
- Let the student know you will have to call her parents.
- Shave ten minutes off the student's next preferred classroom activity.

Problem: ***The student dawdles in the OCT classroom for a prolonged period of time or repeatedly says she is not ready to go back when told her time is up.***

Solution: Require the student to make up the time and academic work she has missed during the time she was not ready to return to her classroom. In other words, make certain the student does not escape what was required in her classroom during the time she was gone.

Problem: ***The student cannot be trusted to walk to the receiving OCT classroom alone, and the receiving teacher's classroom is not within sight of the sending teacher's classroom.***

Solution: In this case, it is essential to have a prearranged agreement with a designated

Box 4-6

Technique Hint

For *younger* students, missing a preferred activity might mean losing time from recess, free time, or story time.

For *older* students, the requirement may be to wait 52 seconds (or some other arbitrary amount of time) at the end of a class before being excused to go to the next class. This puts time and space between the procrastinating student and her peers, making this seem a bigger penalty.

Box 4-7

Technique Hint

Have *younger* students stay in from recess for ten minutes and work on missed assignments.

Require *older* students to complete a special homework assignment related to their missed work. Inform them that you will be contacting their parents about the extra homework and any procrastination.

adult in the school to escort the student. The designated adult can be an aide, the school counselor or psychologist, or an assistant principal who has been trained in this role. Needing an escort is usually rare. Most students will take the OCT hall pass and go to the OCT classroom when they are asked to do so.

Making OCT Even Better

1. The effectiveness of OCT is greatly enhanced when students who have earned it are sent to *different* grade levels to complete it. When feasible, a receiving teacher's OCT classroom that is two or more grade levels below the student's assigned grade is best. For example, a fifth-grade teacher might send her students to a third-grade classroom for OCT. By being "downgraded," students who earn OCT are less likely to have friends in the OCT classroom. Typically, they do not want to go to classrooms where the students are unfamiliar and the environment is foreign. Resist the urge to comment, "If you behave like younger children, then you will have to go to their classroom for OCT." This serves only to humiliate students, making the situation worse.

2. It is desirable for each teacher to form a partnership with two or more receiving teachers to whom they can send students for OCT. For one thing, there may be times when more than one student will earn OCT and need to be sent to a receiving classroom. For another, students will never know ahead of time which classroom they will be sent to until they are given the OCT hall pass and told to go to Mrs. Rhode's classroom. This variation is especially effective when OCT is used with older students.

3. With kindergarten students, the teacher should consider placing an OCT desk and chair in an out-of-the-way place in each kindergarten classroom until the Christmas break. Then, the teacher should partner with receiving teachers and send the kindergartners to other grades for OCT after the Christmas break. This allows very young students a chance to learn the routine in a familiar setting.

4. There is some debate over whether students should work on their assignments while in OCT. We believe that care must be taken not to create an undue hardship on the receiving teacher, who is trying to

teach her own class. However, the sending teacher may give an assignment to the student to work on while in OCT, with no expectation that the receiving teacher will assist with or monitor the work. If the sending teacher chooses not to do this, the student can be given the option to finish an academic assignment (e.g., a math worksheet that has previously been placed in the receiving classroom) before any OCT is earned. If the student completes this "canned" assignment or an assignment the sending teacher has given her, she can raise her hand and ask to return to her classroom early. At this point, the receiving teacher carries out Step 7 (of the implementation steps), asking the student if she is ready to return. If she answers "Yes," the teacher asks the student to complete her Return Contract and go to her classroom with the completed assignment, the Return Contract, and the OCT hall pass.

5. The principal might consider having a party across a grade level (e.g., all sixth-grade classrooms) on a Friday at the end of the month for students who have not earned an excessive number of OCTs during that month. The party should include students who have not earned more than the preestablished number of OCTs for the period of time. Keeping the number a secret right up until the start of the party will motivate students to keep the number low. In addition, a select group of students could plan the party and decide the number of OCTs that students can have and still attend. The party committee should know that the arrangements and OCT number for the month are to be kept secret. Including one or two Tough Kids on the committee will keep their motivation high. It is all right if they know the secret number of OCTs for the month. This knowledge will help them work harder so that they can attend the party. While the party takes place, students who have *not* earned the right to attend may be sent to one of the participating classrooms for that teacher to supervise, while the students who have earned the right may go to the other participating classrooms or to a central location, which will be supervised by the rest of the teachers from that grade level.

> **Box 4-8**
> ## Technique Hint
> Completing an academic assignment is optional for students. If they do it, they can return to their own classrooms faster.

6. The Return Contract contains valuable information to help teachers manage their classrooms. Using the data the contracts

contain, teachers should regularly ask themselves these questions:

- What are the most frequent behaviors resulting in OCT?
- Who most frequently earns OCT?
- Is there a certain time or academic subject during which students are being sent to OCT?
- Is the overall use of OCT decreasing?

Teachers may need to use OCT more frequently at the beginning of the school year. However, if it is being used correctly, the number of OCT occurrences should go down during the school year, with only periodic upsurges after holidays and in late spring.

Box 4-9

Technique Hint

Ask teachers to meet with their OCT partners every few weeks to review all Return Contracts. Brainstorming new ideas to try with chronic OCT users or for the most frequent behavior problems helps teachers to make needed adjustments and changes to the program.

7. It is helpful to have a prewritten letter for teachers to send home to parents explaining the use of OCT before it is implemented. The letter should invite parents to ask questions about the program. The goal is to provide a unified approach to discipline in the school, where school staff and parents are working together.

8. OCT should be combined with procedures adapted from the Unified Discipline Project (White, Algozzine, Audette, Marr, & Ellis, 2001). To use these procedures, the teacher constructs a large posterboard chart with a pocket envelope on it for each student. The pocket envelopes are then numbered. For example, a class of 25 students requires a posterboard with 25 individual pocket envelopes numbered 1–25, each representing a student in the class. The posterboard is then placed at the front of the classroom so that it is easily seen by all students. The teacher places three colored slips of paper in each student's pocket envelope. The top paper slip is green, the middle paper slip is yellow, and the bottom paper slip is red. When a student breaks a classroom rule—including not following the teacher's directions—the green slip is removed by the teacher, leaving the yellow slip showing. Each time a rule is broken, the teacher identifies the violation to the student so that there is no misunderstanding as to why she has lost a slip. For example, the teacher might say, "Lois, that is not following my directions. You lose a green slip." When the green slip is removed, the yellow slip then serves as a warning. If another rule is broken that day by the student, the yellow slip is removed, leaving the red slip showing. The red slip is the signal that the student is to pick up an OCT hall pass and go immediately to the designated OCT classroom. With this procedure, the teacher does not have to tell the student to go to OCT, unless she does not automatically do it. Of course,

before using this procedure, the teacher must specifically teach his class how the program works. This includes explaining that when the red slip is showing, the student must pick up a hall pass and leave for the designated OCT room. Role-playing how the procedures work is a good way to ensure that students understand it. After the student returns from OCT with her Return Contract, the green and yellow slips are placed back in her envelope, and the procedure starts again. At the beginning of each day, all the slips are returned, and each student starts over with green, yellow, and red slips. The advantage of this system is the ease of simply removing individual students' colored slips of paper when classroom rules are broken. The system is visual, so students receive continual feedback as to how well they are following the classroom rules.

Part II of the Suspension Gradient: Prime Time Suspension (PTS)

Why use PTS? Typically, the most rewarding times in school for students are recess, lunch, time spent with friends, and getting out of school at the end of the day. Missing lunch, recess, time with friends, or having to stay when school lets out is generally *not* preferred by students. On the other hand, participating in math drills, health lectures, or spelling tests are the times of the school day that students who earn suspensions enjoy the least. In fact, missing out on these classroom activities is actually rewarding to many students! Remember that all types of suspension are actually forms of time-out behavior management strategies. The idea is to remove students from rewarding environments they enjoy and place them in environments they find less rewarding for their suspension time. An example of the idea behind PTS, then, is to deny students a portion of the time they value and enjoy the most, rather than those they find less enjoyable. Lunchtime and after-school suspensions are the two types of Prime Time In-School Suspensions we discuss in more detail in this section.

When to Use PTS

Prime Time Suspension is effective for both elementary and secondary students. It is often the suspension of choice to use for students who chronically break basic school or classroom rules. This includes students who may want to avoid certain activities, people, or times of day by being assigned an OCT. Examples of basic rule violations for which PTS is appropriate include:

- Tardiness
- Truancy
- Not being prepared
- Not having homework completed

We do not believe it is a good idea to send students to a more restrictive form of ISS than PTS for being truant or tardy. Frequently, truant and tardy students are already trying to miss or avoid class time. It is much more desirable to have these students remain in class, once they are there, and then miss out on their "prime time" favorites such as lunch, recess, or getting out of school on time.

PTS generally works well for annoying, persistent, low-intensity problem behaviors such as those just listed. It works less well for higher-intensity behaviors such as defiance or extreme noncompliance. Thus, if a student is disrupting her class to the point of interfering with other students' learning, then a more restrictive form of suspension than PTS is usually called for. The more restrictive ISS is discussed later in this section.

> **Box 4-10**
>
> ***Remember!***
>
> Use Prime Time Suspension (PTS) for annoying, low-intensity behaviors and the more restrictive forms of In-School Suspension (ISS) for higher-intensity, more serious behaviors.

Bumping PTS Up a Notch

1. One other component should be considered when using either lunchtime or after-school PTS: the use of a Tracking Sheet. Simply being inconvenienced by missing a lunch period or staying after school may not be powerful enough to bring about substantial behavior change for all students. In this case, we suggest adding a tracking requirement to the suspension procedure. Use of a Tracking Sheet requires a student to carry a specially designed form around to her teachers the day after earning and serving PTS time. The purpose of the Tracking Sheet is to document the student's performance the next day. For example, a middle-school student who earns PTS for chronic tardiness would take a Tracking Sheet to each of her seven class periods the following day. Each teacher indicates on the sheet whether the student was on time to her class. The teacher then initials the sheet in the box reserved for her particular class period. A chronically tardy elementary student would carry a Tracking Sheet requiring feedback from her teacher four times during the day, documenting whether she is on time. These four times are:
    - When school starts in the morning
    - After morning recess
    - After lunchtime
    - After afternoon recess

Having this tracking requirement the day after serving PTS strengthens PTS in that students will work to avoid it. We discuss more about how to use the Tracking Sheet later in this section.

2. When a student breaks a rule that is designated as earning PTS, she is given a PTS slip like the one depicted in *Figure 4-3*. (There is also a sheet of PTS slips to copy at the end of this section.) The staff member who assigns the PTS marks on the slip the type of PTS experience the

Figure 4-3

Sample PTS Ticket

Prime Time Suspension Ticket

❑ Lunch ❑ After School

Name ______________________

Date __________ Behavior ______________

Assigned by ______________________

(see rules on back)

student has earned. When a student is given the slip, she is expected to report to that suspension site at the next available opportunity (e.g., the next lunch period or after school that day). Failure to report to the site on the assigned day results in a heavier consequence, which we discuss later in this section. All staff members who assign PTS must keep a list of the names of the students receiving PTS slips that day and turn in the list to the central office prior to the start of the next PTS time. As students show up at their designated PTS sites, their names are checked off on a master list kept for that site each day. Students who miss their assigned PTS sites and times are identified when their names are not checked off on the master lists.

> **Box 4-11**
>
> **Technique Hint**
>
> In one junior high in which the authors worked, Lunchtime PTS was held in the ninth-grade geography classroom with the geography teacher supervising. This teacher volunteered to take on this daily role and was compensated for working through his lunch period. He ate his lunch while the students were eating.
>
> As an additional "perk" for the geography teacher, when dances and other school activities were held, he was *not* asked to supervise and was given this time as an additional prep period in his classroom.

Steps for Implementing Lunchtime PTS

Lunchtime PTS is a very effective procedure for students who hate to miss out on lunchtime with their friends. The steps for implementing this procedure follow.

Step 1: Select a room to serve as the Lunchtime PTS site. A classroom with desks and chairs that is not being used during the lunch period works well. Also arrange adult supervision. Teachers, staff, or aides will often agree to rotate this responsibility.

Step 2: Post the Lunchtime PTS rules in a conspicuous place in the designated room. Rules usually include:

- Show up on time (specify the time).
- Bring your lunch (from home) or a lunch ticket.
- Do what the supervisor asks you to do.
- Do not talk without permission.
- Stay in your seat.

It is also a good idea to have the rules printed on the back of the PTS slips so that students are aware of the expectations before they arrive.

Step 3: As students arrive for their Lunchtime PTS, the supervisor notes their names on the master list of expected students. (A reproducible copy of the Lunchtime PTS Master List is included at the end of this section.) The supervisor also notes the time students arrive (usually, Lunchtime PTS lasts only 20–30 minutes). Students who do not arrive on time or who break any Lunchtime PTS rules are not given credit for serving the PTS. At the end of the PTS, they are informed that they did not receive credit and that they must repeat their PTS following day. Their names are then placed on the new master list for the following day.

Step 4: Assign a student aide or other person to the Lunchtime PTS room each day at the time the PTS begins. Without engaging in other conversation, the PTS supervisor collects lunch tickets from arriving students who had planned to purchase their lunch at school that day. The supervisor gives the student aide or other designated individual the tickets to take to the lunchroom. The aide turns in the tickets and picks up lunches for the PTS students. This may require several trips, unless a rolling cart is available to carry the lunches. Students who have lunches from home should take them to the PTS room.

Step 5: Students are allowed to eat their lunches while serving their Lunchtime PTS. However, once they are finished, they are to remain quietly in their seats until the time is up. The student aide who picked up the lunch trays collects them from the students and returns them to the lunchroom. The supervising teacher passes by each desk with a trash bag or trash can to collect any refuse from students.

Step 6: When the time is up, the supervising teacher lets students know whether they have been given credit for serving their time (i.e., they arrived on time and followed PTS rules). If not, they are told that they must return the following day. The supervising teacher then excuses the students, giving them just enough time to stop at the rest room and their lockers before their next scheduled classes.

Box 4-12

Technique Hint

Always have someone other than the students assigned to Lunchtime PTS pick up and deliver their school lunches. If PTS students are allowed to do this for themselves, they will still have a chance to see their friends and socialize. It is also common for PTS students who are permitted to pick up their own lunches to take an unreasonable amount of time to do so. A common excuse is "The line was really long. I hurried as fast as I could." PTS students who pick up their own lunches often return to the PTS room when their assigned time is almost up.

Step 7: Before secondary students leave the Lunchtime PTS, they are given Tracking Sheets to take around the next day to all their teachers. *Figure 4-4* shows a sample secondary Tracking Sheet. (A reproducible copy of a secondary Prime Time Tracking Sheet is included at the end of this section.) The Tracking Sheets have a place to write in the problematic behavior that earned the students the PTS in the first place. The students are instructed to carry their sheets to all of their classes and obtain each teacher's initials on the forms. The form also has a place for the teacher to indicate whether or not the students engaged in the same behavior again. At the end of the day, students must return the signed Tracking Sheets to a designated person, most often an assistant principal, school psychologist, or counselor.

The Tracking Sheet for elementary students is slightly different from the secondary version, which is signed by several teachers. Those who are tardy, talk out, or do not work should get teacher feedback on their Tracking Sheets at the following times:

- When school starts in the morning
- After morning recess
- After lunchtime
- After afternoon recess

For not being prepared or not having their homework, students should be checked the first thing in the morning of the following

Box 4-13

Technique Hint

For *elementary* students, Lunchtime PTS can be held in a separate room the same way it is held for secondary students. Another option is to require students to sit at an isolated table in the lunchroom with a teacher or other staff member. If they sit with an adult, talking or interacting with the adult or other students is not permitted.

Figure 4-4

Sample Secondary Tracking Sheet

PRIME TIME TRACKING SHEET			
Behavior being tracked:			
Name:			**Date:**
PERIODS	Behavior Rating (Circle One)	Teacher Initials	COMMENTS
1.	Acceptable Unacceptable		
2.	Acceptable Unacceptable		
3.	Acceptable Unacceptable		
4.	Acceptable Unacceptable		
5.	Acceptable Unacceptable		
6.	Acceptable Unacceptable		
7.	Acceptable Unacceptable		

THIS SHEET MUST BE RETURNED TO THE TRACKING SHEET SUPERVISOR AT THE END OF THE SCHOOL DAY BEFORE GOING HOME.

day. In this case, the teacher crosses off all rating times on the sheet, except the first one. *Figure 4-5* shows a sample elementary Tracking Sheet. (A reproducible copy of this sheet is included at the end of this section.)

Figure 4-5
Sample Elementary Tracking Sheet

PRIME TIME TRACKING SHEET			
Behavior being tracked:			
Name:			Date:
Times	Behavior Rating (Circle One)	Teacher Initials	COMMENTS
1. Start of School	OK Not OK		
2. After AM Recess	OK Not OK		
3. After Lunch	OK Not OK		
4. After PM Recess	OK Not OK		

Troubleshooting Lunchtime PTS

While some problems can occur with Lunchtime PTS, they are generally minimal if the procedure has been set up correctly. Some of the more likely problems and their solutions are reviewed next.

Problem: ***Some students in the school have medical conditions such as diabetes or hypoglycemia. What about Lunchtime PTS for them?***

Solution: Make sure that any students with medical conditions have access to the right foods during Lunchtime PTS. They must also be allowed to eat their lunches in a timely manner. Students should *never* be denied their lunches. They are denied only lunchtime with their friends.

Problem: ***A student does not report to Lunchtime PTS after having been given a slip.***

Solution: In this case, the student should be called to the office and informed that her Lunchtime PTS has been increased to two days. An escort (i.e., a counselor, vice principal, school psychologist, etc.) should be made available to see that the student goes from her last class before lunch to the Lunchtime PTS room. The escort should show up about ten minutes before the end of the class to prevent the student from "bolting" when the bell rings at the end of the period. The student should not know ahead of time, however, that an escort will be provided. In addition, the parents should be notified of the problem.

Problem: ***A student does not return her initialed Tracking Sheet to the designated person at the end of the day following her Lunchtime PTS.***

Solution: If the student does not return her initialed Tracking Sheet to the designated person, she is assigned an additional Lunchtime PTS. In other words, she must start completely over with her assigned Lunchtime PTS. She is still required to carry the Tracking Sheet for a day, have it initialed by her teacher(s), and return it to the designated person. In addition, her parents will be notified.

Problem: ***A student returns her Tracking Sheet, but it is missing teachers' initials.***

Solution: If teachers' initials are missing, the student may be given the option to find those teachers at the end of the day before leaving school. If she does not obtain their initials before leaving and turns in her sheet, she must start the process over the following day with a new Tracking Sheet.

Problem: ***A student forges teachers' initials.***

Solution: This is a serious problem. In this case, parents are notified immediately, their input sought, and a more restrictive form of suspension time assigned.

Steps for Implementing After-School PTS

Wanting to leave school and be with their friends is the highlight of the day for most students. After-School PTS is an effective procedure that can be combined with Lunchtime PTS or used by itself. A critical requirement before using After-School PTS is to consider how students attending a school get to and from it. A school to which all students walk is an ideal place for implementation. In the majority of schools, however, at least some busing of students takes place. In such schools, transporting students safely home after completing their After-School PTS time must be prearranged or provided. In any case, when After-School PTS is used, the parents *must* be informed ahead of time that it has been earned, and their agreement obtained as to how their child will return home afterward. Some parents will pick up their child or have a family member or friend do so. In cases where a student lives close to the school, parents may want him to walk home. Other parents will agree to have their child serve the time if the school provides transportation home and if district policy permits this option. If the school does provide transportation home, two designated adults *must* be present when the student is transported, *never* just one adult alone. Providing safe transportation is always critical with After-School PTS, particularly when days are short and it is dark when students are excused. Nevertheless, After-School PTS is a powerful procedure when used correctly. Its advantages are that:

- It can be used in combination with Lunchtime PTS.
- It can be used for behaviors that occur later in the day after lunchtime has passed.
- It is especially effective for tardy or truant students who try to avoid school.

The disadvantages of After-School PTS are that:

- It occurs after the regular school day and requires adult supervision.

- It requires contacting the parents to inform them that their child has earned After-School PTS and that she will be returning home later.
- It sometimes has to be delayed in order to inform the parents ahead of time and to arrange transportation home.

Using After-School PTS for students who are tardy or truant requires these school-avoiders to spend more time in school because of their problematic behavior. The basic steps for setting up After-School PTS are similar to those for Lunchtime PTS.

Step 1: After-School PTS requires a separate room with desks, chairs, and adult supervision, just like Lunchtime PTS. Teachers, counselors, aides, or other staff will often agree to rotate this after-school responsibility.

Step 2: A parent *must* be informed ahead of time that her child will be staying for After-School PTS. A staff member must document the time and date that the parent was contacted and gave permission. If the parent cannot be contacted or does not give permission, the student must not be required to attend After-School PTS. In this case, an alternative type of suspension must be selected, one that takes place during the school day. One alternative is to require the student to make up an equivalent amount of assigned time by attending one or more Lunchtime PTS sessions, beginning the next day.

Step 3: Post the After-School PTS rules in a conspicuous place in the designated room. The rules are usually similar

to the rules for Lunchtime PTS, with just a few adjustments:

- Show up on time (specify the time).
- Do what the supervisor asks you to do.
- Bring your books, assignments, and supplies.
- Talk only with the supervisor's permission.
- Stay awake and stay in your seat.
- Do not bring food or drinks (unless the student has a medical plan that requires it).

It is desirable to print the After-School PTS rules, in addition to the Lunchtime PTS rules, on the PTS slips students receive when they earn PTS time. This way, students are aware of the expectations before they show up to serve their time.

Step 4: Decide how long the After-School PTS program will operate after school has ended for the day. In most schools, this is 30–60 minutes. Let students know beforehand that they are expected to work on their homework assignments during After-School PTS in order to be given credit for the time. If a student has no homework that day, she may read a book. (This is rarely the case for students who earn any type of suspension time.)

> **Box 4-14**
>
> **Technique Hint**
>
> In one school, students assigned to After School PTS often reported that they had left needed books at home, loaned them to friends, or lost them. Their principal solved this problem by keeping a complete set of all the textbooks used in the building in the After-School PTS room. In other words, excuses for not having needed textbooks became irrelevant.

Step 5: As students arrive to serve their After-School PTS, the supervisor notes their names on her master list of expected students. (A reproducible copy of the After-School PTS Master List is included at the end of this section.) The supervisor also notes the time each student arrives. Students who are not on time or who break After-School PTS rules do not receive full credit for serving their time. When students arrive late or break rules, they must be reminded of this point.

At the conclusion of the After-School PTS session, students who were late are reminded that they must return the next day to make up for the lost time. They are then given new PTS slips and their names placed on the new master list for the following day along with the amount of time they must make up. Their parents must be notified again of the additional time to be made up the next day.

> **Box 4-15**
>
> **Technique Hint**
>
> To a student who arrives eight minutes late for After-School PTS, it is appropriate for the supervisor to say, "Cal, you're eight minutes late. You have eight minutes to make up here tomorrow after school."
>
> To a student who breaks an After-School PTS rule, the supervisor might say something like, "Tiffany, you're out of your seat. That's ten minutes here tomorrow." If Tiffany breaks another rule, the supervisor might say, "Tiffany, you're talking without permission. That's ten more minutes tomorrow," and so on.

Step 6: Before secondary students are excused at the end of the After-School PTS session, they receive Tracking Sheets to present to their teachers the next day (see *Figure 4-4*.) The Tracking Sheets have a place to write in the problematic behavior that earned the students the After-School PTS. The students must carry their Tracking Sheets to all of their classes and obtain each teacher's initials on their forms. There is also a place on the Tracking Sheets for teachers to indicate whether or not students engaged in the same behavior again. At the end of the day, students must return the initialed Tracking Sheets to a designated person, most often an assistant principal, school psychologist, or counselor.

Box 4-16

Technique Hint

Elementary students in After-School PTS can sit at their desks in their own classrooms with their teachers using the steps described in this section. As another option, students can spend the time sitting at a desk in a quiet, secluded part of the main office where no interesting activities are taking place. Provision must be made to adequately supervise students during this time, while keeping interactions with other students and adults to a minimum.

The Tracking Sheet for elementary students is the one shown in *Figure 4-5*. The problematic behavior that earned the elementary student the After-School PTS time should be written on the Tracking Sheet. Students are then required to get their teachers' feedback on the sheet the next day at the following times:

- When school starts in the morning
- After morning recess
- After lunchtime
- After afternoon recess

Step 7: The After-School PTS supervisor must have a copy of the written notes that document parental permission concerning how each student will get home when the PTS is over. (These are the notes made by the staff member who called to notify the parents about the After-School PTS the students have earned.) The supervisor must release students only to approved individuals. She must see that parents' instructions are followed. The supervisor must note on the master list the time and the person to whom each student was released and indicate that the parent's instructions were followed.

Troubleshooting After-School PTS

Almost all of the troubleshooting steps for Lunchtime PTS also apply to After-School PTS. The unique issues with After-School PTS are covered below.

Problem: ***A parent agrees that the student can serve After-School PTS, but safe, alternative transportation is not available.***

Solution: Getting the student safely home after completing After-School PTS is critical. The school staff member who notifies the parent of the After-School PTS must document in writing the means by which the student will arrive home and whether the parent agrees with it. In winter, students should not walk home in the dark. Some school districts do not permit school staff to provide the transportation because of safety and insurance issues. However, if it is allowed, a designated staff member should never drive the student home without the presence of a second designated staff member, and only in accordance with district policy. When safe, alternative transportation is not available, After-School PTS should not be used. The student should be assigned a different type of ISS.

Problem: ***On some days, especially when both Lunchtime PTS and After-School PTS are used, there are too many students to have all of them use a Tracking Sheet the next day.***

Solution: Decide how many students attending each of the PTS sessions can be effectively tracked the next day by the staff member assigned that task. For example, you may decide that five students from each session can be tracked. Have the supervisor for Lunchtime PTS place each student's PTS slip in a container. At the end of the session, have her draw that number of PTS slips from the container. Repeat this procedure at the end of After-School PTS. The students whose slips are selected are the ones who are required to carry the Tracking Sheet the next day.

Problem: ***For supervisory or other reasons, the school is not able to provide an After-School PTS every day.***

Solution: Providing After-School PTS every day is the most effective way to go. However, sometimes this is not possible. Another option is to provide After-School PTS two or three times each week (e.g., on Tuesdays and Thursdays or on Mondays, Wednesdays, and Fridays). If After-School PTS is used two or three times per week,

> **Box 4-17**
>
> **Technique Hint**
>
> The advantage to using After-School PTS two to three times per week is that it cuts down on the number of days the procedure has to be run and supervised. The disadvantage of two to three times per week for After-School PTS is that it delays the procedure. For example, if a student has a behavioral problem on Monday, she would not fulfill the PTS procedure until Wednesday. If this same student had a behavioral problem on both Monday and Tuesday, her time in After-School PTS on Wednesday would be increased from one hour to two hours.

it is best to increase each PTS session to a minimum of 45 minutes, up to a maximum of 90 minutes. In this case, when a parent is notified that her child has earned After-School PTS, she is also informed that the time has been assigned for the next scheduled After-School PTS session. Thus, if a student has earned After-School PTS on a Tuesday, and the school provides the sessions three times each week (e.g., Mondays, Wednesdays, and Fridays), the parent is told that the student's assigned time is Wednesday after school.

Problem: ***A student did not show up for After-School PTS on the assigned day. After arrangements were made for her to make up her time at the next scheduled session, she did not show up then either.***

Solution: When a student does not show up for After-School PTS on the assigned day, and she is assigned for the next scheduled session, try to *prevent* her from missing it a second time. Good communication with parents is one way to achieve this. When students have previously missed After-School PTS, parents can be told to expect a note signed by the supervisor, indicating that the student's time has been made up. Parents should be asked for support and assistance when the notes are not taken home. In addition, a staff member can escort repeat "no-shows" from their last class period of the day to the After-School PTS room. Arriving ten minutes before the class is over to avoid letting the student make a run for it is a good idea. If escorting the student from her last class is not successful, it is appropriate to double the time the student has earned and have her make it up in Restrictive In-School Suspension (RISS). We discuss RISS next.

Implementing Restrictive In-School Suspension (RISS)

RISS is the "big gun" of all the ISS procedures. It should be used for the most serious problematic behaviors such as severe defiance, noncompliance, fighting, property destruction, and bullying other students. Additionally, it can be used when students quickly accumulate so much Lunchtime PTS and/or After-School PTS that they cannot reasonably make it up in these formats. It is also appropriate when students do not show up for an assigned After-School PTS session for the second time. When this happens, the amount of assigned time should be doubled, and it should be converted to RISS.

RISS involves more time and effort in the form of adult supervision than other forms of ISS. It also takes students out of their instructional environments for longer periods of time, which is a problem for many students.

We suggest that each time RISS is used, an ABC-RISS Sheet be filled out. The ABC-RISS Sheet will yield valuable information regarding:

- Which students are sent to RISS most frequently
- What behaviors result in RISS the most
- What times of the school day are students most frequently sent to RISS
- Which staff members send students to RISS the most

Step 1: Designate a room to serve as the RISS site. In most cases, an unused classroom with desks and chairs is sufficient. The RISS room should be set up to reduce communication and interaction among students. Options include turning desks to face the walls if space permits or, at the very least, in traditional rows so that students are not facing each other. Arranging effective supervision is critical.

Step 2: Post the RISS rules on the wall in a conspicuous place. Select rules that are similar to those for Lunchtime PTS and After-School PTS. A first rule violation offense should result in the addition of 30 minutes to the RISS time. A second violation should add one hour. A third infraction should double the assigned RISS time. Additional rule infractions should require parental collaboration to determine how the student's time should be made up. During this conference, it is also appropriate to discuss the need for additional interventions.

Step 3: The initial assigned time period for RISS should generally be a minimum of one hour, up to a maximum of one day.

Figure 4-6

ABC-RISS Sheet

Student's Name ______________________ Date __________

Teacher's Name ______________________ Date __________

A Antecedent—What was going on before the behavior?

- Time ______________________
- People ______________________
- Place ______________________
- Event(s) ______________________
- Student's Behavior ______________________
- Down Time ______________________
- Other ______________________

B Behavior—Describe the problematic behavior very specifically, in objective terms, based on what was observed.

____

____

C Consequences—What happened after the problematic behavior occurred? Specifically describe.

- Positive or negative attention from peers or adults ______________________
- Obtained tangible item ______________________
- Escaped a person, situation, or place ______________________
- Avoided a person, situation or place ______________________
- Other ______________________

R Replacement Behavior—What does the student need to do instead?

____

Comments: ______________________

Form filled out by ______________________

Box 4-18

Technique Hint

Many principals have found that they obtain the same results with a half-day or a one-day RISS assignment as with a three-day RISS. For example, if the half-day RISS goes through the lunch period, this can be a particularly powerful deterrent for secondary students. The idea is to assign the least amount of time found to effectively reduce further recurrences of the problematic behavior, with as little waiting to begin the assignment as possible.

If a student is assigned RISS three times, a parental conference is needed to collaborate on a solution.

Step 4: Because RISS is used for the more serious problematic behaviors such as fighting or severe defiance, the student must be escorted to the RISS room by an adult. If the student refuses to go, the adult should wait two or three minutes and restate the request. The escort should not grab or threaten the student under any circumstances. The student should be informed that assigned RISS time does not begin until she is in the designated RISS room, sitting at the assigned desk.

Step 5: On the way to the RISS room, the adult should escort the student to her locker to gather books, study materials, and assignments to which the student has access. The number of items gathered should provide sufficient academic work for the student to do during the length of her assigned RISS. The adult then determines with the student whether she has enough class assignments to occupy her during this time. If there are not enough assignments, the supervising adult can have the student fill out a "Request for Assignment" slip to be delivered to one or more teachers, so that they can provide more work. See *Figure 4-7* for a sample of the form. (A sheet of Request for Assignment slips to copy is included at the end of this section.)

Box 4-19

Technique Hint

In one school in which the authors worked, the office kept a complete set of the school's textbooks on hand to loan students for RISS use. The books were loaned when students reported they had left their books at home, loaned them to friends, or lost them. **In other words, excuses for not working on assignments were eliminated!**

Step 6: When a student enters the RISS room, she is directed to a desk and asked to begin working on her assignments.

Step 7: After the student has begun the assigned RISS time, an ABC-RISS Sheet is filled out for the incident by the adult who placed the student in

RISS. A new sheet is filled out every time a student is assigned and placed in RISS. The A, B, and C parts of the sheet are:

- The **A** (antecedents) section is for recording the time, the place, the people who were present, or the other events that were happening when the student engaged in the problematic behavior.
- The **B** (behavior) section is for describing the problematic behavior.
- The **C** (consequences) section is for recording the events that immediately followed the problematic behavior. This may include events such as receiving peer attention, arguing with the teacher, or leaving the classroom.

The ABC-RISS Sheets should be compiled and reviewed at least weekly by a designated adult such as the assistant principal or a counselor. These sheets contain a wealth of information, such as which students are coming to RISS most often, what events (antecedents) are commonly "setting the stage" or "triggering" the problematic behavior, and what the rewards or payoffs are for students who engage in such behavior. For example, evaluating the ABC-RISS Sheets may reveal that a student's problematic behavior helps her avoid a disliked class. Or, it may show that there are consequences such as receiving peer attention or escaping a particular social or academic situation. *Figure 4-6* shows an ABC-RISS Sheet. (A full-size ABC-RISS Sheet to copy is included at the end of this section.)

Step 8: During the time students are making up their assigned RISS time, provision must be made for them to have rest room breaks periodically. This should be done while classes are in session, rather than during recess or between classes so as to avoid contact with other students. A designated office staff member should come to the RISS room every hour or so to escort students, one at a time, to the rest room and back. Likewise, for students who are serving RISS time during the lunch period, provision must be made for them to eat lunch in the RISS room. This can be accomplished by operating the RISS room in a manner similar to that of the Lunchtime PTS. Another option

Figure 4-7

Request for Assignment Form

Request for Assignment

____
(Teacher's Name)

________________________ has been assigned to RISS today. Please send the assignment for ____________________
Date

to the office as soon as possible so that the student can work on it while making up the RISS time.

Thank you for your help.

is to escort the RISS students to the lunch detention room. They follow the Lunchtime PTS procedures just as the other students who are assigned there do. If this option is selected, students are escorted back to the RISS room at the end of the lunch period.

Step 9: When a student's RISS time is completed, and before being excused, she is given a Tracking Sheet (this is the same Tracking Sheet described for Lunchtime PTS and After-School PTS). The student takes this sheet to classes the next day. The student's teachers must initial the sheet, indicating that she did not engage in problematic behaviors in their classes. At the end of the day, the student returns the Tracking Sheet to the RISS supervisor. The supervisor then staples it to the student's ABC-RISS Sheet before filing them for documentation and future reference.

Troubleshooting RISS

Problem: ***A student continues to be defiant or noncompliant, or continuously tries to interact with other students, disrupting the RISS room.***

Solution: After the student has broken RISS rules three times—or if the student does not stop her problematic behavior—she should be removed from the RISS room to a separate, supervised site. This site is usually in or close to the principal's office. The student may serve out her RISS time in this location, unless she continues to violate RISS rules. If she continues, her parents must be called to pick her up, and a parent conference must be scheduled before the student is readmitted. Further action should be collaboratively planned.

Problem: ***A student sleeps or does not work on assignments while serving RISS time.***

Solution: The student should be informed that her time does not begin until she is actively working on her assignments. The supervising adult should remain calm and unemotional, and avoid threats, reprimands, and negative comments. In fact, the adult should act like there is all the time in the world and that it doesn't matter when the student's time begins to count. Many students are used to receiving a lot of attention for this kind of behavior, and they would rather have negative attention than no attention. The adult should be prepared to wait out the student. Any time spent sleeping will count as additional time to be made up.

Problem: ***The school does not have a spare room that can be used as the RISS site.***

Solution: When a separate room is not available, some schools have built three-sided plywood "carrels"—that are hinged so they can be folded up when not in use—that can be placed in supervised environments such as another classroom or a library. The carrels are set up in an out-of-the-way space in the room when they are needed. A student desk and chair are placed in each one when they are in use. When a decentralized RISS program is set up using carrels, office staff must maintain responsibility for assigning and monitoring students and providing them with rest room breaks and lunch. The teacher in whose room a carrel is set up should have no responsibility except to report to the office when the student breaks RISS rules. In this case, the office staff will remove the student to serve the time in a quiet place in the office.

Problem: *No trained staff members are available to supervise the RISS program.*

Solution: If staff are available, but not trained, training can be provided. A building administrator must closely supervise the initial operation of the RISS room. If no one is available, or if effective training cannot be provided, RISS must not be used.

Problem: *A student is repeatedly being sent to RISS.*

Solution: After earning RISS three times, the student's ABC-RISS Sheets and Return Contracts must be reviewed and evaluated. Is there a particular time, adult, peer, or class with whom the student is having the most problems? If there is a pattern to the student's RISS placement, some type of accommodation or intervention is warranted. The student may be incapable of completing the required academic work. Or, a particular teacher or peer may be contributing to or triggering the problematic behavior. If the problem is a deficit in academic skills, special help in the form of accommodations or tutoring may be needed. If the student is having problems during transition or unstructured times (e.g., on the school bus; before school; in the hallways, rest rooms, or lunchroom), then an individualized program may be needed. Possible programs include setting up a Home Note program or developing a contract with the student. If a particular teacher or peer is usually involved in the incidents, a problem-solving session led by a counselor, school psychologist, or administrator should be scheduled with these individuals.

Problem: *A teacher overuses RISS, sending many more students to RISS than her colleagues.*

Solution: The principal or assistant principal should schedule a meeting with a teacher who overuses RISS. In the meeting, the administrator reviews with the teacher the ABC-RISS Sheets of the students the teacher has sent to RISS. The teacher may need help with a classroom behavior management program. Or, it may be that she doesn't intervene soon enough with problem behaviors, and many of them escalate to higher levels that are then much more difficult to handle. The administrator should also assess whether the teacher needs some type of assistance or whether she is selectively trying to "get rid" of her most challenging students.

Box 4-20

Technique Hint

The meeting with a teacher who overuses RISS should be conducted by a school administrator and *not* just the RISS supervisor. Some teachers who overuse the program believe it is their right to frequently send students to RISS for even minor behavior problems. This is not a right, but an abuse, of the procedure.

Problem: *Special education students are frequently sent to RISS.*

Solution: Caution is needed when using RISS with a special education student who has an Individualized Education Plan (IEP). If the student is repeatedly (i.e., ten times) sent to RISS, and the special services listed on her IEP are not available in the RISS setting, each day of placement in RISS counts as a suspension. When an eleventh RISS placement is made, a change of special education placement is considered to have taken place. Under such circumstances, federal regulations must be observed. These issues are covered more fully in Section 5, the legal section of this Briefcase, where disciplinary removal of special education students is discussed.

Making RISS Even Better

Once a student has successfully completed RISS time, a copy of her ABC-RISS Sheet and her Return Contract are sent home to her parents. They should be called either ahead of time to let them know to expect these forms or afterward to make certain they received them.

Special Cases and Techniques

In this section, we emphasized In-School Suspension (ISS) programs on a gradient from least restrictive to most restrictive. We began with Other Class Time-Out (OCT), moved to Lunchtime and After-School Prime Time Suspension (PTS), and finally discussed Restrictive In-School Suspension (RISS). However, there are several special cases and techniques that school administrators should consider when developing additional suspension (time-out) programs and selecting other undesired consequences for their schools. Special cases can include settings such as lunchrooms, field trips, or the playground at recess time. They can also include explosive crises situations in which a student is so out of control that placing her in an ISS program will only make the situation worse for her and for the other students in the room. There is also the ubiquitous Out-of-School Suspension (OSS). We review these special suspension techniques and cases next.

Out-of-School Suspension

There is a place for OSS. However, this technique is frequently overused, especially for minor behavior problems. Other less-restrictive ISS techniques that we have reviewed are frequently more effective for these minor behavior problems. When is OSS warranted? If the behavior of a student is truly dangerous and threatening to other students or staff in the school, then OSS should be considered. Similarly, if a student violates the "safe school" standards of your district by bringing a weapon or controlled substances to the school, then OSS should be used. Many school districts now have zero-tolerance levels for safe school violations and mandate OSS for these behaviors. It should be noted that specific legal mandates governing the use of OSS differ for students with disabilities who have IEPs from those for students without disabilities. These mandates must be adhered to and are discussed in more detail in Section 5, the legal section of this Briefcase.

As we have said, we prefer not to use OSS for many problematic behaviors because it takes students out of their learning environment and often places them in unsupervised or undersupervised situations in the community.

For many students, this is *not* an undesired consequence. However, we suggested that a parent conference is needed before a student is allowed back in school for a number of situations:

- When a student consistently violates the rules in the ISS room and continues to be highly noncompliant
- When a student will not go to the suspension environment when repeatedly told to do so by staff
- When a student forges a teacher's initials on the Tracking Sheet
- When a student refuses to return to class after the suspension period

The suggested parental conference for readmission of the student is used as a last resort in these situations, and only after other options have been tried first.

Can OSS be completely eliminated? Probably not, because some school district policies call for it in certain situations, and a few situations do warrant it. But, OSS can be *dramatically* reduced. It should *not* be used as the first technique of choice for most problematic behavior. It should be used sparingly, and reserved for when student and staff safety are at stake. It is also appropriate as a last resort when a student continues to engage in intense, defiant behavior or continues to violate the rules in the less-restrictive forms of ISS we have suggested.

Explosive Crises

If a student has an explosive episode in school and continues to engage in out-of-control behavior, it is a mistake to use OCT, Lunchtime PTS, After-School PTS, or RISS. A student who continues such behavior will be disruptive in almost any school environment in which she is placed. It is *critical* to remain calm and unemotional and to talk slowly in a quiet voice when dealing with an out-of-control student. It is imperative to *not* threaten the student, argue with her, lecture her, or attempt to have the last word. **Model the very behavior you want from the student**—regardless of her behavior—and avoid getting into a power struggle with her!

- If you judge the situation to be one in which the student may be looking for a way out and is likely to comply, you may make a quiet, calm statement such as, "Let's go down to the office for a while"; "Come with me to the office"; or "I need you to come with me."
- If the situation is one in which the student may lose face by backing down, consider removing the other students and teachers who are nearby. You might say, "Mrs. Ruedas, this would be a good time to take the class to the library for a while" or "Mr. Evans, Callie and I need to have some time by ourselves. Please

ask these other students to go with you." Then, once the audience is gone, quietly and calmly ask the student to come with you. If the student does not respond, appear to remove your attention from the student for a few minutes, refrain from speaking, and make the request again. When the adult refrains from behaving in an angry manner and continues to talk slowly, quietly, and calmly, *even the most agitated student will usually deescalate after several interactions.*

- Once you have the student in the office, invite him to take a seat. You might simply say, "Please sit down," or "Have a seat and take a few minutes before we talk." After a nonconfrontive cooling-off period, it is likely the student will not only be more compliant and cooperative but also willing to discuss the problematic behavior.

Field Trip and Bus Problems

Problematic behavior during field trips or special activities in public places off the school campus can be daunting. Most of the time, it is impractical to use the techniques we have suggested when in public or while on trips. One approach we like is to buy a handheld tape recorder and have the adult in charge take it along on these occasions. If a student

> **Box 4-21**
>
> **Technique Hint**
>
> An effective, practical resource for administrator use with explosive, crisis situations is *Administrative Intervention*, developed by staff at Boys Town in Omaha, Nebraska (Black & Downs, 1993). The techniques illustrated in this book include how to handle the crisis, gain compliance from the student, and solve problems by teaching the appropriate social behavior the student should have used in the situation. All of this is accomplished through the *teaching interaction technique*, which also shapes and teaches an apology sequence for the student to deliver to the person involved in the original, upsetting incident. The Boys Town *Administrative Intervention* is an invaluable tool for use in both elementary and secondary settings. The program's effectiveness is well documented in the research.

has a temper tantrum, argues vehemently, or uses profane language, the adult turns on the tape recorder and records the incident. In many cases, the problematic behavior will stop right there! If not, after returning to school, have the student listen to herself on the tape recorder and then assign her to OCT or Lunchtime or After-School PTS. This will let students know that being off the school campus does not mean there are no undesired consequences for problematic behavior; the consequences may simply be delayed. If you do decide to use this technique, be sure the supervising adult explains it fully to students before leaving the school.

Box 4-22

Technique Hint

In some cases, it may be appropriate to play the taped episode for the student's parents.

A variation of this technique can be used on the school bus. Disruptive behaviors, arguing, and yelling can be recorded by the bus driver. The tape is then given to the student's teacher, and the procedures just outlined are carried out. We suggest that the recorded student with the problematic behavior be given a behavior Tracking Sheet to carry the next day. The bus driver also must initial the form, indicating the status of the student's behavior on the bus that day.

Recess Problems

When playground rules are broken at recess, it is not always convenient or practical to use the same time-out or ISS procedures that are used at other times. One approach is what we call Soda-Pop Bottle Suspension. Here is how to use this procedure:

- Gather two one-liter plastic soda-pop bottles that are empty and clean. Fill one with sand. Connect the bottles so that the two openings are touching, using a short plastic PVC connector pipe like the ones used with lawn sprinkler systems. Glue the bottles and PVC connector to each other securely. This will make a large hourglass-type fixture. (Repeat this procedure two more times to make three hourglass fixtures.)
- Spray-paint three circles in an out-of-the-way place on the playground. The area you select must be one that will be supervised.
- At the beginning of recess, place the three soda-pop bottle configurations inside the circles.
- If a student breaks recess rules, inform her that she has Soda-Pop Bottle Suspension. Escort her to one of the circles and ask her to turn over one of the bottle hourglasses, standing it on its empty-bottle end. Tell the student that when the sand finishes draining (this will take only a few minutes), she may ask the playground supervisor for permission to leave the circle and return to the regular recess activities. The student may leave the circle *only* after the playground supervisor excuses her.

Figure 4-8
Soda-Pop Bottle Suspension

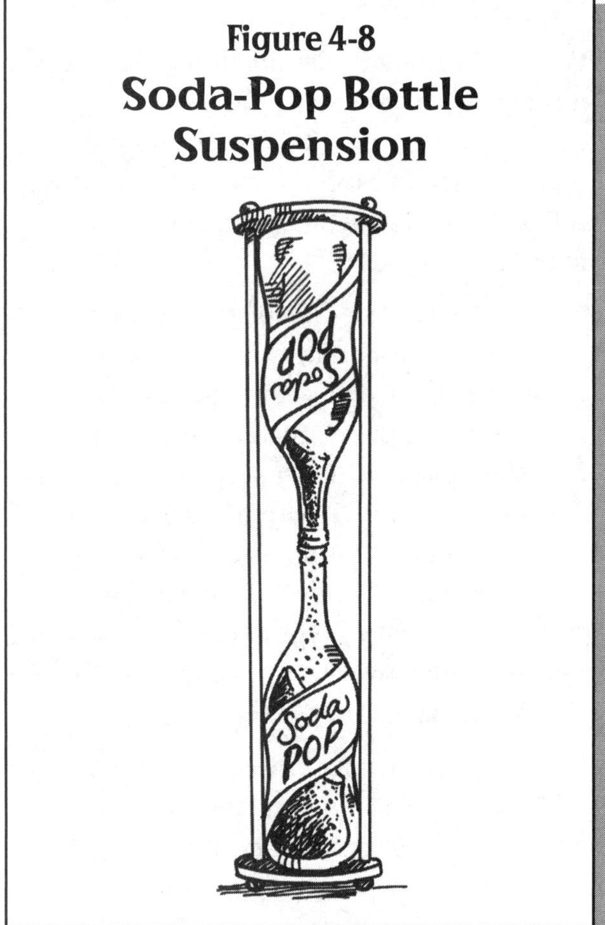

Lunchroom Problems

Lunchroom problems can involve noise levels, messes with food, or breaking school or lunchroom rules. For students who create problems in the lunchroom, a specific table can be designated for lunchroom suspension. This table should be as isolated as possible from other tables and must be supervised by an adult. The lunchroom suspension table has only three special rules:

1. Eat your lunch.
2. Stay in your assigned seat.
3. Do not interact, talk, or socialize with other students.

When students break lunchroom rules, remain excessively noisy after being given a warning, or purposely make a mess, they should be asked to take a seat at the designated table. We recommend that students who are assigned to the lunchroom suspension table spend the entire lunch period there, not leaving until they are excused by the supervising adult. Of course, students who have lunchroom problems can also be assigned to Lunchtime PTS instead of a designated table in the lunchroom.

Box 4-23
Technique Hint

The lunchroom suspension procedure is not designed for students who accidentally spill or drop food and are willing to clean up after themselves. It is for those students who throw or purposely spill or drop food or drinks or for students who accidentally make a mess but do not willingly clean it up.

Special School Suspension

This form of in-school suspension can be used for specific problems such as fighting, bullying, or anger management. Special School Suspension requires the student to attend a class where a specific lesson is taught to address the primary referral problem. For example, if fighting on the playground is a problem, then a student might be required to attend the Suspension School where recess rules are reviewed and alternatives to fighting and anger management are taught for the next three recess periods. An alternative for secondary students is to attend Suspension School for three consecutive lunch periods. In any case, the Suspension School should be assigned *as soon as possible* after the problematic behavior has occurred. Likewise, the required class sessions should take place close in time to each other.

When Special School Suspension is assigned, it is important to have a trained staff member (e.g., school psychologist, counselor, social worker) teach a well-defined, specific curriculum lesson for the problematic behavior (e.g., anger management, bullying). Effectiveness will also be enhanced if the staff member teaching the class assigns hands-on homework relating to the special curriculum lesson. Generally, Special School homework consists of students' practicing the strategies they have learned in the class *after* they have left for the day and *before* they attend the next session the following day. This means requiring students to try out the strategies in the real world in their own environments. The students then report back on their use of the strategies at the next class.

Restitution

This procedure requires students to compensate people or repair damage done during their problematic behavior. For example, cleaning graffiti off walls is a form of restitution for defacing them. Another is having students work in the school on some constructive task unrelated to the problematic behavior. For stealing, in addition to returning or replacing the stolen item, elementary students may be assigned to pick up trash on the playground. Secondary students may be required to pick up trash after games or special events. Sweeping the halls, weeding, or planting flowers are other options for making restitution. If a student has destroyed property and doesn't have the money to pay to replace what he has destroyed, these types of jobs can be assigned a certain dollar rate until the amount of the destroyed property is reached. The idea behind effective restitution is to have the student *make things even better* than they were before the problematic behavior occurred.

Community Service

This strategy involves the student working at a pre-approved agency to perform a needed task or service. Community service forms of suspension generally occur after school or on weekends. Community service may be of the student's choosing—and approved by the principal—or assigned to the student through a pre-approved agency to perform a specific task or service. It is not uncommon for community service to be ordered by a court as part of a sentence for illegal behavior that occurred on school property.

Work Crew

With this technique, the student works at an assigned task over a period of days. It can include restitution for damaging school property or part of a community service sentence because of an illegal behavior. With work crews, the student performs a specific task before school, after school, or on weekends under the direct supervision of an adult.

Modified Suspension

With this form of OSS, the student is permitted to attend a shortened school day for critical core academic classes. Generally, the student is not allowed to participate in lunch or extracurricular periods. This approach is particularly appropriate when a student has had serious behavioral difficulties during unstructured periods of time. It can also be used as an intermediate step for allowing a student to return to school after an OSS.

Saturday School

Saturday School requires the student to attend school on Saturday morning as the result of problematic behavior during the school week. (You may recall the use of Saturday School in the movie *The Breakfast Club*. Please don't run your Saturday School like this vice-principal did!) Although Saturday School can be effective, it has some limitations:

- It is not as effective as other ISS procedures outlined in this Briefcase.
- Its use delays implementation. A student who displays problematic behavior on Monday has to wait until Saturday for the undesired consequence.
- Saturday School requires at least two staff members to supervise on a valued weekend day.

> Box 4-24
>
> **Technique Hint**
>
> Suspension techniques are most effective when they occur immediately after the problematic behavior occurs.

Referral for Evaluation

Such referral for possible special education eligibility consists of evaluating learning potential (i.e., IQ), achievement, and social/emotional areas. This referral requires written parental permission. Initiated by the special education team, it notifies the parent that the student has been referred and the major area of educational concern. It also includes a Permission to Evaluate form, which must be signed and returned by the parent before the evaluation can begin.

Referral to Law Enforcement

At the principal's discretion, law enforcement in the local municipality may be contacted to investigate suspected violations of local, state, and federal law.

School Psychologist

Referrals to the school psychologist may be made for a specific purpose (e.g., to determine whether an effective classroom management system was in place in a classroom prior to an incident) or a more general purpose (e.g., to interview the student to determine whether other referrals should be made). When making a referral, be as specific as possible with the school psychologist as to what information you need.

School Violence Risk Assessment

Referrals for School Violence Risk Assessment should be made in the event that a student expresses homicidal thoughts or ideas toward school staff or other students. A principal should contact her district administrative supervisor to discuss the referral and obtain support to have it conducted. Referred students, pending parental or guardian consent, must complete a comprehensive psychiatric and psychological evaluation by qualified mental health professionals. It is recommended that these professionals include a licensed psychologist and a psychiatrist. A psychoeducational evaluation by the school's psychologist should be part of the assessment. The purpose of the assessment is to determine the level of risk posed by the identified student and to assist in determining an appropriate educational placement for the student.

Truancy School

Principals may want to establish an ongoing Truancy School to which they may assign students. The instructor—often a school counselor or psychologist—addresses goal setting, communication, and legal ramifications of truant behavior. Typically, the class meets once each week for three weeks after school hours. Parents of the students are required to attend.

Summary

Suspension is one of the most widely used and abused discipline techniques in schools today. In elementary schools, it has generally involved placement in the school's central office. In secondary schools, suspension has most often taken the form of Out-of-School Suspension. In these cases, suspension has often been viewed as "retribution" for problematic behavior, with no effort to assess how effectively it changes the problematic behavior. The emphasis is generally on having a student serve her time.

In this section, we emphasized that it is not appropriate to view suspension as retribution but rather to use it as a behavior management strategy. When implemented in this way, suspension can systematically reduce problematic behavior. Essential data are collected to assess its effectiveness. When data are evaluated regularly, areas in need of attention can be identified on an ongoing basis. Then, needed changes and adjustments can be made, maintaining and ensuring program effectiveness.

In effect, suspension is a time-out procedure whereby students are removed from a rewarding environment and placed in a less rewarding environment as a result of their problematic behavior. If the general school environment is punishing, frustrating, and negative for students, no amount of suspension will result in improved behavior. In fact, students will often purposely misbehave in order to be placed in suspension programs, particularly if they can avoid a negative school environment and be with their friends in suspension.

We also emphasized that when suspension techniques are used, every effort should be made to return the student to the instructional environment as soon as possible. If students spend long periods of time in suspension environments, they miss large amounts of valuable instructional time. Usually, they can ill afford to lose this time. Also, small amounts of suspension time are more effective than large amounts.

Suspension program use should be tailored to the severity of the problem behavior. In other words, we do not believe in using more restrictive forms of suspension for small, less severe behavior problems. We suggest viewing suspension on a gradient, along the dimensions of time and place. For less severe behavior problems, we recommend placing students in suspension programs close to the classroom. These programs include Other Class Time-Out or Prime Time Suspension, involving lunch or after-school time. For more serious problem behavior, we recommend a program that involves a longer time period and removal from the classroom (i.e., Restrictive In-school Suspension). The purpose of using suspension as a behavior management strategy is that the least restrictive form for the least amount of time will result in changing the student's behavior.

Other Class Time-Out Hall Pass

Student's Name ______

Sending Teacher ______

Receiving Teacher ______

Time Sent ______ Date ______

Other Class Time-Out Hall Pass

Student's Name ______

Sending Teacher ______

Receiving Teacher ______

Time Sent ______ Date ______

Other Class Time-Out Hall Pass

Student's Name ______

Sending Teacher ______

Receiving Teacher ______

Time Sent ______ Date ______

Other Class Time-Out Hall Pass

Student's Name ______

Sending Teacher ______

Receiving Teacher ______

Time Sent ______ Date ______

Other Class Time-Out Hall Pass

Student's Name ______

Sending Teacher ______

Receiving Teacher ______

Time Sent ______ Date ______

Other Class Time-Out Hall Pass

Student's Name ______

Sending Teacher ______

Receiving Teacher ______

Time Sent ______ Date ______

Other Class Time-Out Hall Pass

Student's Name ______

Sending Teacher ______

Receiving Teacher ______

Time Sent ______ Date ______

Other Class Time-Out Hall Pass

Student's Name ______

Sending Teacher ______

Receiving Teacher ______

Time Sent ______ Date ______

Other Class Time-Out Hall Pass

Student's Name ______

Sending Teacher ______

Receiving Teacher ______

Time Sent ______ Date ______

Other Class Time-Out Hall Pass

Student's Name ______

Sending Teacher ______

Receiving Teacher ______

Time Sent ______ Date ______

Other Class Time-Out
RETURN CONTRACT

My Name ____________________ Time ______ Date ______

Teacher Who Sent Me ____________________

Teacher Who Received Me ____________________

Problem behavior that earned my OTC____________________

____

What I will do next time instead ____________________

____

____

❑ (check) Yes, I am ready to go back to my own classroom.

❑ (check) I would like to talk to my teacher.

____

Student's Signature

Other Class Time-Out
RETURN CONTRACT

My Name ____________________ Time ______ Date ______

Teacher Who Sent Me ____________________

Teacher Who Received Me ____________________

Problem behavior that earned my OTC____________________

____

What I will do next time instead ____________________

____

____

❑ (check) Yes, I am ready to go back to my own classroom.

❑ (check) I would like to talk to my teacher.

____

Student's Signature

Prime Time Suspension	Prime Time Suspension
❑ Lunch ❑ After School	❑ Lunch ❑ After School
Name ______	Name ______
Date ______ Behavior ______	Date ______ Behavior ______
Assigned by ______ (see rules on back)	Assigned by ______ (see rules on back)
Prime Time Suspension	**Prime Time Suspension**
❑ Lunch ❑ After School	❑ Lunch ❑ After School
Name ______	Name ______
Date ______ Behavior ______	Date ______ Behavior ______
Assigned by ______ (see rules on back)	Assigned by ______ (see rules on back)
Prime Time Suspension	**Prime Time Suspension**
❑ Lunch ❑ After School	❑ Lunch ❑ After School
Name ______	Name ______
Date ______ Behavior ______	Date ______ Behavior ______
Assigned by ______ (see rules on back)	Assigned by ______ (see rules on back)
Prime Time Suspension	**Prime Time Suspension**
❑ Lunch ❑ After School	❑ Lunch ❑ After School
Name ______	Name ______
Date ______ Behavior ______	Date ______ Behavior ______
Assigned by ______ (see rules on back)	Assigned by ______ (see rules on back)
Prime Time Suspension	**Prime Time Suspension**
❑ Lunch ❑ After School	❑ Lunch ❑ After School
Name ______	Name ______
Date ______ Behavior ______	Date ______ Behavior ______
Assigned by ______ (see rules on back)	Assigned by ______ (see rules on back)

PTS Rules

Lunch PTS

- Show up on time.
- Bring your lunch, lunch ticket, or lunch money.
- Follow the supervisor's directions.
- Talk only with permission.
- Stay in your seat.

After School PTS

- Show up on time.
- Follow the supervisor's directions.
- Bring books, assignment & supplies.
- Talk only with permission.
- Stay in your seat.
- No food or drinks.
- Stay awake to receive credit.

PTS Rules

Lunch PTS

- Show up on time.
- Bring your lunch, lunch ticket, or lunch money.
- Follow the supervisor's directions.
- Talk only with permission.
- Stay in your seat.

After School PTS

- Show up on time.
- Follow the supervisor's directions.
- Bring books, assignment & supplies.
- Talk only with permission.
- Stay in your seat.
- No food or drinks.
- Stay awake to receive credit.

PTS Rules

Lunch PTS

- Show up on time.
- Bring your lunch, lunch ticket, or lunch money.
- Follow the supervisor's directions.
- Talk only with permission.
- Stay in your seat.

After School PTS

- Show up on time.
- Follow the supervisor's directions.
- Bring books, assignment & supplies.
- Talk only with permission.
- Stay in your seat.
- No food or drinks.
- Stay awake to receive credit.

PTS Rules

Lunch PTS

- Show up on time.
- Bring your lunch, lunch ticket, or lunch money.
- Follow the supervisor's directions.
- Talk only with permission.
- Stay in your seat.

After School PTS

- Show up on time.
- Follow the supervisor's directions.
- Bring books, assignment & supplies.
- Talk only with permission.
- Stay in your seat.
- No food or drinks.
- Stay awake to receive credit.

PTS Rules

Lunch PTS

- Show up on time.
- Bring your lunch, lunch ticket, or lunch money.
- Follow the supervisor's directions.
- Talk only with permission.
- Stay in your seat.

After School PTS

- Show up on time.
- Follow the supervisor's directions.
- Bring books, assignment & supplies.
- Talk only with permission.
- Stay in your seat.
- No food or drinks.
- Stay awake to receive credit.

PTS Rules

Lunch PTS

- Show up on time.
- Bring your lunch, lunch ticket, or lunch money.
- Follow the supervisor's directions.
- Talk only with permission.
- Stay in your seat.

After School PTS

- Show up on time.
- Follow the supervisor's directions.
- Bring books, assignment & supplies.
- Talk only with permission.
- Stay in your seat.
- No food or drinks.
- Stay awake to receive credit.

PTS Rules

Lunch PTS

- Show up on time.
- Bring your lunch, lunch ticket, or lunch money.
- Follow the supervisor's directions.
- Talk only with permission.
- Stay in your seat.

After School PTS

- Show up on time.
- Follow the supervisor's directions.
- Bring books, assignment & supplies.
- Talk only with permission.
- Stay in your seat.
- No food or drinks.
- Stay awake to receive credit.

PTS Rules

Lunch PTS

- Show up on time.
- Bring your lunch, lunch ticket, or lunch money.
- Follow the supervisor's directions.
- Talk only with permission.
- Stay in your seat.

After School PTS

- Show up on time.
- Follow the supervisor's directions.
- Bring books, assignment & supplies.
- Talk only with permission.
- Stay in your seat.
- No food or drinks.
- Stay awake to receive credit.

PTS Rules

Lunch PTS

- Show up on time.
- Bring your lunch, lunch ticket, or lunch money.
- Follow the supervisor's directions.
- Talk only with permission.
- Stay in your seat.

After School PTS

- Show up on time.
- Follow the supervisor's directions.
- Bring books, assignment & supplies.
- Talk only with permission.
- Stay in your seat.
- No food or drinks.
- Stay awake to receive credit.

PTS Rules

Lunch PTS

- Show up on time.
- Bring your lunch, lunch ticket, or lunch money.
- Follow the supervisor's directions.
- Talk only with permission.
- Stay in your seat.

After School PTS

- Show up on time.
- Follow the supervisor's directions.
- Bring books, assignment & supplies.
- Talk only with permission.
- Stay in your seat.
- No food or drinks.
- Stay awake to receive credit.

Lunchtime PTS
Master List

Supervisor____________________ Date____________________

Student's Name	Arrival Time	Tally of Rules Broken	Successful Completion?	Reassigned?
1.				
2.				
3.				
4.				
5.				
6.				
7.				
8.				
9.				
10.				
11				
12.				
13.				
14.				
15.				
16.				
17.				
18.				
19.				
20.				
21.				
22.				
23.				
24.				
25.				
26.				
27.				
28.				
29.				
30.				

SECONDARY PRIME TIME TRACKING SHEET

Behavior being tracked:			
Name:		Date:	
PERIODS	Behavior Rating (Circle One)	Teacher Initials	COMMENTS
1.	Acceptable Unacceptable		
2.	Acceptable Unacceptable		
3.	Acceptable Unacceptable		
4.	Acceptable Unacceptable		
5.	Acceptable Unacceptable		
6.	Acceptable Unacceptable		
7.	Acceptable Unacceptable		

THIS SHEET MUST BE RETURNED TO THE TRACKING SHEET SUPERVISOR AT THE END OF THE SCHOOL DAY BEFORE GOING HOME.

SECONDARY PRIME TIME TRACKING SHEET

Behavior being tracked:			
Name:		Date:	
PERIODS	Behavior Rating (Circle One)	Teacher Initials	COMMENTS
1.	Acceptable Unacceptable		
2.	Acceptable Unacceptable		
3.	Acceptable Unacceptable		
4.	Acceptable Unacceptable		
5.	Acceptable Unacceptable		
6.	Acceptable Unacceptable		
7.	Acceptable Unacceptable		

THIS SHEET MUST BE RETURNED TO THE TRACKING SHEET SUPERVISOR AT THE END OF THE SCHOOL DAY BEFORE GOING HOME.

ELEMENTARY PRIME TIME TRACKING SHEET			
Behavior being tracked:			
Name:			**Date:**
Times	**Behavior Rating** (Circle One)	**Teacher Initials**	**COMMENTS**
1. Start of School	OK Not OK		
2. After AM Recess	OK Not OK		
3. After Lunch	OK Not OK		
4. After PM Recess	OK Not OK		

ELEMENTARY PRIME TIME TRACKING SHEET			
Behavior being tracked:			
Name:			**Date:**
Times	**Behavior Rating** (Circle One)	**Teacher Initials**	**COMMENTS**
1. Start of School	OK Not OK		
2. After AM Recess	OK Not OK		
3. After Lunch	OK Not OK		
4. After PM Recess	OK Not OK		

After-School PTS
Master List

Supervisor________________________________ Date________________________________

Student's Name	Arrival Time	Tally of Rules Broken	Successful Completion?	Reassigned?	Release Time	Released To	Parent Instructions Followed?
1.							
2.							
3.							
4.							
5.							
6.							
7.							
8.							
9.							
10.							
11							
12.							
13.							
14.							
15.							
16.							
17.							
18.							
19.							
20.							
21.							
22.							
23.							
24.							
25.							
26.							
27.							
28.							
29.							
30.							

Request for Assignment

____
(Teacher's Name)

_________________________ has been assigned to RISS today. Please send the assignment for ____________________
Date

to the office as soon as possible so that the student can work on it while making up the RISS time.

Thank you for your help.

Request for Assignment

____
(Teacher's Name)

_________________________ has been assigned to RISS today. Please send the assignment for ____________________
Date

to the office as soon as possible so that the student can work on it while making up the RISS time.

Thank you for your help.

Request for Assignment

____
(Teacher's Name)

_________________________ has been assigned to RISS today. Please send the assignment for ____________________
Date

to the office as soon as possible so that the student can work on it while making up the RISS time.

Thank you for your help.

Request for Assignment

____
(Teacher's Name)

_________________________ has been assigned to RISS today. Please send the assignment for ____________________
Date

to the office as soon as possible so that the student can work on it while making up the RISS time.

Thank you for your help.

Request for Assignment

____
(Teacher's Name)

_________________________ has been assigned to RISS today. Please send the assignment for ____________________
Date

to the office as soon as possible so that the student can work on it while making up the RISS time.

Thank you for your help.

Request for Assignment

____
(Teacher's Name)

_________________________ has been assigned to RISS today. Please send the assignment for ____________________
Date

to the office as soon as possible so that the student can work on it while making up the RISS time.

Thank you for your help.

ABC-RISS Sheet

Student's Name ______________________ Date ____________

Teacher's Name ______________________ Date ____________

A Antecedent—What was going on before the behavior?

- Time ______________________
- People ______________________
- Place ______________________
- Event(s) ______________________
- Student's Behavior ______________________
- Down Time ______________________
- Other ______________________

B Behavior—Describe the problematic behavior very specifically, in objective terms, based on what was observed.

____

____

C Consequences—What happened after the problematic behavior occurred? Specifically describe.

- Positive or negative attention from peers or adults ______________________

  ____
- Obtained tangible item ______________________
- Escaped a person, situation, or place ______________________

  ____
- Avoided a person, situation or place ______________________

  ____
- Other ______________________

R Replacement Behavior—What does the student need to do instead?

____

Comments: ______________________

Form filled out by ______________________

Section 5

Legal Issues and Solutions

Whose Job Is This Anyway?

- One of your favorite teachers makes the evening news because she duct-tapes a plastic bag full of cat feces to a student's desk as punishment for using profane language.
- The assistant principal has a sexual assault charge filed against him for "patting down" a female student suspected of possessing drugs.
- Your custodian loses his cool and "gets into it" with a student who is kicking the Coke machine that ate his money.
- You suspend several students for sexual harassment. One of them is protected under Section 504 and files a complaint with the Office for Civil Rights for disparate discipline.
- The superintendent calls you to check out the allegation that your special education teacher is locking students in "coffins."
- A student in your diesel mechanics class urinates in the corner of the shop. When he fails to comply with several requests to clean it up, the teacher does it, using the student as a mop.
- A student with Asperger's syndrome drops his pants in calculus class for who-knows-what reason. You suspend the student for three days until the special education IEP Team can meet and adjust his program. The student's father—who is an attorney (of course)—informs you that you cannot suspend his son for any reason because the

behavior is a direct manifestation of his disability.

Sound familiar? We could go on. These are all situations that have actually happened. If you are a principal and you haven't had any of these experiences yet, rest assured that it is only a matter of time. When the media call about your teacher, the police investigate the assistant principal, Child Protective Services looks into the situation with the custodian, the Office for Civil Rights shows up for an on-site investigation, the superintendent demands an explanation at the board meeting, the attorney subpoenas information, or a hostile parent starts browbeating you over your special education procedures, whom do you think they will ultimately hold responsible? That's right. You, the PRINCIPAL! Stay tuned, however; help is on the way in this section.

Answers to Common but Tricky Questions

We start by answering some of the most common, but tricky, questions you are likely to encounter in your role as principal.

General School Questions

Question: ***Can a school require that students be tested for drugs?***

Answer: Yes, in *some* circumstances. Suspicionless drug testing was recently upheld by the Supreme Court (*Board of Education of Independent School District No. 92 of Pottawatomie County et al. v. Earls*, 2002). Under this decision, random testing of students participating in extracurricular, competitive activities is permissible under the Constitution so long as the testing procedures are reasonable. Courts are currently divided on the issue of whether random drug testing of students in other extracurricular activities is allowed (*Vernonia School District v. Acton*, 1995; *Todd v. Rush County Schools*, 1998; *Trinidad School Dist. No. 1 v. Lopez*, 1998). Principals are cautioned not to act without the direction of their school district's policy with respect to drug testing. Such a policy must include:

- The rationale for initiating drug testing
- Specific definition of the groups to be tested, including the frequency and numbers
- Methods to be used
- Costs, and who is responsible for those costs

- A system in place to counsel students and parents
- Procedures to sanction those who test positive

Question: ***Can a school establish a dress code?***

Answer: School boards have the right to establish dress codes. Principals should defer to their school boards to decide what constitutes appropriate dress in their communities, within constitutional limits. Courts have traditionally left these types of decisions up to the reasonable discretion of local school boards and typically determine only whether there is a reasonable basis for the dress code. However, clothing or speech that is vulgar, indecent, lewd, or plainly offensive may be banned in schools (*Bethel School District v. Fraser*, 1986). The citizens of the community, through their elected representatives on the school board along with the school officials appointed by them, make the decision as to what is vulgar, indecent, lewd, or plainly offensive clothing or speech. People will always differ about the level of crudeness that should be tolerated before a school principal acts. However, it is the job of the principal to make the call as to what would be offensive to a reasonable person in his community.

Question: ***Can a school ban blue (or whatever color) hair?***

Answer: Caution! The Fourteenth Amendment guarantees individuals the right to exercise control over personal appearance. Check, or ask your district's attorney to check, case law in your circuit before banning certain hairstyles or colors. They must be perceived as *clearly disruptive* before disciplinary action can be taken.

Question: ***Can a student be banned from distributing literature (e.g., religious, political, sexual) messages on the school campus?***

Answer: *Use extreme caution!* The legal decision in *Tinker v. Des Moines Independent School District* (1969) states that, "students do not shed their constitutional rights at the front door and enjoy, to a great extent, the right to express themselves in school." However, students' rights to free speech are not absolute. School officials *do* have the authority to place certain restrictions on students' First Amendment rights. The court in the *Tinker* case established that schools can restrict speech if the speech causes a material and substantive disruption to the school environment. Before taking action to limit free speech on

your campus, check your district's policy and consult a district-level administrator and possibly legal counsel. In recent years, there has been a wide range of tolerance in our society, backed up by case law.

Question: ***What is the legal standard for a hostile educational environment?***

Answer: Under federal civil rights law, a hostile educational environment exists only when the student making the complaint is a member of a protected class (i.e., a racial minority or a student with disabilities). The student must show that he has been subjected to unwelcome communication or behavior that substantially interferes with his education or creates an intimidating, hostile, or offensive educational environment. In order to prevail in his claims, the student must prove that the district failed to rectify the problem after receiving adequate notice and that there is a continuing problem.

Question: ***A coach cuts a player (a Section 504 eligible student) from the baseball team for lack of teamwork and a poor attitude. Does this amount to discrimination under Section 504?***

Answer: The coach must have a *legitimate, nondiscriminatory* reason for cutting the student from the team. If the coach can produce evidence that similar students without disabilities have been cut for the same reason, there is then a rationale for the action that is nondiscriminatory. The student cannot be cut solely on the basis of his disability. However, the coach should maintain written documentation of everything concerning his actions.

Question: ***What should you do if a parent hangs around the school excessively, day after day (e.g., the parent wants to know everything a teacher is doing in class, spends time in the faculty lounge, and so on)?***

Answer: While parental involvement in students' education is almost always encouraged, there are cases today where parental over-involvement is a major problem! We know of one parent who camped out in a school day after day, attempting to dictate every detail of her daughter's school day. This parent spent hours in the faculty room and lay down in front of doorways and in foyers, crying and wailing that school officials were insensitive to her needs. Fortunately, cases even remotely resembling this one are still the exception; however, they seem to be occurring with increasing frequency and can cause extreme disruption in a school. There are specific days and instances when parents and other relatives are invited and encouraged to come to school to participate in some way with their children. Parents may also be invited to attend meetings with school staff for a particular purpose. **Under state and federal law—including the Individuals with Disabilities Education Improvement Act (IDEA) of 2004—parents and guardians do NOT have the right to attend school with their children.** Certainly, parents can be invited by a teacher or a school to observe or assist in a classroom or other setting. Rules implemented by school administrators should clearly indicate that consent to be present at school may be withdrawn without notice and that a parent's continued presence at the school after consent has been withdrawn will be dealt with under state and local laws relating to trespassing. See *Table 5-1* for more information about parents who hang around the school.

Threats

Question: ***How do you determine whether a student makes a* serious *threat?***

Answer: Courts have consistently held that for speech or expression to be considered threatening, others who hear or read the alleged threat must reasonably consider that a threat has been made. In the ninth circuit, it was determined that speech or expression is a threat if a reasonable person would view the alleged threat to the person to whom it was communicated as a serious expression of intent to harm or assault (*Lovell v. Poway Unified School District*, 1996). This decision demonstrates that the courts are often willing to give school officials the benefit of the doubt when they use their best judgment to protect the safety of the school community.

Table 5-1

When Parents Hang Around the School

Permitted access to a part of the school does not mean access to *all* areas of the school. The principal can restrict visitor access to only those parts of the school that are reasonably associated with the purpose of the visit. For example, access to attend a basketball game does not mean access to areas of the school that are not immediately adjacent to the gymnasium.

Access to public school property and activities is governed by law, including the U.S. Constitution, federal and state statutes, and local government ordinances. Local school administrators are encouraged to become familiar with these laws and ordinances so they can act with confidence in developing guidelines and implementing procedures relating to access of schools and school activities.

The principal has the authority to limit or control access to any school facility or activity carried out under his direction. This includes authority to take reasonable steps to prevent contraband from being transported onto school grounds or to a school-sponsored activity. The principal also has the right to restrict or prohibit access by individuals who are not specifically authorized or required by law to be present on school grounds or at school activities.

Question: ***Can a school discipline a student for creating a threatening Web site?***

Answer: School officials have justifiable reason to discipline a student who expresses a serious threat to the safety of those in the school environment or to cause serious harm, even if the expression did not originate at school. This can include a threatening Web site. School officials must assess the meaning of the information and carefully consider the protections given to student speech and expression. However, creating a derogatory Web site is not, in and of itself, illegal. The line is crossed with a Web site when it rises to the level of the legal definition of defamation of character. Basically, if a Web site does not pose a serious threat to someone's safety, the site's creator can say anything she wants to say about anyone. If the Web site content does rise to the level of defamation of character, however, there may be legal consequences.

Attorneys

Question: ***If an attorney shows up unexpectedly for a meeting (e.g., an IEP meeting for a special education student or any other kind of meeting), what should you do?***

Answer: Inform the visiting attorney that the school will require representation also. Give him the name and number of the district's attorney and tell him that all interaction between him and the district's attorney must go through the proper channels. If this does not persuade the visiting attorney from sitting in on the meeting, let all parties know that the meeting must be scheduled for another time when the district's counsel can be present.

> **Box 5-1**
>
> Principals have little to gain and *much to lose* by trying to meet alone with attorneys. Get backup from your school district when attorneys unexpectedly show up and try to participate in your meetings.

Question: ***If a visiting attorney gets belligerent and browbeats your staff, what can you do?***

Answer: Above all, do not become emotionally involved. Insist firmly, but politely, that the tone must remain civil. If the tone persists after making this request a maximum of two times, end the meeting, and reschedule it.

"And if you can't afford an attorney we will supply one for you at no cost."

Gay and Lesbian Students

Question: ***Are gay and lesbian students protected under Section 504?***

Answer: Sexual orientation is specifically excluded from protection under Section 504. However, examine your state and district policies closely to determine whether sexual orientation has been included in them. Whether protected under Section 504 or not, sexual orientation should be covered in district harassment policies. Complaints and bullying based on sexual orientation must be taken seriously. School administrators put themselves at risk for liability if they are indifferent to complaints based on sexual orientation.

Question: ***Must a school allow clubs for gay/straight alliances?***

Answer: *The Equal Access Act* (EAA; 1984), forbids schools that have allowed a "limited open forum" from denying access for meetings based on religious, political, or any other content. Schools that allow one noncurriculum club to meet on school grounds have created a limited open forum and must then allow any other club to meet. To deny access to a student group, the school must demonstrate that at least one of the following is true:

- The meeting would materially and substantially interfere with the orderly educational activities in the school
- The meeting would be a threat to order, discipline, and the well-being of students

Court cases have shown that this burden of proof is very difficult for schools to demonstrate. Therefore, the only sure way to disallow some student clubs is to disallow *all* nonacademic student clubs. The text of the *Equal Access Act* can be viewed online at http://www.usdoj.gov/crt/cor/byagency/ed4071.htm// and at http://www4.law.cornell.edu/uscode/20/.

Zero-Tolerance Policies

Question: ***Are harsh penalties imposed under a school's or school district's zero-tolerance policy unconstitutional in that they amount to "cruel and unusual punishment" under the Eighth Amendment?***

Answer: The school or district must satisfy all of its due process obligations to the student, including those pertaining to notification and a hearing. Once this has been completed, courts have generally ruled in favor of school districts, even if the punishments are extremely harsh (*Ratner v. Loudon County Public Schools*, 2001). Keep in mind that the due process provisions are different for special education students protected under IDEA and other students protected under Section 504.

The Family Educational Rights and Privacy Act (FERPA)

FERPA, a federal law, is the acronym for the Family Educational Rights and Privacy Act (1974). FERPA defines "educational records" as records that are directly related to the student and maintained by a school. A "record" itself, as defined by FERPA, is "any information recorded in any way, including, but not limited to, handwriting, print, computer, media, video or audio tape, film, microfilm, and microfiche." Under FERPA, schools cannot release information other than "directory information" without prior written notice to the parents.

IDEA (2004) for special education students also incorporates and references FERPA. It provides for additional privacy protections for students who receive special education and related services. In particular, when special education students reach the age of majority at 18—and their rights under IDEA transfer from their parents to them—their rights regarding educational records also transfer. However, a school must provide any notice specified under the due process requirements of IDEA to *both* the student and the parents after this transfer takes place (*Letter to Schaffer*, 2000).

Answers to Commonly Asked FERPA Questions

Question: ***What is directory information?***

Answer: Directory information is information about a student that is not generally considered to be harmful or an invasion of privacy. Directory information includes but is not limited to:

- Name, address, telephone number, and e-mail address
- Date and place of birth
- Photographs from school publications
- Participation in officially recognized activities
- Field of study
- Weight and height of athletes
- Enrollment status (full-time or part-time)
- Degrees and awards received
- Dates of school attendance
- Most recent, previous school attended
- Grade level

Directory information cannot include student numbers, social security numbers, or status of a student as to disability, race, national origin, limited English proficiency, poverty, or homelessness.

Question: ***Are there any exceptions to education records?***

Answer: Records kept in the "sole possession" of the maker of the record and not revealed to anyone else are not considered educational records. For example, notes about a student made by a school psychologist in his daily planner *that have not been shared with anyone* else are not considered educational records. The minute the notes are shared with anyone, however, they become educational records.

Question: ***Under what conditions do you have to obtain a parent's consent before education records may be disclosed?***

Answer: Except for specific exceptions, a parent must provide a signed and dated written consent before the school may disclose the child's education records. The consent must:

- Specify the records to be disclosed;
- State the purpose of the disclosure; and
- Identify to whom the disclosure may be made.

Question: ***Are disciplinary records protected?***

Answer: The U.S. Department of Education has consistently held that discipline records are education records (*Letter to Watkins*, 2003; *Letter to Pasadena Unified School District*, 1999). However, many state and district courts have held that they are not (*Hardin County Schools v. Foster*, 2001). More recently, courts have found that FERPA preempts state law (*Caledonian-Record Publishing Co. Inc. v. Vermont State Colleges*, 2003; *Rim of the World Unified School Dist. v. Superior Court of the County of San Bernardino*, 2002). Given these decisions, it is advisable to treat discipline records as protected records.

Question: ***May disciplinary records be transferred to another school?***

Answer: Sometimes. FERPA states that nothing within it prevents a district from including appropriate information concerning disciplinary action taken against a student for conduct that posed a significant risk to the safety or well-being of that student, other students, or members of the community. School officials must use good judgment in determining what behavior constitutes a significant risk. Under the No Child Left Behind Act (2001), school districts must have a procedure in place for the transfer of disciplinary records regarding suspension and expulsion to any school for any student who is enrolled or wishes to attend the school.

Question: ***Are law enforcement records protected under FERPA?***

Answer: Law enforcement records are *not* education records under FERPA. Law enforcement records can be disclosed to others without parental consent. They are records that are created by a law enforcement unit, for a law enforcement purpose, and maintained by the law enforcement unit.

Question: ***Are there any times when a parent's prior written consent is not required?***

Answer: Education records are permitted to be disclosed without a parent's prior written consent:

- To school officials with a legitimate educational need to know
- To schools in which a student seeks or intends to enroll
- To federal, state, and local educational authorities conducting an audit
- In connection with financial aid, such as for college
- To organizations conducting studies on behalf of schools
- To comply with a court order or subpoena (a reasonable effort should be made to notify the parent)
- To a state's juvenile justice agency
- In the event of a health or safety emergency (If a principal is approached by a community agency representative who demands a student's education records, insist that he provide a letter on his agency's letterhead requesting the records and including a justification of the health or safety issue.)

Question: ***What do you do if you receive a subpoena or a court order to produce documents?***

Answer: FERPA allows a district to disclose protected information to a court if a judge requests the records or issues a subpoena. In this case, the school must attempt to notify the parent in order to give the parent an opportunity to seek protective action.

Question: ***Do noncustodial parents have FERPA rights to inspect their children's education records?***

Answer: Schools must give *full* FERPA rights to *both* parents, unless one of the parents provides a copy of a court order or other legally binding document, such as a divorce decree, that specifically states otherwise.

Question: ***What happens when a student turns 18?***

Answer: Generally, parents lose their FERPA rights when their child turns 18. At that point, the student is considered an "eligible student" and becomes entitled to all of the FERPA rights. However, FERPA allows a school to disclose education records to parents if the student is considered a dependent under Section 152 of the Internal Revenue Code. The provisions of the federal tax law find an elementary or secondary school student to be a dependent when the parents provide more than half of his support.

Question: ***If a parent demands a copy of his child's education records "right now," do you have to drop everything and copy them?***

Answer: No. A school has up to 45 calendar days to provide educational records once they have been requested. However, we suggest that you provide them as soon as is practical. Basically, there should be nothing secret in education records. You may charge a reasonable cost for the copies. However, if charging the parent effectively prevents him from receiving the copies he has requested (e.g., he has a low income), you should not charge for them.

Question: ***If a parent demands that something be taken out of his child's file, do you have to comply?***

Answer: Maybe. A parent should identify the portion of the record he believes contains inaccurate or misleading information. You must then decide within a reasonable time whether to change the record as requested. If you decide not to change the record, you must inform the parent of his right to a hearing. You are the designated "records manager" in the school, unless the school district has appointed someone else to make these decisions. A good guideline to use is if the information is not critical to the education records, take it out and do not argue about it. Remember: It is always important to document the request regardless of your decision!

Question: ***May parents inspect and review test protocols?***

Answer: If a student receives special education services, the Office for Special Education Programs (OSEP) states that a parent has the right to inspect and review, but not obtain copies of, their child's test protocols. This right does not extend to blank test protocols that have not yet been used for the child.

Question: *May parents of a victimized child be informed of the results of a school's investigation, as well as the disciplinary action taken against the other student, without violating FERPA?*

Answer: As an administrator, you must assure parents that "appropriate action has been taken." Parents who request such information may inspect, review, or be informed of only the specific information related to their child's records. Disciplinary records containing other students' names must be appropriately edited prior to their release.

Question: *Is media-taping or photographing students a violation of FERPA?*

Answer: No. Video or audio images of students are not education records. Education records are "records, files, documents and other materials that contain information directly related to the student and are maintained by an education agency." FERPA does not establish an individual right to privacy in this case.

Box 5-2
Technique Hint

Caution! Take care in circumstances where students are photographed and identified as having disabilities in the presence of other students who also have disabilities (e.g., they are IDEA eligible). Doing so discloses that others in the room are also eligible, and eligibility is considered an education record.

Question: *Is "peer grading" a violation of FERPA?*

Answer: No. The U.S. Supreme Court decision *Falvo v. Owasso* (2002) stated:

> The federal statute that prohibits release of student education records without parental consent does not outlaw the practice of "peer grading," in which students score each other's tests and papers.

However, the decision did *not* give the go-ahead for teachers to post graded work with student names or to ask students to call out their scores. These practices should be avoided. Similarly, teachers should treat grade books and student work confidentially.

Box 5-3
Additional FERPA Resources for Principals

Technical assistance and advice for principals:

Family Policy Compliance Office
U.S. Department of Education
400 Maryland Ave., SW
Washington, DC 20202-5920
(202) 260-3887

Informal technical assistance:
FERPA@ed.gov

Web site: www.ed.gov/policy/gen/guid/fpco/ferpa/index.html

Parent and Guardian Custody Issues

The right of parents to exercise control over their children's education is a fundamental, constitutional right. Parental rights in traditional families are usually fairly straightforward. However, such families are fast becoming the exception, not the rule! In nontraditional families, the right of a parent or guardian regarding a child's education may be affected by custody orders. Principals need to be aware of laws governing which parent has the legal authority to make educational decisions.

Custody issues are significant for IDEA-eligible students as well. Parents of students with disabilities have a right to participate in their children's evaluation, program development, and educational placement.

> **Box 5-4**
>
> **Definitions**
>
> **Parent:** Mother, father, or legal guardian.
>
> **Custody:** The legal right and responsibility for raising a child and personally supervising the child's upbringing, especially the right to keep the child in a residence.
>
> **Guardian *ad litem* (Lat. "guardian at law"):** The person appointed by the court to look out for the best interests of the child during the course of legal proceedings.
>
> **Parent under IDEA:** Students with disabilities are subject to the definition of "parent" under IDEA:
>
> - Natural or adoptive parents
> - Guardian (other than the state, for children who are wards of the state)
> - Person acting in the place of a parent
> - Surrogate parent
> - Foster parent (in some states)

Answers to Parent and Guardian Questions

Question: ***When can a foster parent be considered a parent?***

Answer: A state may allow a foster parent to act as a parent for a student with a disability under IDEA if both the following are true:

- The natural parents have relinquished their right to do so
- The foster parent has an ongoing, long-term parental relationship, is willing to make the educational decisions, and has no conflict of interest

Question: ***Who can be a "person acting as a parent"?***

Answer: A person can act as a parent if he has an ongoing, long-term parental relationship, is willing to make the educational decisions, and has no conflict of interest. Such a person might be a grandparent, a stepparent with whom the child lives, or a person who has been designated by the state as responsible for the child. For students who are IDEA-eligible, states may expand or limit their definition of "persons acting as parents."

Question: ***What should the district do about students who live with relatives?***

Answer: States and local school districts have the discretion to allow an aunt, uncle, grandparent, or sibling over the age of 21 to act as a guardian. Typically, a relative must have a universally recognizable familial label, such as stepparent or other blood relative.

Question: ***Are parental rights always transferred to the student at the age of majority?***

Answer: Upon reaching the age of majority (i.e., 18 years old), if a student is a dependent under the U.S. tax code, his parents maintain the right to receive all notices sent by the school district. Under such circumstances, they also have the right to access the student's educational records. They do not, however, retain the right to make educational decisions for the student. Parental rights are transferred to the student, unless he has been found incompetent by a court.

Question: ***Which school district has responsibility for educating a student when the noncustodial parent lives in a different school district?***

Answer: A student's school district of residence is that of the custodial parent, regardless of whether he is in general education or IDEA-eligible. That school district is responsible for his educational costs, unless another adult has been assigned by a court as his legal guardian. For a student with disabilities, the district in which the noncustodial parent lives has no responsibility to contribute to the expense of the student's educational program in the custodial parent's school district.

"I'm Rocky's dad, I got custody, and I'm taking Rocky to Sturgis for two weeks."

Question: ***What are the rights of divorced parents who share joint legal and physical custody?***

Answer: Parents who share equally in the legal and physical custody of their child have equal rights to make educational decisions on the child's behalf, unless a court order specifies otherwise. This is also the case for IDEA-eligible children. See *Table 5-2* for an explanation of the types of child custody.

Box 5-5

Types of Child Custody

Legal Custody: Legal custody is the "bundle" of rights, duties, and responsibilities of a parent regarding the child. All significant decisions made for a child are made by a parent with legal custody. Custody agreements approved by a court, sometimes known as *decrees*, may be present if a parental couple is separated, divorced, has never been married, or is no longer living together.

Physical Custody: Physical custody is the right of a parent to have the child live in the same residence as the parent.

Sole Custody: Sole custody means that only the *custodial* parent has physical, as well as legal, custody of a child. The noncustodial parent has visitation rights, although not always.

Joint Custody: Joint custody means that parents live separately but share the physical and legal custody of their child. The details of exactly how the physical and legal custody are blended are specified in the couple's divorce decree. When disputes arise, school officials must examine the stipulations of the divorce decree.

Table 5-2

Noncustodial Parents' Participation in Educational Decisions

A noncustodial parent is not entitled to participate in educational decisions and processes related to general education or IDEA, unless the custodial parent agrees to the participation.

Examples of educational decisions:

- Medical decisions
- Emergency contact
- Medication administration
- Permission to participate in extracurricular activities
- Checkout or pick-up from school
- Permission for field trip participation
- Dietary restrictions
- Classroom accommodations
- Disciplinary actions
- Schedule changes
- Notification of meetings
- Consultation with teachers
- Enrollment in school
- School visitations, unless invited to a specific activity

Examples of educational decisions related to IDEA:

- Consent for initial evaluation
- Consent for initial placement
- Notification requirements
- Participation in IEP team decisions

Conducting Investigations in the School Setting

What course work did you take to prepare for conducting investigations in the school setting? Conducting an investigation properly may be one of the most overlooked aspects of a school administrator's formal and informal training. Thorough knowledge about conducting an investigation is needed to provide a factual basis for all kinds of important—and possibly controversial—decision-making. Such decision-making includes that related to determining appropriate disciplinary consequences, other necessary administrative action, and referrals to law enforcement. During an investigation, enough information must be gathered to direct and support decision-making. An investigation may be triggered by:

- Misconduct
- Allegations of sexual harassment
- Destruction of property
- Drug or alcohol issues
- Safety concerns
- Theft
- Possible violations of the law

An investigation provides documentation for justifying decisions, possible litigation, and graduated disciplinary actions.

Who Conducts School Investigations?

Investigations in schools should be initiated by the building principal or appropriate district-level administrators. Generally, the principal or assistant principal is responsible for conducting investigations at the school level.

However, other employees may be designated by the administration as investigators. It is critical for investigators to:

- Respect the privacy rights of students, parents, and employees while gathering enough factual information to support or dismiss a presenting issue
- Collect information in a timely manner while ensuring thoroughness
- Protect the legal rights of all those who are involved

What Are Some of the Legal Bases for Conducting Investigations?

There may be many legal reasons for conducting investigations. We describe a few of them here.

1. **Discrimination**—Federal and state laws prohibit discrimination and harassment

based on race, religion, color, national origin, ancestry, disability, medical condition, marital status, age, and sex. Title VII of the Civil Rights Act (1964), the Americans with Disabilities Act (1990), and the Age Discrimination in Employment Act (1967) all create a risk of liability if a school district knew or should have known about a possible violation and failed to act on it. Liability may be limited by conducting a timely, thorough investigation and then taking appropriate action.

2. **Safety and Health**—Federal and state laws regulate health and safety in schools and impose a duty on school officials to investigate accidents and reports of safety concerns. Two of them are:
   - The Occupational Safety and Health Administration (OSHA) of 1965, which requires school officials to do whatever is reasonably necessary to protect the safety and health of employees and students
   - Workers' Compensation programs that require school officials to document accidents in the workplace leading to workers' compensation claims
3. **Safe and Drug-Free Schools**—The Safe and Drug-Free Schools (SDFS) Act of 2001 requires school officials to provide an educational environment that is free of alcohol, drugs, and weapons.

What Are Some Pitfalls to Avoid?

Before conducting an investigation, you should be aware of some of the common pitfalls. These include:

1. **Privacy**—Federal and state laws seek to balance the interests of school officials to maintain a safe and orderly educational setting with the rights to privacy and free expression by students and employees. Students and employees are protected by the U.S. Constitution, statutes, and common law that can all impact a school investigation. As you conduct an investigation, inform all individuals you interview that disclosure on their part of private facts relevant to the case under investigation may be an invasion of privacy. Also, explain to them that such disclosure may result in personal liability. Along the same lines, investigators must not reveal details of the *investigation to any witnesses or other employees*.
2. **Defamation**—During an investigation, school officials may be given false or damaging information about others by the people they are interviewing. School officials generally have *qualified privilege* to pass on defamatory information to others who have a legitimate need to know. This privilege does not extend to information disclosed to others who do *not* have a legitimate need to know. Thus, investigators as well as witnesses should be discouraged from disclosing information regarding the investigation to others who do not have the need to know.
3. **False Imprisonment**—False imprisonment involves confining or restraining another individual. Be aware that the risk of liability for false imprisonment may exist during an investigation. Students may claim false imprisonment if they are restrained, detained, locked in a room, or blocked from leaving a room.

Box 5-6

Technique Hint

Immediately contact the police in cases involving safety issues when a student refuses to submit to questioning or a search. Do ***not*** attempt to physically coerce the student to comply with a demand.

4. **Assault and Battery**—Remember: One person's idea of discipline may be another person's idea of assault and battery. Assault is considered to have occurred when an individual *fears* that an investigator is going to harm him physically. Battery is considered to have taken place when harmful touching occurs. Avoid claims of assault and battery by maintaining a professional demeanor, limiting physical contact with the student, and arranging for a witness to be present during all of your interviews.

How You Can Prepare for the Investigation?

Whenever considering conducting an investigation, work through the steps outlined here before the investigation begins. See *Table 5-3* for a summary of the 11 steps.

1. **Determine the need for an investigation.** Determining whether to conduct an investigation is a significant decision. Investigations take time, disrupt the educational environment, and often do not turn out the way you thought they would. The success of an investigation is determined by how fairly all participants think they have been treated. If, as a school administrator, you have already investigated an issue and a school patron or employee remains dissatisfied, this may be the time to ask your district office to conduct an independent investigation

Table 5-3

Preparing for an Investigation

1. Determine whether there is a need for an investigation, and be able to articulate that need.
2. Determine the specific objective of the investigation.
3. Review the advantages and disadvantages of conducting an investigation.
4. Determine the individuals who potentially can serve as investigator(s) for the case.
5. Develop an initial witness list.
6. Develop a list of documents to be inspected during an investigation.
7. Develop an investigation plan.
8. Determine the questions to be asked of each witness to be interviewed.
9. Make certain you have a secure place to store investigation information.
10. Gather enough information to cover the scope of the investigation.
11. Maintain interagency collaboration with law enforcement.

into the matter. Some situations that may trigger an investigation are:

- An allegation of policy violation
- An allegation of misconduct
- An allegation of illegal activity
- An anonymous complaint
- A complaint registered with an outside agency
- Suspicion of misconduct
- A complaint of harassment or discrimination
- A "red flag" case

2. **Determine the objective of the investigation.** Brainstorm with colleagues to find out what they perceive as the goal of the investigation. *Never* initiate an investigation to justify a decision that has already been made and acted upon. Investigations rarely turn out exactly the way all who are involved would like them to. Some common objectives of investigations are to:
   - Provide a factual basis for a decision that must be made
   - Determine whether conduct violates district policy
   - Determine responsibility or guilt in an incident
   - Identify students or employees who have violated the law
   - Identify areas where the school or district could improve
   - Restrict adverse publicity
   - Limit liability
   - Create a record for possible litigation
3. **Identify the advantages and disadvantages of an investigation.** Carefully consider and weigh the advantages and disadvantages of conducting an investigation. Explore other ways the issue might be addressed. Some disadvantages to consider are:
   - Notoriety
   - Disruption of the school
   - Discovery of a systemic problem
   - Potential litigation
   - Adverse publicity
4. **Identify potential investigator(s).** In many cases, the issue that is the subject of investigation will determine who should be assigned to conduct it. For example, if a sexual harassment issue is being investigated, appoint a male/female team. Allow assigned investigators access to legal advice as they need it during the investigation. Whatever the gender or expertise of a particular school or district staff, major considerations when assigning an investigator are integrity, patience, honesty, credibility, and writing skills. Other important qualities in an investigator include:
   - The ability to maintain confidentiality
   - Knowledge of the regulations of the Family Educational Rights and Privacy Act (FERPA) and the Government Records Access and Management Act (GRAMA; 1992)
   - Knowledge of district policies
   - Knowledge of school law
5. **Develop an initial witness list.** Begin an initial list with the names of the accused

and the accuser. Evaluate witnesses based on their credibility, vested interests, and relationship with the accused or accuser. Some witnesses may have a specific piece of information that can be collected through a written statement or by collecting a document. Ask all witnesses if they are able to identify others who may know something about the situation. Modify the witness list as you discover additional witnesses. Retain the witness list for your records.

6. **Determine documents to be inspected.** In other words, identify any documents that might contribute to the investigation. Examples of helpful documents are:
   - Internet surfing activity, e-mail, cell phone records
   - Notes in lockers, backpacks, desks, or textbooks
   - Teacher logs, disciplinary records, law enforcement records
   - Personnel files
   - Prior administrators' notes
   - Security camera videotapes
7. **Develop an investigation plan.** Plan the order in which witnesses will be interviewed, taking into consideration opportunities that witnesses may have had to collaborate on their statements. Consider the informal relationships that students, teachers, and members of the community may have developed that could create problems.
8. **Develop questions to be asked of each witness.** We suggest that you use the same set of questions for each witness. This helps cover all of the issues that must be addressed as well as bring consistency to the investigation.
9. **Secure all information.** Lock investigative notes and materials in a secure place; confidentiality is *absolutely critical*. Materials that are left out may be scrutinized or tampered with by anyone with access to offices, conference rooms, or other areas where materials are located. Go out of your way to secure the information!
10. **Consider the scope of the investigation.** Gather enough information to either take appropriate disciplinary action or make an appropriate referral to law enforcement. When a violation of law is reasonably expected, you must *immediately* contact law enforcement.
11. **Collaborate with law enforcement.** To ensure the best investigation involving violations of law, work cooperatively with law enforcement agencies.

How Should You Conduct the Interviews?

Conduct the interviews as quickly as possible, but not before preparing the investigation plan. Keep in mind these steps as witnesses are interviewed:

1. **Be consistent in your introduction.** When stating the purpose of the interview, be as general as possible, letting the witness do most of the talking. Inform the witness that confidentiality will be maintained in accordance with FERPA and GRAMA. Ask the witness if he has any questions regarding the process. Be sure to obtain the witness's name and other identifying demographic data as needed to maintain

complete and accurate documentation throughout the investigation.

2. **Be objective.** Maintain constant awareness of your own body language. Again, allow the witness to talk with as little response from you as possible. A witness can easily be led by an investigator's emotional response to what he has said. Your job is to gather information and facts as accurately as possible, without influencing the witness. Convey the impression that you are taking this incident seriously and treat all who are involved with respect.
3. **Avoid arguments.** Avoid doing or saying anything that threatens, coerces, or confronts a witness. Remember: Witnesses have the right to leave if they choose to do so. Make the witness feel as comfortable as possible. Rely on your prearranged set of questions to stay on track.
4. **Avoid questions that can be answered with "yes" or "no."** Structure the wording of your questions in a manner that will elicit descriptive, elaborative statements from the witnesses.
5. **Do not lead the witness.** Avoid asking questions that hint at the answer you want or expect. Leading questions give the witness an easy way to respond and the investigator an inaccurate account of what really happened. Take time to listen to the witness.
6. **Be sure to get all the relevant facts.** As you question each witness, double-check to make certain you have asked each person:
   - What happened?
   - What time did the incident occur?
   - Where did the incident take place?

Box 5-7

Technique Hint

In some instances, it may be a good idea to call all students involved in an incident at the same time to minimize their ability to collaborate on their response to questions or statements. We've listed some ideas to help limit the problems in calling multiple students at the same time.

1. When calling multiple students (or staff), make certain that they are separated physically and visually. Be sure to make allowances for parents coming in and out of your interview area to contact their children.
2. Make arrangements for each student to be monitored by an adult while waiting to be interviewed. If possible, have more than one administrator interview students, using the same set of questions.
3. When calling students who are suspected of carrying evidence on their person, send them to a room other than the office of the principal, assistant principal, counselor, or attendance monitor to minimize alarm. Provide for an adult to chaperone the student and to note any stops at potential areas where evidence could be discarded.
4. For students who have difficulty writing, provide them with a recording device to make their statements. Have the recorded statements transcribed later. Do not let a student's inability to produce a written statement limit your ability to gather the information you need.

- Who was close by?
- Who else might have witnessed the incident?
- How did the incident unfold?

7. **Practice reflective listening.** To make certain that you correctly understand what the witness has conveyed to you, restate what he just said. Ask the witness if your understanding is accurate before moving on.
8. **Summarize.** Write a summary statement of what each witness said for your records. It may be advisable in some circumstances to provide the witness with your summary statement and ask him to review, add, or make needed changes before signing it. This may be particularly helpful when you think the witness has the potential of being influenced by others to change the account at a later date.
9. **Request a written, signed statement.** A written, signed statement from a witness is often a useful tool to substantiate his account later on. However, written, signed statements can be problematic when a student or employee is not comfortable writing and is constrained by a lack of writing ability or language barriers.
10. **Develop a hypothesis based on the facts.** After you have completed your investigation, develop a hypothesis or informed guess as to what occurred. The hypothesis should be based on the collected evidence, including documents and witness interviews. Write a concise narrative of the incident, including all of the relevant facts and information. In cases where an investigation narrative is used as evidence in a court proceeding, rest assured that the focus will shift from what actually happened to any inappropriate references made to witnesses if derogatory references are part of the investigation record!

Box 5-8

Technique Hint

In your investigation narrative, avoid the use of slang as well as derogatory or inflammatory language when referring to individual or groups. Examples of terms to avoid include:

- *druggies*
- *jocks*
- *cowboys*
- *goths*
- *gangsters*
- *tree huggers*
- *potheads*
- *nerds*

11. **Convene a team to determine an appropriate response.** Once you have a credible hypothesis statement, call together the appropriate staff or other officials to determine an appropriate response to the investigation. If a disciplinary consequence is to be imposed, make certain that it is consistent with those given to students who committed similar infractions.

Guidelines for Student Searches

Do it right! The U.S. Supreme Court has said that if a search of a student is not conducted properly, evidence of a crime or other prohibited behavior that is discovered during the investigation will be subject to the *exclusionary rule*. The exclusionary rule says that evidence of a crime that is obtained from an unreasonable or an improperly performed search cannot be used to prove the guilt of a student and, therefore, *cannot* be used to punish the student.

Can a principal or police officer search students, their lockers, or their cars without the student's permission? Exactly what is considered a search anyway? What about the use of metal detectors? These are some of the issues we cover in this section.

What Is a Search?

The Fourth Amendment to the Constitution protects students from unreasonable searches by public school officials on school property, on school buses, and at school events. Under the Fourth Amendment, a search occurs when a legitimate expectation of privacy by the student is invaded. When is a student's expectation of privacy legitimate? It is legitimate if the student's conduct indicates an actual or even perceived expectation of privacy and the student's perceived expectation of privacy is one that society would accept as reasonable. A student may have a legitimate expectation of privacy in the following examples. Thus, depending on the circumstances, these may be searches:

- Examining a student's items in places that are not in the open and exposed to public view
- Physically examining or patting down a student's body or clothing, including the student's pockets
- Opening and inspecting personal possessions such as purses, backpacks, bags, books, notes, calendars, appointment books, and closed containers
- Handling or feeling any closed, opaque item to determine its contents when it cannot be determined by the item's shape or other publicly visible physical properties
- Using any extraordinary means to enlarge the view into closed or locked areas, containers, or possessions

What Is *Not* a Search?

A student may have no legitimate expectation of privacy in the following examples. Thus, depending on the circumstances, these may *not* be searches:

- Observing an object after a student denies owning it

- Observing an object a student has abandoned with no apparent intention to retrieve it
- Observing any object in plain view, publicly exposed
- Detecting anything exposed by means of sight, smell, touch, taste, or hearing, as long as school officials are in a place in which they have a right to be and they have not used extraordinary means to detect the object

General Search Rule

School officials do *not* need to establish the more strict standard of *probable cause* applicable in criminal procedures. They need only *reasonable grounds* to justify a search on school grounds, school buses, and at school events. However, student searches by school officials are justified *only* if the following two requirements are met:

1. **The search is reasonable at its inception.** The search must be justified at its beginning. A student search is justified when there are reasonable grounds for suspecting that the search will reveal a specific criminal law or school rule violation.
2. **The search is reasonable in scope.** The search must be reasonably related in scope to the circumstances that justified the principal's decision to search in the first place. In other words, a search is permissible when the way the search is conducted is reasonably related to the objectives of the search and not excessively intrusive, given the type of infraction and the age and sex of the student (*New Jersey v. T.L.O.*, 1985; *Edward v. Rees*, 1989).

What Are Reasonable Grounds?

To conduct a lawful search, a principal must have *reasonable grounds* to believe **all** of the following:

1. A criminal law or school rule has been or is being violated.
2. A particular student has committed a criminal law or school rule violation.
3. The suspected criminal law or school rule violation is of the kind for which there is physical evidence.
4. The evidence being sought would be found in a particular place associated with the student suspected of breaking the criminal law or school rule violation.

Reasonable grounds means a school official conducting the search must be able to *put into words* the reasons a particular student is suspected of a criminal law or school rule violation. *It must be more than a hunch or suspicion!*

Examples of factors that, by themselves, may constitute reasonable grounds to search, depending on the circumstances, include:

- Someone observes a criminal law or school rule violation in progress.
- Someone observes a weapon or part of a weapon.
- Someone observes an illegal item.
- Someone observes an item reasonably believed to be stolen.
- There is an odor of tobacco, marijuana, alcohol, or other prohibited substance.
- There is a positive alert by a drug-sniffing dog.

- The student appears to be under the influence of alcohol or drugs. (Note: A witness must be able to describe the exact conduct that caused him to believe the student was under the influence of alcohol or drugs.)
- The student admits to a criminal law or school rule violation.
- The student fits the description of the suspect and is in the proximity of a recently reported criminal law or school rule violation.
- The student flees from the vicinity of the recent criminal law or school rule violation.
- There is information from a reliable source that the student is committing, has committed, or is about to commit a criminal law or school rule violation.
- The student uses threatening words or behavior suggesting there is imminent and substantial risk of injury.
- The student gives oral or written voluntary consent to conduct a search. The consent cannot be the result of fraud, duress, fear, or intimidation.

What Are *Not* Reasonable Grounds?

The following factors by themselves do not likely constitute reasonable grounds to search. However, some combination of these factors—along with other identifiable circumstances—may be used to support reasonable grounds to search:

- The student appears to be lying. (Note: The witness must be able to describe the exact conduct that caused him to believe the student was lying.)
- The student runs when the school official approaches.
- Another student turns in evidence incriminating the student.
- The student to be searched has a history of previous, similar violations (e.g., student was previously disciplined for a similar violation or criminal offense or was already the subject of an investigation for a similar infraction or criminal offense).
- The student became nervous or agitated when approached. (Note: The witness must be able to describe the exact conduct and why it caused him to be suspicious of the student).

In an emergency, a school official can search, if necessary, to avoid imminent substantial injury.

General Guidelines for Conducting a Search

Once reasonable grounds to conduct a search have been established, follow these general guidelines:

1. **Move the student to a private area.** Personally escort the student to be searched to the office or other private location. Maintain uninterrupted visual contact with the student from the time he is stopped to the time the search location is reached. This is necessary to ensure that the student does not abandon any contraband.
2. **Always watch the student's hands.** If a student is suspected of having a weapon

or drugs, he may try to discard them if the opportunity arises. This can occur any time, from when the student is told to accompany the school official to the office up to and including the time when he is actually in the office and being searched. Never allow a student to follow a staff member where the student cannot be observed.

3. **Always have a witness.** Have another school official present from the beginning of the search until the evidence has been obtained. This will strengthen the case brought against the student and will protect the searcher from charges of improper conduct.
4. **Make sure that the searcher is of the same gender as the student.** The witness must be of the same gender, too. This protects the rights of the student as well as those of the searcher from claims of impropriety.
5. **Conduct the search in a private area.** Perform the search in a discreet manner so as to cause the least amount of embarrassment possible. Only the searcher, the witness, and the student should be present. A student must never be searched in front of another student. Carry out the student search in a private area where there will be no interruptions.
6. **Tell the student what you are looking for.** Give the student a chance to surrender the item. Before beginning the search, ask the student if he has anything in his possession that violates criminal law or school rules. If the student hesitates, tactfully advise him that you have reasonable suspicion that he does possess such an item. Then explain that you plan to conduct a search and that it would save everyone time and unnecessary embarrassment if he cooperates. This type of questioning by a school official is not a custodial interrogation requiring *Miranda* warnings (*Edward v. Rees*, 1989; *Jensen v. Reeves*, 1999).
7. **Proceed reasonably, one step at a time.** The student should first remove all outer clothing, such as coat, sweater, hat, and shoes. He should then be asked to remove all objects from his pockets. These items should be laid aside until the student search is complete. Conduct the search on the side of the student's body, working from top to bottom on each side. *Do not stop if contraband is found.* Continue until all places have been searched. Next, focus on the items that have been set aside. Items that could conceal contraband should also be searched. Remember: The scope of the search must be reasonably related to the circumstances that justified it in the first place as well as to the item that is being sought.
8. **Confiscate any item that violates a criminal law or school rule.** This includes any item that provides evidence of a criminal law or school rule violation. Each confiscated item should be placed inside a separate, sealed envelope. Each envelope should be marked to include a description of the item taken, the date and time it was confiscated, the source of the item, the name of the person who confiscated the item, and the name of the person who witnessed the search. Confiscated evidence should be secured in a locked storage area with restricted access. The confiscated evidence should be transferred

to police or to other appropriate officials in a timely manner.

Different Kinds of Searches

Generalized School Searches

Generally, some level of individualized suspicion is necessary for a search to qualify as reasonable under the Fourth Amendment. However, courts have upheld *generalized searches*—that is, searches conducted on all or on random students. For example, courts have found that requiring students to pass through metal detectors as they enter the school building to be reasonable under certain circumstances. Three criteria are used to determine whether a suspicionless search will pass legal muster:

- The nature of the privacy interest on which the search intrudes
- The nature of the intrusion
- The nature and immediacy of the school's concern and the efficacy of the actions used to address that concern

School administrators need to know that the more intrusive the search, the greater the degree of individualized suspicion required. In undertaking either an individualized search or a generalized search, administrators must be prepared to state the reasons for undertaking the search. A general rule is that the more intrusive the search, the more likely it will constitute a Fourth Amendment violation.

Point-of-Entry Searches

These searches take place when school officials require students to open their backpacks for inspection before entering the school building or when leaving a specific location in the school, (i.e., the school library). Requiring all students to undergo this form of search is considered a somewhat greater intrusion on privacy than does the use of metal detectors. This is because this point-of-entry inspection allows school officials to look inside closed containers. Although requiring a student to open a closed container for inspection clearly is considered a search under Fourth Amendment purposes, this inspection is permitted, provided that school officials follow certain rules designed to minimize the degree of intrusion on the student. The intrusion may be decreased by following policies and procedures similar to those used with metal detectors (which is discussed next):

- Students have adequate notice and an expectation of the search.
- School officials request permission for the search from the students.
- School officials inform students that they are free to leave before entering a specific location if they do not wish to consent to the search or that they may check their bags or briefcases at a designated location.
- The search is visual only, and the individual conducting the search does not touch the student's property.
- Police officers do not conduct the search, and its purpose is not to gather evidence for a criminal prosecution.

Point-of-entry inspections are not to be used by school employees as a means to search particular students who are suspected of carrying drugs or weapons. If a school staff member suspects a student has weapons or drugs, the search must be conducted in accordance with the *reasonable suspicion* standard. (See Police Officer Searches, following.)

Metal Detectors

Random searches using metal detectors are reasonable administrative searches. However, the search may not be used as a pretext to target specific students or groups of students. Principals should adopt the following procedures if they use metal detectors:

- Request that all students empty their pockets and other belongings of all metal objects before the search takes place.
- Request a second walk-through when the metal detector is activated.
- Use a handheld (wand) metal detector, if available, to focus on and discover the location of the metal source if a second activation results.
- Expand the scope of the search if the activation continues or is not explained. If no less restrictive alternatives remain available, a limited pat-down search might then be necessary.
- Escort the student to a private area for a more intrusive search.
- Have any further search—such as a frisk or a request to open purses or book bags—conducted by a school official of the same gender as the student, using the standard search guidelines discussed earlier.

Car Searches

A search of a student's car on school property by school officials is governed by the reasonable suspicion standard. Schools can require an application for parking lot access. If a school adopts such an application process, it should provide each student and his parent with a copy of the application. The application should have a written statement on it that notifies students and their parents of the school's policy on car searches (*People in the Interest of P.E.A.*, 1988).

Locker Searches

The search of a student's locker by school officials is lawful, at least where there exists reasonable grounds that evidence of a criminal law or school rule violation will be found in it. If school authorities have made it clear that possession of lockers is *nonexclusive against the school and its officials*, a locker search may also be justified in the absence of sufficient reasonable grounds (*Zamora v. Pomeroy*, 1980; *Singleton v. Board of Education*, 1995; *In the Interest of Isaiah B.*, 1993). Thus, we advise principals to include in their school code of conduct the statement that **"possession of a locker is nonexclusive against the school and its officials and is, therefore, subject to search at any time for any reason."**

Police Officer Searches

Police officers are held to a higher standard for conducting a search than are school officials. If any police officer whose duties normally are performed elsewhere comes to the school and initiates a search there or gets school officials to do so on his behalf, both the police officer *and* the school officials may be held to a higher standard than the reasonable grounds standard that generally applies. That higher standard is *probable cause*. Probable cause means that it is more likely than not that the police will find the evidence for which they are looking. The *reasonable grounds* standard that applies to searches conducted by school officials, on the other hand, requires only that school officials be able to articulate why evidence of a criminal or school violation may be found. The higher probable cause standard is not necessarily applicable if police are merely present during the school's investigation or if they assist but do not conduct the search (*State v. Twayne*, 1997; *People in the Interest of P.E.A.*, 1988). However, local judges and individual prosecutors have varying views on this issue, and it is best to involve police in the search only when there is a significant safety risk or when the search will be conducted using the probable cause standard.

Drug Testing

Random urinalysis drug testing of students participating in extracurricular athletics has been approved by courts as long as the testing procedures are reasonable. Currently, courts are divided on the issue of whether random drug testing of students participating in other extracurricular activities is allowed (*Vernonia School District v. Acton*, 1995; *Todd v. Rush County Schools*, 1998; *Trinidad School Dist. No. 1 v. Lopez*, 1998).

Strip Searches

Strip searches of students in a school setting by school officials are generally considered *unreasonable*. School officials must be able to articulate reasonable grounds for conducting a strip search of a particular student instead of a less intrusive search. Caution here! A strip search is *always unreasonable* for a minor infraction and should be considered only for infractions that present an imminent threat of substantial harm (e.g., because of possession of weapons or other dangerous contraband). Keep in mind that what may constitute reasonable grounds for a search of a locker or even a pocket or purse may fall well short of reasonableness for a strip search (*Cornfield v. Consolidated High School District*, 1993; *Knop v. Northwestern School District*, 1998; *Kennedy v. Dexter Consolidated Schools*, 1998). **School officials considering a strip search are well advised to consult first with local law enforcement for additional guidance.**

Drug-Sniffing Dogs

The sniffing of a student, his locker, or his car by a drug-detection dog is *not* considered a search. A positive alert by a drug-detection dog is reasonable grounds to search (*Zamora v. Pomeroy*, 1980).

Surveillance

This may involve watching an area by use of either video cameras or the naked eye. It is permissible as long as the area or activity being surveyed is considered a common area and open to the public. Two examples of common areas are parking lots and hallways, in which students are not considered to have a reasonable expectation of privacy. If a school official has the right to monitor the activities of a particular common area, the monitoring of that area can be done using video surveillance. Successful legal defense of surveillance searches is more likely if the school has posted signs that warn that all people in a certain area are subject to video-camera surveillance.

On a somewhat different note, it is usually permissible for school officials to make observations from concealed, stationary locations. For example, a school official's limited observation of a student in the school rest room using a one-way mirror does not violate the student's Fourth Amendment rights (*United States v. Katz*, 1967). However, school officials should be cautious when conducting surveillance in rest rooms or locker rooms because some courts have held that there is a greater expectation of privacy in these areas. When a rest room stall is equipped with a door, individuals in the stall are accorded a reasonable expectation of privacy (*Ward v. State of Florida*, 1994). If a school conducts surveillance in a rest room or a locker room, students should be observed only by designated school officials or security personnel of the same gender as the students under surveillance. There should also be signs posted that warn students that surveillance cameras may be observing them.

Listening to or Recording Private Conversations

Generally, this is not permissible without the consent of one of the participants in a conversation (*Stern v. New Haven Community Schools*, 1981). The only exception is when conversations can be heard with the "naked ear."

The Plain View Doctrine

This permits school officials to confiscate items they come upon during the course of performing their duties without violating the Fourth Amendment as long as two conditions are present:

- At the moment the items come into view, the school officials are legitimately present and have not already violated a student's Fourth Amendment rights.
- It is immediately apparent to the school officials that they are observing evidence of a rule infraction or a crime.

Field Trips and School-Sponsored Events

Courts have generally found searches conducted before or during field trips or school-sponsored events to be more reasonable than searches taking place during normal school activities. This is because a wider variety of activities takes place on field trips than on school grounds. Although the search may technically take place off school grounds, the same search-and-seizure rules apply during these events. Educators' authority over students is expected to extend to wherever students go while under the educators' supervision. For example, after giving advance notice to students and their parents, it is considered reasonable to search students' luggage before a school-sponsored trip. *Table*

5-4 summarizes the required student-search standards for various types of searches.

Table 5-4

Summary of Student Search Standards

Search Area Justification	Expectation of Privacy	Required
Person or property	Yes	Reasonable grounds or consent
Car	Yes	Reasonable grounds or consent
Locker	No	No justification required if "nonexclusive" notice given
Abandoned property or student denies ownership	No	No justification required
Plain view	No	No justification required

Weapons

Dangerous and criminal student misconduct frequently involves the use of weapons. Familiarity with the definition of weapons under federal and state laws is a prerequisite to determining when disciplinary sanctions may be properly imposed by a school or school district for dangerous and criminal misconduct.

Definition of Weapon (Gun-Free Schools Act)

Guns, by and large, are covered under the Gun-Free Schools Act (1994), although not all types of guns meet the statutory definition of "weapon" under this act. Knives and other instruments of violence are not considered weapons at all, for purposes of this particular law. The term "weapon" is defined as meaning the same thing as a "firearm," which in turn is specifically defined as one of the following:

- Any weapon (including a starter gun) that will be, is designed to, or may readily be converted to expel a projectile by the action of an explosive
- The frame or receiver of any such weapon
- Any firearm muffler or firearm silencer
- Any destructive device (the term does not include an antique firearm)

An unloaded bullet is not a "weapon" or even a "dangerous weapon" for purposes of federal law. Although there appears to be no principled reason that a school district could not sanction possession of bullets in the same way it sanctions possession of guns, that was not the case in *M.K. v. School Board of Brevard*

County (1998), which upheld the student's challenge to his expulsion for loose bullets discovered in his book bag. The school district's disciplinary code, though detailed and legalistic, did not cover the student's particular misconduct.

Definition of Weapon (School's Disciplinary Code)

A state or school district may define a weapon more broadly than the federal Gun-Free Schools Act, triggering disciplinary consequences for possession. It is important to check your local district policy as well as your state's law for guidance regarding facsimile weapons, bombs, knives (including knives with blades of less than 2½ inches), incendiary devices, razor blades, box cutters, and the like. These items are *not* covered under IDEA for students with disabilities. If your district does not have a policy that covers this area, it needs to get one!

Definition of Weapon (IDEA)

In IDEA, the term "weapon" is defined consistently with the phrase "dangerous weapon" under the definition of weapon in the United States Code. The code states:

> a weapon, device, instrument, material, or substance, animate or inanimate, that is used for, or is readily capable of, causing death or serious bodily injury, except that such term does not include a pocket knife with a blade less than 2½ inches in length.

For further information regarding weapons, see the "Weapons/Drugs/Serious Bodily Injury" discussion in the Disciplinary Removal Flowchart and Summary part of this section.

Unloaded Guns

Unloaded guns are always weapons, as indicated in *M.K. v. School Board of Brevard County* (1998) and *McLaughlin v. United States* (1986). In *McLaughlin*, an unloaded handgun that was used to commit an assault during a bank robbery was found to be a dangerous weapon. Both of the definitions of weapons in the federal Gun-Free Schools Act and the definition of dangerous weapon under the United States Code do not expressly require that a gun be loaded. It is the potential for harm that is the issue, not just whether the gun can actually be used at any particular moment that seems to be the requirement to meet the definition.

Background of Legalities Relating to Discipline

Principals are responsible for maintaining a safe and orderly learning environment. Along with this responsibility comes the expectation that the school principal will identify, initiate, facilitate, and maintain behavior management systems schoolwide, as well as within classrooms and for high-risk populations, including the school's Seven Percent Students. A myriad of local, state, and federal laws and regulations affect discipline practices in schools. Next, we offer some general guidance for administrators who find themselves daily in the middle of the situations we described at the beginning of this section. Many of us can easily pull from our memory bank an image of a school principal who doled out discipline with the stroke of a paddle. Obviously, those days are long gone!

Discipline has topped the list of public concerns in education for 30 years. Discipline and drugs now have equal billing in the Gallup Poll (Northwest Regional Educational Laboratory, 2004). Why? Because school discipline must be maintained in order for learning to take place. Also, in an increasingly violent society, schools must be safe havens for students. During the same 30 years, a body of case law dealing with discipline has become well developed; these cases initially began by dealing with general education issues. After passage of the Education for All Handicapped Children Act in 1975, courts were also called into service to determine the extent to which discipline was related to IEPs of students with disabilities. Various components from these cases formed the core of practices and procedures to be considered when disciplining *all* students—students with disabilities, in particular.

The Principal's Seven Deadly Sins of Discipline

As you work through the process of identifying and implementing behavior management systems within your school, there are some well-practiced "sins" that will render your discipline less effective and that can ultimately result in serious legal problems. You should be aware of them up front so they can be avoided.

1. **No rules**—The All-School Rules we recommend in this Briefcase should establish the minimum acceptable standard of behavior in your school. These rules must be appropriately developed, publicly posted, thoroughly explained, and consequated. The behavioral expectations and standards of All-School Rules *must be specifically taught*. Without All-School Rules, students have no parameters for their behavior. It is also safe to say that without them, the difference between your idea of expected behavior and your students' ideas of expected behavior will quickly be identified!
2. **No consequences**—Students must know ahead of time exactly what will happen when they follow the All-School Rules (positive consequences) and when they choose *not* to follow them (undesired consequences). In the absence of both positive and undesired consequences, compliance with rules is eroded, and rules then have no meaning.
3. **Inconsistency**—Both positive and undesired consequences *must be applied consistently* when they are earned. When students follow the All-School Rules, they need to receive feedback letting them know that they have behaved appropriately. The Principal's 200 Club, discussed in Section 3, is an example of a behavior management system that can be used effectively to provide feedback. Conversely, when students choose *not* to follow the All-School Rules, similar undesired consequences for similar misbehavior must be the standard applied for *all* students. (The exception to this standard is when a student has purposely been placed on an individualized Behavior Intervention Plan tailored to his needs.) Inconsistency is not only bad practice, but it can also be interpreted as a violation of Section 504 for eligible students.
4. **Emotional involvement**—The benefit of established All-School Rules and

predetermined positive and undesired consequences is that students and staff understand ahead of time what will happen when rules are violated. When students exhibit unacceptable behavior, do not internalize it or take it personally. Overreacting to misbehavior *always* make things worse!

Box 5-9

Educators who are not in charge of themselves have no business being in charge of students who are not in charge of themselves.

—Unknown

5. **Empty threats**—"Say what you mean, and mean what you say." Nothing diminishes compliance with All-School Rules faster than making empty threats to students without following through when they are broken. *Not following through* teaches the student in question that he can do whatever he wants—at least part of the time—and it also teaches the same lesson to his friends and peers. They will be well aware that nothing happened when the student broke one or more rules. Do not threaten a student that you will take action for breaking rules. Rather, when he chooses not to follow a rule, identify the problem behavior (e.g., "That's not following Mrs. Bowen's directions") and then follow through with the predetermined undesired consequence.
6. **Escalating the behavior**—No situation is so bad that inappropriate administrative handling of it can't make it worse! When intervening with students, always calmly *identify the behavior that prompted you to intervene in the first place* rather than *the behavior the student exhibited* when you intervened. Usually, a lot of adrenaline is pumping and emotions are running high when discipline is called for and staff intervene with students. Under these conditions, the possibility of the situation escalating out of control is great. Your job is to intervene calmly, responsibly, and professionally, and *not make things worse!* (See Explosive Crises in Section 4 for further information.)
7. **Maliciousness ("I'm gonna get this kid")**—The purpose of behavioral intervention is to teach and guide as well as to reduce the likelihood that inappropriate behavior will occur again. The mantra of the malicious principal is, "I'm gonna give this kid enough rope to hang himself." Malicious principals meet their own needs, not the needs of students. In our view, they have absolutely no business being principals.

The Seven Deadly Sins of Discipline remind us what we should avoid as we discipline students in our schools. They also provide some general guidelines we should follow as we discipline all students. Remember, however, that about 10% of the students in your school are protected by IDEA 2004 because of their special education eligibility. Another 10%–25% are eligible for protection under Section 504. Requirements under IDEA and/or Section 504 afford these students significantly greater protections than those without disabilities when it comes to discipline. These protections are discussed in more detail later in this section.

Disciplinary Requirements for All Students When Removal Is Selected as a Disciplinary Consequence

The school administrator is generally responsible for schoolwide discipline and must make decisions regarding disciplinary consequences. When students violate school rules, the school administrator is the one who responds and must make a series of decisions that provide due process protections for all students. When the administrator decides to select removal as a disciplinary consequence, it is assumed that the school has adequate and effective alternative consequences to deter rule-violating conduct and that these have been considered. It is also assumed that removal from school is the appropriate consequence for the particular case at hand.

If the administrator has considered the alternatives and removal is the appropriate consequence in the case, the administrator must be prepared to answer the question "Does the behavior exhibited warrant the penalty of removal from school?" Factors to consider in answering this question include:

- For students with disabilities, is the penalty consistent with those imposed on students without disabilities for the same or similar offenses?
- Is the penalty consistent with acceptable district penalties?
- Have mitigating circumstances surrounding the offense been considered?

Box 5-10
Disciplinary Removal Flowchart

We walk you through general and specific guidelines on all the major facets of removing students—protected as well as nonprotected—from school as a disciplinary consequence in the coming pages in narrative form. However, because there are many ways to conceptualize how these components fit together, we also provide a one-page graphic representation of the process in the form of a Disciplinary Removal Flowchart at the end of this section. Following the flowchart, we also provide a succinct written summary of it, which indicates the pages in this section where you can find detailed information related to each specific topic regarding removal. The flowchart and its summary review the information related to disciplinary removal that we cover in this section. They also provide different ways of looking at the necessary information while emphasizing efficiency and practicality.

Is the Student Protected?

The student is protected by IDEA 2004 discipline procedures if:

1. The student is eligible for special education under IDEA.

2. The student is an eligible individual under Section 504.
3. The school had knowledge that the student had a disability before his behavior that precipitated disciplinary action.

The student is *not* protected by IDEA 2004 discipline procedures if:

1. The parent has not allowed an evaluation of the student.
2. The parent has refused special education services.
3. The student has been evaluated and found not to be eligible under IDEA 2004.

For students *not* protected, the school administrator is free to proceed with notification to parents, ensuring that they have been informed of their rights:

1. Due process procedures in connection with *suspensions of ten school days or less* include:
   - Oral or written notice of the charges to the student and parents
   - An explanation of the evidence school administrators have
   - An opportunity for the student to present her explanation of the incident
2. For removals of more than ten days, the student is entitled to a hearing in which he can present his side of the story and ask questions of school officials.

A school district is considered to have knowledge that a student has a disability if:

- The parent of the student expressed concern in writing to the principal or the teacher that the student is in need of special education.
- The parent requested an evaluation of the student.
- The teacher of the student or other educational staff expressed specific concerns regarding the student's behavior in accordance with the school district's child-find procedures.

See *Table 5-5* for documentation that could indicate that students have special education needs.

Table 5-5

Possible Sources of Documentation That Indicate a Student Is in Need of Special Education Services

- Office referrals
- Low academic achievement (e.g., failing classes, low test achievement scores, lacking credit for graduation)
- Truancy referrals
- Teachers' notes and records
- Information from parents or medical records

Short-Term Removal

The school must document short-term removals of all students, including both students with disabilities and students without disabilities. There are three reasons this documentation is critical:

1. If charged with a civil rights violation of disparate disciplinary treatment under Section 504 (a very common complaint), the school must provide documentation that the proposed disciplinary consequences are similar for students with disabilities and those without disabilities.
2. A running total of the number of school days a student with disabilities has been removed in a year is critical for decision-making related to educational change-of-placement issues.
3. The data requirements of the Office for Civil Rights, the Office for Special Education Programs, the Safe and Drug-Free Schools Act, the No Child Left Behind Act, and the Gun-Free Schools Act demand it.

Parent Contact

Best and defensible practice suggests that once the decision is made to immediately remove a student from the school environment, the parents must be contacted. The purpose of the parent contact is to:

1. **Inform them that their child has been involved in a violation of school rules.** Parents need to know that their child has been involved in a serious behavioral problem at school, that it will be investigated, and that their child must be removed from school. Removing a student from school without informing the parents is asking for trouble! This notification must be documented.
2. **Determine what immediate action should be taken.** Usually, students are not removed from school until a parent conference can be held. However, other available options include different forms of ISS and referral to law enforcement (and possible removal by an officer).
3. **Make an appointment for a parent conference.** The initial parent conference needs to take place as soon as possible. What should you do if you can't convince a parent to come in? After three attempts to get the parent to come to school—including sending a certified letter requiring a signature—we suggest contacting your local social services agency and following through on filing educational neglect charges against the parent.

Box 5-11

Immediate Action

Take immediate action to remove the student from school as discussed with the parent.

Proposed Consequence Determined

Before a principal meets with the parent(s) and the student, a proposed consequence must be determined. The most critical factor to consider is the consistency of this consequence with those imposed on other similarly situated students for the same or similar offenses. It is important to base the number of days of removal on rationale that is consistent for all students. Some school districts have developed standards of discipline that guide administrators in determining consequences.

Box 5-12

Caution!

The number of days of proposed removal may have to be adjusted for special education students eligible under IDEA and students eligible under Section 504 to meet the specific requirements of these laws.

Parent Conference

The parent conference should be held as soon as possible after the behavioral incident. The principal or assistant principal, the parent(s), and the student usually participate in the meeting. The purpose of the parent conference is to:

1. Inform the student and parent(s) of the allegations or charges against the student. If the student or parent(s) disagrees, the administrator must share the documented evidence used to substantiate the student's involvement in the incident.
2. Inform the student and parent(s) of the disciplinary consequence being proposed.
3. Ask and answer questions regarding the incident, the penalty, and the process.

When Students Must Be Removed

A great deal of discussion in this Briefcase has focused on our belief that OSS is overused and often ineffective as a disciplinary consequence. We have also talked about collecting disciplinary and office referral data as another tool to help target specific times, days, behaviors, students, and locations related to rule-breaking in a school. Regularly identifying these data points allows you to respond effectively with appropriate interventions so that the need to use removal from school as a disciplinary consequence is greatly reduced. Even with these supports in place, there may still be situations when you conclude that removal is necessary. In these cases, following the Top Ten Rules for Removal (for either OSS or expulsion) can provide general guidance regarding best, and legally safe, practice when removing a student as a disciplinary consequence. The Top Ten Rules for Removal apply to all students in a school.

Top Ten Rules for Removal

1. ***All* students have some procedural due process rights related to removal.**

   In *Goss v. Lopez* (1975), the U.S. Supreme Court set out to accommodate the competing interests of the student and the school system. According to the Court, the student's interest was to avoid unfair or mistaken exclusion from the educational process. The interest of the school was the maintenance of the discipline and order that are essential for education. To balance these interests, the Court specified due process procedures in connection with *suspension of ten days or less* to include:

   - Oral or written notice of the charges to the student and the parents
   - An explanation of the evidence that school authorities have and an opportunity for the student to present his explanation of the incident

For removal of more than ten days, the student is entitled to a hearing at which he can present his side of the story and ask questions of school officials.

2. **Principals must keep accurate records on suspensions for *all* students.**

   It is critical that discipline data be collected and be easily retrievable for all students. Not only are these data valuable in planning behavior interventions within the school, but they are also required for several federal reports: the Office for Civil Rights, the Safe and Drug-Free Schools Act, the Gun-Free Schools Act, the No Child Left Behind Act, and the Individuals with Disabilities Education Act. Further, data on cumulative days of suspension must be readily available for principals to determine whether an additional assignment of suspension is a change of placement for students with disabilities.

3. **For students with disabilities, the due process rights for concurrent or cumulative suspensions of ten days or less are the same as for students without disabilities.**

   Principals have almost total discretionary authority for suspensions of ten days or less. To avoid claims of disparate discipline, school administrators should ensure that similar infractions result in a similar number of days of suspension, regardless of a student's protected status.

4. **Consequences involving removal are the same for students with disabilities as they are for students without disabilities. However, the total number of days of suspension may have to be modified for special education students with disabilities in order to comply with IDEA.**

   Yes, it is true that students with disabilities have significantly more due process rights than students without disabilities. However, when making a determination as to how many days of suspension are appropriate for students with disabilities, administrators must start at the same place as they would for a student without disabilities. The question is "What would the consequence be if the student were not disabled?" The administrator must then work through the additional due process rights of the student with a disability to determine whether the same number of days may be imposed.

5. **Educational services must be provided to students with disabilities in special education on the 11th day of removal.**

   Whether concurrent or cumulative, and whether or not it amounts to a change of educational placement, educational services for students with disabilities as listed on their IEPs must be provided on the 11th day of removal. This requirement underscores the need for very careful record keeping.

6. **If the parents agree, no further due process is required.**

   If the parents of a special education–eligible student agree with a change of educational placement for disciplinary reasons—as well as with the educational services provided—there is no need for further due process. This includes a Functional Behavior Assessment (FBA), a Behavior Intervention Plan (BIP), and whether the behavior in question is a

Box 5-13

Is the Removal a Change of Placement Under IDEA 2004?

A disciplinary consequence or sanction is a change of placement if:

1. The student is removed for more than ten consecutive school days.
2. The student is subject to a series of removals that total more than ten cumulative days that constitute a pattern of removal. In deciding whether a pattern of removal exists, the IEP team must consider the following questions:
   - Is the student's behavior similar to or different from previous behavior that warranted suspension?
   - What is the length of time for each removal?
   - What is the total amount of time out of school?
   - What is the proximity of the removals, one to another?

The overall question is:

Are the removals preventing the student from receiving an appropriate education?

manifestation of the student's disabilities. Remember, however, that parents reserve the right to withdraw their consent at any time!

7. **A principal can change the educational placement of a student with disabilities for weapons and drug violations or other violations that are not a manifestation of the student's disabilities.**

   One of the primary provisions of IDEA is to allow a principal to change the placement of a student with disabilities for weapons or drug violations to an alternative setting. In this case, a principal may change the placement for 45 calendar days even if the behavior in question is a manifestation of the student's disabilities. He may change it to the same number of days as for a student without disabilities if the behavior is *not* a manifestation of the student's disabilities. In keeping with previous case law, a principal cannot change the educational placement of a student with disabilities when the behavior is a manifestation of his disabilities, beyond what we have specified here. Manifestation determination is fully discussed in detail in Section 6.

8. **A manifestation determination must be made prior to the school's final determination of educational change of placement for a student with disabilities.**

Where a change of placement is proposed, the manifestation determination determines the number of days a student with disabilities can be removed from school. More information regarding making a manifestation determination is provided in Section 6.

9. **A Functional Behavior Assessment and a subsequent Behavior Intervention Plan must be completed for students**

with disabilities when their educational placement is changed or when removals from school total more than ten days in a year.

Remember: Not only does a change of educational placement trigger an FBA and a BIP, but so do removals totaling more than ten days. (See Section 6 for detailed information regarding how to conduct an FBA and a BIP.)

10. **Principals should develop alternatives to Out-of-School Suspension.**

    As we have mentioned in previous sections, it is very helpful to have effective alternatives to OSS in place so that you can avoid many, if not most, of the pitfalls discussed here! Section 4 provides step-by-step information as to how to set up and implement many of these alternatives.

Answers to Suspension Questions

Question: *Can students be suspended from extracurricular activities as a disciplinary consequence?*

Answer: Students have no constitutionally guaranteed right to participate in extracurricular, including interscholastic, activities. Participation in extracurricular activities is a privilege, and the U.S. Constitution protects only liberty and property interests.

Question: *If a student is suspended toward the end of the year, may he be excluded from the graduation ceremony?*

Answer: Yes. Participation in the graduation ceremony has generally been viewed by courts as a privilege, not a right. Although students have a property interest in a diploma, they have no similar claim to participation in the graduation ceremony.

Question: *If a student is suspended from a parochial school for a safe-school violation, can he be denied enrollment in a public school?*

Answer: Caution! Many states permit school districts to apply a suspension from another school or school district where the offense would be grounds for excluding the student from the school district where the student seeks to enroll. Most courts have held that unless your state specifically addresses this issue, public schools may not deny entry into public schools of students who have been suspended from parochial schools (*Hamrick by Hamrick v. Affton School District Board of Education*, 2000).

What Is Section 504?

Section 504 is the common term used to refer to Section 504 of the Rehabilitation Act of 1973. Section 504 is a federal anti-discrimination law designed to protect the rights of individuals with disabilities in programs and activities that receive federal funds from the U.S. Department of Education. Both Section 504 and IDEA fall under the auspices of the department as well as the Office for Civil Rights, which is responsible for ensuring compliance with Section 504.

Section 504 requires a school district to provide a "free appropriate public education" (FAPE) to each qualified student with a disability who is in the school district's jurisdiction, regardless of the nature or severity of the disability. FAPE consists of the provision of regular or special education and related aids and services designed to meet a student's individual needs. (See *Table 5-6* for the definition of "disability.")

Table 5-6

Definition of Disability Under Section 504

The definition of "disability" under Section 504 is considerably broader than that included under the Individuals with Disabilities Education Act (IDEA) for students who qualify for special education services. Section 504 states:

> *No otherwise qualified individual with a disability in the United States ... shall solely by reason of her or his disability, be excluded from the participation in, be denied the benefits of, or be subjected to discrimination under any program or activity receiving Federal financial assistance.*

What Is the Relationship Among Section 504, IDEA, and the Americans with Disabilities Act (ADA)?

Section 504 prohibits discrimination on the basis of disability in programs or activities that receive federal financial assistance from the U.S. Department of Education. The ADA prohibits discrimination on the basis of disability by state and federal governments. Neither Section 504 nor the ADA provides any type of funding to meet its requirements. IDEA, on the other hand, is a grant statute that attaches many specific conditions to school districts that receive IDEA funds.

Students Protected Under Section 504

Section 504 covers qualified students with disabilities who attend schools receiving federal financial assistance. However, to be protected under Section 504, one of the following must be determined to be true for the student:

1. Has a physical or mental impairment that substantially limits one or more major life activities.
2. Has a record of such an impairment
3. Is regarded as having such an impairment.

Section 504 requires that school districts provide FAPE to qualified students in their jurisdictions who have a physical or mental impairment that substantially limits one or more major life activities. An extensive list of common Section 504 accommodations is included at the end of this section.

Answers to Section 504 Questions

Question: ***How does the Office for Civil Rights become involved in disability issues within a school district?***

Answer: Anyone can file a complaint with the regional OCR office.

Question: ***What services are available for students who qualify under Section 504?***

Answer: Section 504 provides no funding. However, school districts are required to provide students with disabilities appropriate education services designed to meet their individual needs to the same extent as the needs of students without disabilities are met.

Question: ***What does it mean to be "out of compliance" with Section 504?***

Answer: A school district is out of compliance with Section 504 when it violates any provision of Section 504.

Question: ***What is a physical or mental impairment that substantially limits a major life activity?***

Answer: The determination of whether a student has a physical or mental impairment that substantially limits a major life activity must be made on an individual basis by persons knowledgeable about the child. Section 504 defines a physical or mental impairment as any physiological disorder or condition, cosmetic disfigurement, or anatomical loss affecting one or more of the following body systems: neurological; musculoskeletal; special sense organs; respiratory, including speech organs; cardiovascular; reproductive; digestive; genitourinary; hemic and lymphatic; skin; endocrine; or any mental or psychological disorder such as mental retardation, organic brain syndrome, emotional or mental illness, and specific learning disabilities.

Major life activities, as defined in Section 504, include functions such as caring for one's self, performing manual tasks, walking, seeing, hearing, speaking, breathing, learning, and working. Our list is not exhaustive; other functions can be considered major life activities for purposes of Section 504.

Question: ***Once a student is identified as eligible for services under Section 504, is that student entitled to services forever?***

Answer: No. The protections of Section 504 apply only to students who meet the definition of persons with disabilities. If a school reevaluates and determines that a student no longer qualifies, the student is no longer eligible for services under Section 504.

Question: ***Are current, illegal drug users excluded from protection under Section 504?***

Answer: Generally, yes. Section 504 excludes from the definition, and from 504 protection, any student who is currently engaged in the illegal use of drugs (with exceptions for students in rehabilitation programs).

Question: ***Are current users of alcohol excluded from protection under Section 504?***

Answer: No. Section 504's definition of a student with a disability does not exclude users of alcohol. However, Section 504 allows schools to take disciplinary action against students with disabilities who use drugs or alcohol to the same extent as students without disabilities.

Question: ***What is an evaluation under Section 504?***

Answer: Section 504 requires school districts to individually evaluate a student before classifying the student as having a disability. The amount of information required is determined by a multidisciplinary committee gathered to evaluate the student. The committee should include persons knowledgeable about the student, the meaning of evaluation data, and the placement options. The committee members must determine if they have enough information to make an informed decision as to whether or not the student has a disability. Section 504 requires that school districts draw from a variety of sources in the evaluation process so that the possibility of error is minimized. The information obtained from all such sources must be documented, and all significant factors related to the student's learning process must be considered. These sources and factors may include aptitude and achievement tests, teacher recommendations, physical condition, social and cultural background, and adaptive behavior.

Question: ***Must school districts consider "mitigating measures" used by a student in determining whether the student is eligible under Section 504?***

Answer: Yes. A school district must consider a student's use of what are called mitigating measures in determining whether the student is substantially limited in a major life activity. Mitigating measures are devices or practices that a student uses to correct or reduce the effects of his mental or physical impairment. Examples include corrective eyeglasses and medications. Someone who experiences no substantial limitation in any major life activity when using a mitigating measure does not meet the definition of a person with a disability and would not be entitled to FAPE under Section 504.

Question: ***Who decides whether a student has a substantial limitation?***

Answer: The determination of substantial limitation must be made by the student's Section 504 team on a case-by-case basis.

Question: ***Are there any conditions or illnesses that automatically qualify a student for protection under Section 504?***

Answer: No. An impairment in and of itself does not qualify a student for protection under Section 504. A student's impairment must substantially limit one or more major life activities in order for him to qualify for protection under Section 504.

Question: ***Is a medical diagnosis sufficient as an evaluation?***

Answer: No. A physician's medical diagnosis must be considered among other sources in evaluating a student with a disability or a student believed to have a disability that substantially limits a major life activity.

Question: ***Who makes the ultimate decision regarding a student's eligibility for Section 504?***

Answer: Section 504 requires that the eligibility determination be made by a group of persons, including those knowledgeable about the meaning of the evaluation data as well as about placement options. If a parent disagrees with the determination, he or she may request a due process hearing.

Question: ***How often must a student be reevaluated under Section 504?***

Answer: Periodic reevaluation is required. It may be conducted in accordance with the IDEA regulation that requires reevaluation at three-year intervals—or more frequently if conditions warrant—or if the child's parent or teacher requests a reevaluation.

Question: *How should a school district regard a temporary impairment?*

Answer: The issue of whether a temporary impairment is substantial enough to be a disability must be resolved by the student's Section 504 team at the school, taking into consideration both the duration, or expected duration, of the impairment and the extent to which it actually limits a major life activity.

Question: *If a student qualifies under IDEA and Section 504, must a school district develop both an IEP under IDEA and a Section 504 plan?*

Answer: No. If a student is eligible under IDEA, he must have an IEP. The accommodations needed under Section 504 should be included in the IEP. All students covered under IDEA are also automatically covered under Section 504.

Question: *Must a school district develop a Section 504 plan for a student who either "has a record of disability" or is "regarded as disabled?"*

Answer: No. In elementary and secondary schools, unless a student actually has a disabling condition that substantially limits a major life activity, the fact that the student "has a record of a disability" or "is regarded as disabled" is insufficient, in and of itself, to trigger those Section 504 protections that require the provision of FAPE. The phrases "has a record of a disability" and "is regarded as disabled" are meant to apply to the situation in which a student either does not currently have or never has had a disability but is treated by others as such.

Question: *What is the receiving school district's responsibility under Section 504 toward a student with a Section 504 plan who transfers from another school district?*

Answer: If a student with a disability transfers to a school district from another district with a Section 504 plan, the receiving district should review the plan and the supporting documentation. If the group of people serving as the Section 504 team at the receiving school district—including persons knowledgeable about the meaning of the evaluation data as well as the placement options—determines that the plan is appropriate, the district is required to implement it. If the district determines that the plan is inappropriate, the district must evaluate the student as required by Section 504 and determine the educational program that is appropriate.

Question: *What are the responsibilities of regular education teachers with respect to implementation of Section 504 plans? What are the consequences if the district fails to implement the plans?*

Answer: Regular education teachers *must* implement Section 504 plans when those plans govern the teachers' treatment of students for whom they are responsible. If teachers fail to implement the plans, such failure can cause their school district to be in noncompliance with Section 504 and subject to its penalties, including the potential loss of all federal funds. All teachers who need to know the contents of individual students' Section 504 plans must be informed *ahead* of time about the contents that pertain to them and about their binding obligation to carry them out. The principal of a school in which teachers are not provided this information places himself and his school district in an unconscionable position. Once informed, a teacher who refuses to implement a student's Section 504 plan may even be subject to a civil lawsuit that could jeopardize his personal property and possibly even his retirement.

Question: ***Must a school district obtain parental consent prior to beginning a Section 504 evaluation?***

Answer: Yes. The OCR has interpreted Section 504 as requiring school districts to obtain parental permission for initial evaluations. If a district suspects that a student needs, or is believed to need, special instruction or related services and parental consent is withheld, districts may use due process hearing procedures to override the parents' denial of consent for an initial evaluation.

Question: ***What are some commonly used, reasonable accommodations?***

Answer: We have included examples of potential, reasonable Section 504 accommodations at the end of this section.

Table 5-7
Summary of Discipline Under Section 504

Protections for students eligible under Section 504 *only* (and *not* IDEA) are the same as they are for students protected under IDEA with these exceptions:

1. **Provision of educational services during school removal**—Section 504 regulations do not contain any provisions similar to IDEA's Individual Alternative Education Setting provision, and the OCR has not published guidance extending these provisions to Section 504–only students. Therefore, if a district does not provide services to students without disabilities for removals beyond ten days, then services do not need to be provided to Section 504–only students.
2. **Functional Behavior Assessment (FBA) and Behavior Intervention Plan (BIP)**— Section 504 regulations do not contain any provisions similar to IDEA's *mandatory* FBAs and BIPs. However, conducting FBAs and BIPs may be a good idea anyway when a student has recurring behavior problems.
3. **Discipline of a student addicted to alcohol or use or possession of alcohol**— A student who is currently using alcohol may be disciplined in the same manner as any other student, regardless of whether that student is disabled on the basis of alcoholism.
4. **Discipline of students with disabilities who are current drug users for possession of drugs in violation of district policy**—Section 504 excludes those students who are currently engaged in the illegal use of alcohol or drugs from eligibility.

Note: Provisions for students protected under IDEA are described in more detail later in this section.

Our nonexhaustive list includes specific modifications that are environmental in nature as well as modifications that are related to lesson presentation, assignments and worksheets, test-taking, organization, behavior, and other special considerations.

The Principal's Quick-and-Dirty Guide to the Individuals with Disabilities Education Act

Now that we've covered more general information, we are going to plunge deeper into the unique world of special education. To be sure, the devil is in the details when it comes to discipline for students who qualify for special education services. Ignoring the details is a dangerous way to do business!

The special education process is designed to make sure that each student with a disability under the Individuals with Disabilities Education Act (IDEA) has an educational program that is individualized to meet his needs. This includes the discipline part of his educational program. The Individualized Education Program is a written plan developed by the student's IEP Team. This plan outlines the individualized education that is to be delivered to him by the school district. As the principal, you are the leader of the team that makes decisions about the student's educational program. *Table 5-8* summarizes how to get the most out of IEP meetings.

Pitfalls for Principals

Avoid these common statements when dealing with the behavioral problems of special education–eligible students. These are big mistakes!

1. **"Don't worry about the paperwork. Let's get down to the real issues."**

   The *procedural problem* of not having the student's paperwork in order is easy pickings for parents' attorneys. Starting with proper written *prior notice of the meeting* and providing parents with a *parents' rights* brochure—as well as ensuring that parents truly understand their rights—principals must make sure that all the **i**'s are dotted and the **t**'s are crossed. This is often referred to as "being in compliance" in the world of special education. Courts have determined that the most basic foundation for determining that an appropriate educational program (FAPE) is being provided to a student is compliance with the procedures outlined in IDEA (*Board of Education of the Hendrick Hudson Central School District v. Rowley*, 1982). In Rowley, the court outlined a two-part test to determine whether the IDEA requirements were being met:

   - Is the IEP in compliance under IDEA?
   - Is the IEP reasonably calculated to confer educational benefits?

2. **"We have decided to place your child in the Resource (or whatever) program."**

   Never say this! It broadcasts to the world the fact that you have already determined the student's educational placement along the continuum of services before the IEP Team has even discussed the possible placement. The IEP Team members, however, should not come to the IEP meeting with no idea of where the student might be placed. In any case, the school must not finalize the student's placement (*G.D. v. Westmoreland*, 1991). It is a bad

Table 5-8
How to Get the Most Out of IEP Meetings

Hold a pre-meeting with staff who will be in the IEP meeting:

1. Determine who will lead out in the discussion and the order in which other staff will be called upon to present information during the actual meeting.
2. Decide what information each staff member in attendance will present and gain agreement to stick to this plan.
3. Obtain agreement by staff to avoid editorializing, preaching, getting on soapboxes, and describing war stories. Ask staff to stick to the facts and present information in a professional manner. Give staff examples of what you want and what you do *not* want in these areas.
4. Assign someone on the IEP team to serve as scribe during the actual meeting.
5. Assign someone to make sure all forms are organized and available at a moment's notice.
6. Know something about the "style" of the parents with whom you will be dealing, and prepare the team to work effectively with them. Have a plan for what will happen if the parents become combative, refuse to sign documents, or walk out.

Avoid mistakes in the meeting:

1. Determine ahead of time where the meeting will be held and what the seating arrangement will be. Make an effort to see that everyone feels comfortable.
2. Begin the meeting by saying something positive about the student and giving a recent, positive anecdote about him. This will help to set the tone for the meeting, put everyone at ease, and break the ice.
3. Review the student's IEP, his strengths and limitations, goals, and placement in everyday terms.
4. If the meeting comes to an impasse, do not feel like you have to bring everything to a conclusion.
5. Stay calm.
6. Do not let any issues become personal.
7. Remember—signing the IEP means that each person participated in, but not necessarily agreed with, everything in the document. If parents will not sign, make certain that everyone else does, and record that the parents were involved with the meeting and chose not to sign.
8. If parents become belligerent, warn them that you will cancel the meeting if the behavior continues.
9. If the belligerent behavior continues, inform the participants that the meeting is no longer serving the purpose for which it was called, and end it. Schedule another day when people are calmer.

idea to even sound like a decision has been made before the IEP meeting.

3. **"We just don't have those services in our district."**

   Services required by the student and written into his IEP must be based on the individual needs of the student—not the availability of the services (*Leconte*, 1998). In other words, lack of service availability is no excuse under IDEA.

4. **"We can't afford to provide those services."**

   The federal Office for Special Education Programs has stated time and time again that a lack of sufficient resources and personnel is not justification for the failure to provide FAPE to a student (*Letter to Anonymous*, 1998).

5. **"We're changing Kate's therapy from five times a week to once a week."**

   Schools must provide proper *written prior notice* to parents whenever the district proposes to initiate or change, or refuses to initiate or change, the identification, evaluation, or educational placement of a student. (For further documentation, refer also to *Myles S. v. Montgomery County Board of Education*, 1993.)

6. **"This IEP should take only about 15 minutes."**

   Never hurry through an IEP meeting. Make sure that enough time is planned for and taken to ensure that all components of the IEP, as specified under IDEA, are addressed and documented. Inadequate and insufficient IEPs are begging for trouble!

7. **"I sure am glad Li's going to a private school. That's one less IEP I have to worry about."**

   If Li is eligible for services under IDEA, the school must develop an appropriate IEP and offer FAPE despite the fact that his parents are planning to send him to a private school. The only way to prevent parents from coming after you for reimbursement later is to show that the school is ready, willing, and able to provide FAPE, should the parents want to take advantage of the offer.

8. **"Let's see. The vote is 11 to 2 in favor of the district. Parents, you're outnumbered."**

   Decisions at IEP meetings are to be made by consensus, not by a majority vote. The IEP meeting is intended to be a communication vehicle between the parents and the school. In cases where consensus cannot be reached, the Local Educational Agency (LEA) representative—you or your designee—breaks the deadlock.

Remember, however, that parents have the right to seek resolution of their disagreements by initiating a due process hearing under IDEA.

9. **"We've already evaluated A.J., so we're not going to pay for an independent evaluation."**

   Parents have a right to obtain an independent evaluation, at public expense, if they believe the school's evaluation is *not* appropriate and if, indeed, it is not appropriate. Examples of an inappropriate evaluation might include the school's relying on only one test rather than multiple measures for making a determination or using a test for a purpose for which it is not designed. If the school strongly believes that its evaluation is appropriate, the district must initiate its own due process hearing to show that its evaluation is appropriate. If it is not willing to file for a due process hearing, the district must pay for the parents' appropriate evaluation.

10. **"We agree that Andre needs that placement, but all of our programs are full. We'll have to put him on a waiting list."**

    Don't even go there—unless you have a death wish! When it comes to special education needs, there is no such thing as a waiting list. Once the IEP Team determines that a student needs a particular placement, you must somehow make it happen. Legally, you will not win this case if Andre's parents challenge it. They can place their child in a private school with an appropriate program and then ask you to pay for it. Adding the costs of the private school to the attorneys' fees can be extremely expensive.

11. **"He had the free will not to engage in the problematic behavior. Of course, it's not a manifestation of his disability."**

    IDEA specifies the circumstances and criteria to be used in making a manifestation determination related to the student's behavior. This decision must be made by the IEP Team, including the parents; thus, no individual can make this decision. Further, as a principal, you are well advised never to place yourself in the position of attempting to sway the decision of the other IEP Team members. An honest decision must be made by the team, based on the information presented at the IEP meeting. See *Table 5-9* and *Table 5-10* for examples of what not to say—as well as what to say—at IEP meetings.

Additional Questions and Answers About Protected Students

Question: ***What should you do if parents show up for a special education IEP meeting with media?***

Answer: The individuals attending an IEP meeting should be only those people with a particular knowledge of, or a legitimate interest in, the student. The media is neither of these; they are only after a story. If the media show up, postpone the meeting. You are legally obligated to protect the student's privacy under FERPA. Stay calm, and speak softly and unemotionally. In no case should you engage in a shouting match with the parents or the media; this serves only to inflame the situation.

Table 5-9

Phrases to Avoid at IEP Meetings

"We can't do that."

In fact, there's almost nothing that an IEP cannot do. Keep an open mind, and give every idea due consideration. Avoid snap judgments.

"We don't do that in our district."

Avoid making arbitrary decisions denying parental requests. The student's individual needs must determine what will be done for him by the school district.

"We never do that."

There is an exception to every rule.

"We only do ... "

This is a phrase that parents should not and do not want to hear.

"We don't believe in ... "

Unless you have a sound reason and an alternative, avoid this phrase.

"That never works."

Avoid this phrase unless you can give a sound, data-based rationale for making it. Also, unless the rest of the IEP team believes that what the parents are requesting might be harmful to the student, there may be times when they agree to try the parents' request for a time-limited trial period to see how it works.

"No student gets more than this amount of service."

Again, this is a no-no. Decisions must be made on an individual basis. Do not include or exclude students as a group from any service.

"It costs too much to do that."

Cost cannot be the determining factor as to what services are provided to the student.

"It takes too much time to do that."

It is up to the IEP team to determine how much time is needed to meet the student's needs and provide the services she requires. This must be determined individually.

"It goes against district policy."

Before saying this to anyone, make sure you can back it up with chapter and verse. Student requirements on an IEP almost never go against district policy.

Question: ***Does the 2004 IDEA reauthorization allow IEP Teams to exempt students with disabilities from high-stakes tests?***

Answer: No. The Department of Education Office for Civil Rights (OCR) has stated that the IEP Team determines how—not whether—students with disabilities participate in testing programs. The basis for OCR interpretation is that IDEA 2004 requires school districts and states to develop

Table 5-10
Ten Things Parents Like to Hear at School Meetings

1. Their child's name.
2. "We are all here on (child's name) behalf."
3. "We'll make a program that works for (child's name)."
4. "You are the experts on (child's name)."
5. "It's refreshing to see parents taking such an interest in their child."
6. Five positive things about their child, sincerely stated.
7. "All children have positive attributes. What are some of (child's name)?"
8. Something specific about their child (e.g., "I spoke to José just yesterday in the lunchroom. He seemed very excited about the basketball game").
9. "I can tell that (reading, respect, manners, good grooming) is a priority for you at home, because your child shows that at school."
10. While making eye contact with the child, saying, "Take a good look at your parents. They are your greatest advocates."

alternative assessments to make the same high-stakes requirements (OCR, 2000).

Question: *If the state requires passing a high-stakes test for a high school diploma, does a student with disabilities who meets his IEP goals, but fails the test, have a right to his diploma under IDEA or Section 504?*

Answer: Most courts have stated that neither IDEA nor Section 504 prevents states from withholding diplomas to students with disabilities who fail high-stakes tests, as long as these students have access to the accommodations that are specified in their IEPs.

Question: *What happens when a student is referred for special education services during disciplinary proceedings?*

Answer: If a referral for special education services is made any time after the student is already involved in disciplinary proceedings, and the referral is considered appropriate, the special education evaluation must be conducted in an expedited manner.

Question: *Must a student who possibly may be protected "stay put" in his current educational placement during disciplinary proceedings pending evaluation to determine eligibility?*

Answer: No. The student stays in the assigned disciplinary placement (which may include removal from school without services) until the special education evaluation and eligibility determination have been completed.

Question: *Does a student who has been removed from special education services have enhanced disciplinary protections?*

Answer: Maybe. The following case sheds some light on this issue:

A high school student who was qualified as Emotionally Disturbed was withdrawn from special education services at the request of his parents. Subsequently, the student committed a series of violent acts against students and staff. The school removed the student for the remainder of the year without the special protections of IDEA. The Court held that the student was protected, since there was never a determination that the student was no longer qualified for services (*Jeffrey S. v. School Board of Riverdale District*, 1995).

Therefore, a student who has been served by special education services, but whose IEP Team has determined that he no longer qualifies for services, may not be protected. A student who has been taken out of special education services for one reason or another, but who still meets eligibility standards, is an eligible student with disabilities. He merely does not receive services at the present time.

Summary

In this section, we presented answers to tricky legal questions, discussed the parameters of the Family Educational Rights and Privacy Act, talked about parent and guardian custody issues, and defined and discussed weapons in the school setting. We have provided specific information about conducting an investigation, student searches, legalities relating to discipline, advice regarding removal from school, determining disciplinary consequences, and parent conferences. Additionally, we presented information related to Section 504 and the Individuals with Disabilities Education Act. We think this information will serve you well as you navigate the treacherous "white-water" situations with which school administrators are expected to effectively grapple today—and, we hope, keep you off the local news channel and out of the newspaper!

Examples of Potential Section 504 Accommodations

Environmental Modifications

- Seat student near teacher.
- Stand near student when giving directions or presenting lessons.
- Increase the distance between desks.
- Seat student near positive role model.
- Avoid placing student near distracting stimuli (e.g., high-traffic areas, windows, heating system).
- Adjust class schedules.
- Use a study carrel.
- Modify student's work area with barriers.
- Alter location of personal or classroom supplies for easier access or to minimize distraction.
- Provide opportunities for movement.

Lesson Presentation

- Monitor the rate (e.g., slow the rate of presentation) at which you present material.
- Give additional presentations:
  - Repeat original presentations
  - Provide simpler, more complete explanation
  - Give additional examples
- Model skills in several ways.

- Make consequences more attractive:
  - Increase feedback
  - Provide knowledge of results
  - Chart performance
  - Reward approximations
- Recognize and give credit for student's oral participation in class.
- Pair students to check work.
- Provide peer tutoring.
- Provide peer to read aloud, listen.
- Provide peer note-taker (copy / carbon copies).
- Provide peer to monitor assignments.
- Provide student with an overview of the lesson (i.e., tell student what to expect and why) BEFORE beginning the lesson.
- Provide written outline (e.g., chapter outlines, study guides).
- Write key points on the board.
- Repeat and simplify instructions.
- Have student restate or write directions/ instructions.
- Break longer presentations into shorter segments.
- Schedule frequent, short conferences with student to check for comprehension.
- Allow student to tape lesson.
- Provide consistent review of any lesson BEFORE introducing new information.
- Have student orally review key points.
- Highlight important concepts to be learned in text or material.
- Avoid use of abstract language (e.g., metaphors, idioms, puns).
- Paraphrase material using similar language.
- Use visual aids (e.g., charts, graphics, pictures) to supplement verbal information.

Assignment/Worksheet Modifications

- Allow student to obtain and retain information using:
  - Cassette / tape recorder
  - Typewriter
  - Interviews / oral reports
  - Projects
  - Calculator
  - Dictation
  - Computer
- Provide additional guided practice:
  - Require more responses
  - Lengthen practice sessions
  - Schedule extra practice sessions
- Increase amount of time allowed to complete tasks.
- Reduce amount of work, as opposed to allowing more time.
- Break work into smaller segments.
- Teach time-management skills (e.g., using checklists, prioritizing time, prioritizing assignments).
- Set realistic and mutually agreed-upon expectations for neatness.
- Simplify complex directions.
- Give written directions to supplement verbal directions.

- Give worksheets one at a time.
- Provide materials appropriate to student's current functioning level (e.g., lower reading and difficulty level).
- Space practice and drill sessions over time.
- Allow student to tape assignments/ homework.
- Provide study skills training/learning strategies.
- Allow student to type, record, or give answers orally instead of in writing.
- Reduce amounts of copying from the board and textbooks; provide student with written information.
- Use self-monitoring devices.
- Give clear, concise directions for homework assignments.
- Reduce homework assignments.
- Require fewer correct responses to achieve grade.
- Provide structured routine in written form.
- Avoid purple dittos.

Test-Taking Modifications

- Give frequent, short quizzes; avoid long exams.
- Allow open-book exams.
- Give exams orally.
- Give take-home tests.
- Allow student to give test answers on tape.
- Allow extra time for exams.
- Read test items to student.
- Give more objective items (i.e., fewer essay responses).

Organizational Modifications

- Establish daily routine and strive to maintain it.
- Provide peer assistance with organizational skills.
- Provide student with extra set of books for home.
- Provide student with an assignment notebook.
- Provide rules for getting organized.
- Teach goal-setting skills.
- Teach decision-making/prioritizing skills.
- Teach time-management skills.
- Check homework daily/supervise writing of homework assignments.
- Set short-term goals for work completion.
- Give assignments one at a time.
- Give written assignments with expected dates of completion on which the student needs to focus.
- Avoid cluttered, crowded worksheets by using techniques such as:
  - *Blocking* (block assignments into smaller segments)
  - *Cutting* (cut worksheets into fourths, sixths, or eighths, and place one problem in each segment)

- *Folding* (fold worksheets into fourths, sixths, or eighths, and place one problem in each segment)
- *Color-coding, highlighting, or underlining* (emphasize important information on which the student needs to focus)

- Set aside a specific time for cleaning desks, lockers, organizing notebooks, etc.
- Provide student with file folders, notebooks, or trays in which to place his workbooks to prevent misplaced assignments/books.

Behavioral Modifications

- Implement contracts for behavior/ academic goals.
- Post rules, reminder goals on desk, wall.
- Establish eye contact prior to directions and instructions.
- Use precision commands.
- Provide frequent, immediate, positive feedback (e.g., increase verbal reinforcement to ___ per hour).
- Use self-monitoring strategies.
- Use positive reinforcements (i.e., rewards/privileges).
- Increase immediacy of rewards.
- Avoid lecturing.
- Use nonverbal cues to stay on-task.
- Implement a classroom behavior management system.
- Anticipate problems and use preventive strategies.
- Praise specific behaviors.
- Allow legitimate opportunities to move or to stand while working.
- Provide a "stop-and-think" place.
- Allow short breaks between assignments.
- Change tasks every ____ minutes.
- Ignore minor inappropriate behaviors.
- Supervise during transition times.
- Provide recess control (e.g., list details).
- Provide structured recess program.
- Speak softly in nonthreatening manner if student is agitated.
- Look for signs of stress build-up, and provide encouragement or reduce workload.
- Allow student an opportunity to "save face."
- Encourage anger control (e.g., encourage student to walk away; use calming strategies).
- Look for opportunities for student to display leadership role in class.
- Send positive notes home.
- Use mild, consistent consequences.
- Give student choices.
- Meet with the student and the student's parents.
- Meet with the student's other teachers.
- Provide alternative workspace.
- Implement beeper tape and reinforcement menu.

Special Considerations

- Monitor medication issues such as:
  - Who the student's physician is
  - What the name of the student's medication is
  - What the correct dosage of the medication is
  - When the dose is administered
  - Who administers the dose
- Adjust attendance policies (according to time needed at home and in the hospital).
- Adjust schedule or shorten day.
- Provide rest periods.
- Adapt physical education requirements.
- Develop health care and emergency plan.
- Provide transportation to and from school.
- Allow extra time between classes.
- Provide locker assistance.
- Modify activity level for recess, physical education, etc.
- Monitor and provide additional supervision for field trips.
- Assist with carrying books, lunch trays, etc.
- Consider assistive technology.
- Make accommodations for special dietary needs.

Disciplinary Removal Flowchart and Summary

Although the following flowchart may be somewhat visually overwhelming, the beauty of a flowchart is that there is *one way* in and *one way out*. In this case, we prompt you along the way with symbols on the flowchart and short explanations in the summary. The summary also guides you back to the appropriate pages in Section 5 for more detailed explanations. Many of you will not look at this information until you need it. When you do, here is our advice:

1. **Go step-by-step through the process.** If you are uncertain of a step, refer to the summary and, if needed, the specific pages on which the material is presented more fully.
2. **Be sure you understand every step of the process.** Do it right! Remember: You are ultimately responsible for the disciplinary removal procedures followed in your school. The summary is cross-referenced to pages in Section 5.

Remember:

1. Follow the arrows on the flowchart. The process flows in one direction.
2. The process contains all the steps required to make decisions. In practice, many steps will take place simultaneously.

IDEA 2004 (NPRM) DISCIPLINARY REMOVAL PROCEDURES

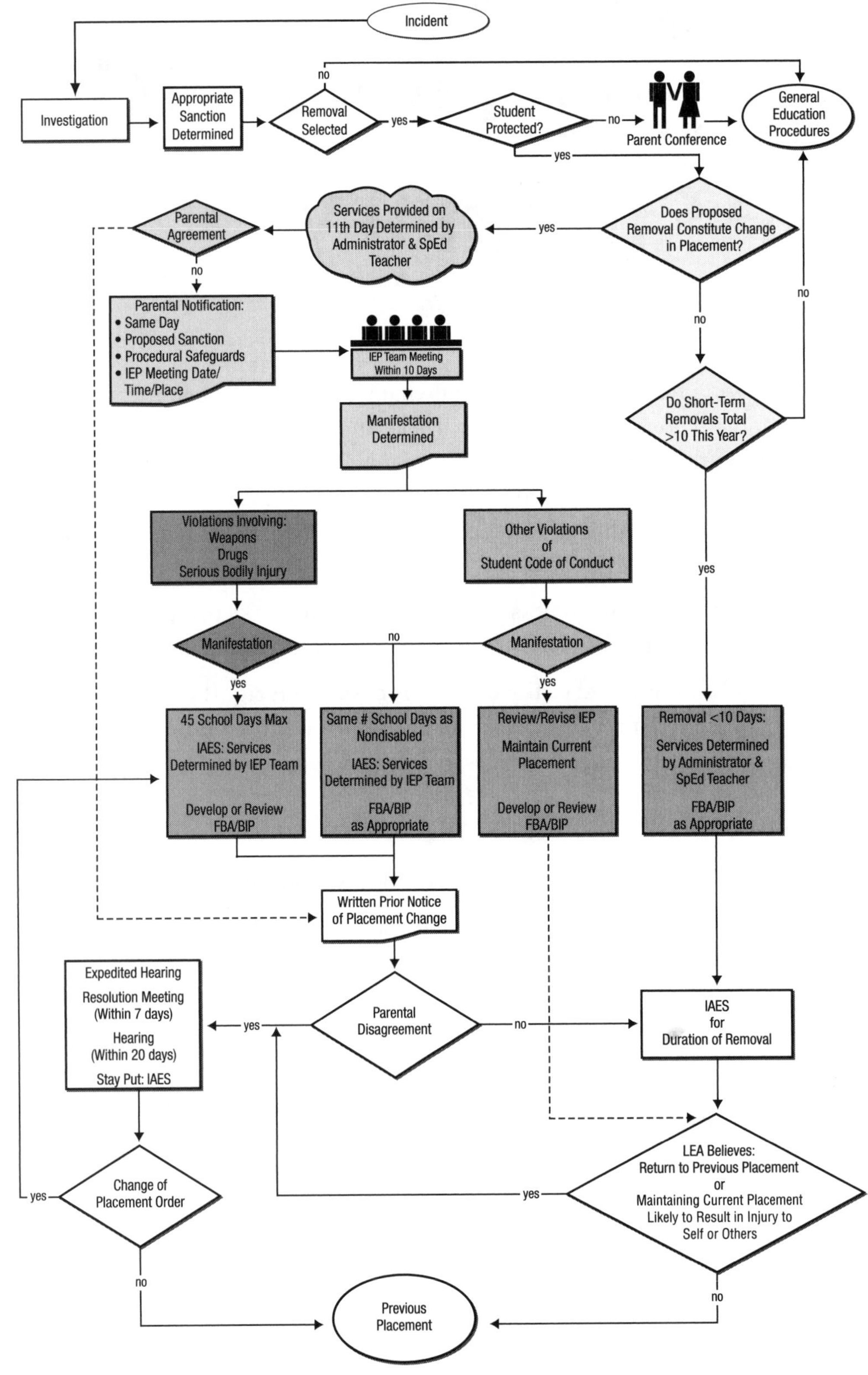

IDEA 2004 (NPRM) DISCIPLINARY REMOVAL PROCEDURES

Incident occurs subject to administrative intervention.

Investigation

Administration conducts an investigation sufficient to develop a hypothesis of nature, extent and culpability relative to incident.

Appropriate Sanction Determined

Administrator determines appropriate sanction consistent with prior sanctions administered to similarly situated students.

IF REMOVAL IS NOT SELECTED, as an administrative sanction, then the administrator may proceed to administer the sanction.

A student is protected by IDEA 2004 discipline procedures if:

1. The student is eligible for special education under IDEA.
2. The student is an eligible student under Section 504.
3. The school had knowledge that the student had a disability before the behavior that precipitated the disciplinary action (§300.533).

Basis of knowledge:

a. The parents expressed concern in writing to administrative personnel or a teacher that their child is in need of special education (300.533(b)(1)).
b. The parents requested an evaluation of their child (300.533(b)(2).
c. The teacher of the child or other educational personnel expressed specific concerns regarding the child's behavior in accordance with the district's child find procedures (300.533(b)(3).

A student is *not* protected by IDEA 2004 discipline procedures if:

1. The parents of the child have not allowed an evaluation of their child (§300.534(c)(1)(i)).
2. The parent has refused special education services (§300.534(c)(1)(i)).
3. The child has been evaluated and was found not to be eligible under IDEA (§300.534(c)(2)).

Parent Conference

IF THE STUDENT IS NOT PROTECTED: Initiate parent conference.

The purpose of the meeting is to:

1. Inform the student and the parent of the charges. If the student or the parent disagree, share with them the evidence utilized to make the determination.
2. Inform the student and the parent of the disciplinary sanction being proposed.
3. Ask and answer questions regarding the incident, the penalty and the process.

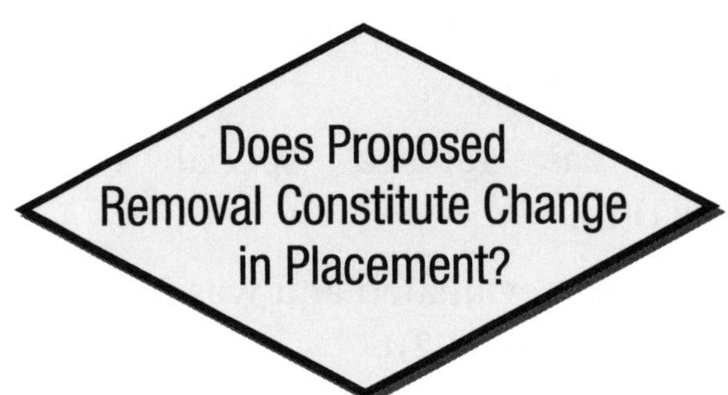

The school administrator must propose a sanction for students with disabilities consistent with relevant disciplinary procedures applicable to students without disabilities.

The school administrator must then determine whether the proposed sanction constitutes a change of placement pursuant to IDEA 2004.

A sanction constitutes a change of placement if:

1. The student is removed for more than ten consecutive school days (§300.536(a).
2. The student is subject to a series of removals that total more than ten cumulative days that constitute a pattern of removal. The IEP Team must consider:
   a. If the behavior is similar or different from previous behavior that warranted suspension.
   b. The length of each removal.
   c. The total amount of time out of school.
   d. The proximity of the removals, one to another (300.536(b)(1–3).

The overall question is: Are the removals preventing the student from receiving an appropriate education?

SHORT-TERM REMOVALS

If a student is suspended for not more than ten consecutive (or cumulative) school days, school personnel may remove a student with a disability in the same way they would remove a student without a disability (§300.530(b)).

After a student with a disability has been suspended for ten days in the same school year, if the current suspension is for not more than ten consecutive school days and is not a change of placement, school personnel and the students's special education teacher determine services, if any, to be provided (§300.530(4).

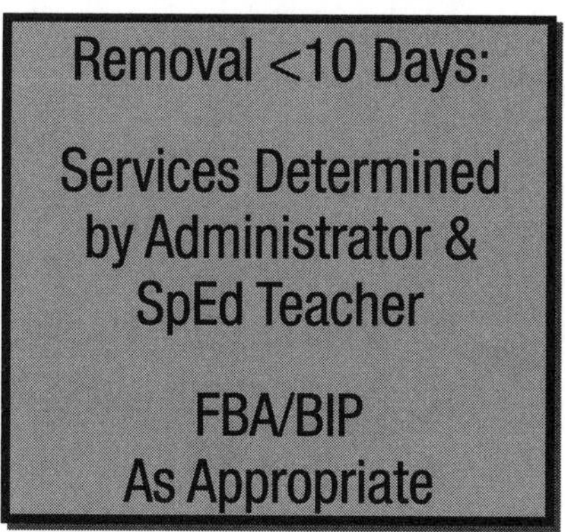

After services have been determined by the administrator and the student's special education teacher (§300.530(b)(2)) and duration of suspension has been determined, the student is subject to the sanction and returns to the previous placement at the end of the suspension.

A Functional Behavior Assessment (FBA) and a subsequent Behavior Intervention Plan (BIP) should be initiated as deemed appropriate (§300.530(d)(1)(ii).

LONG-TERM SUSPENSION

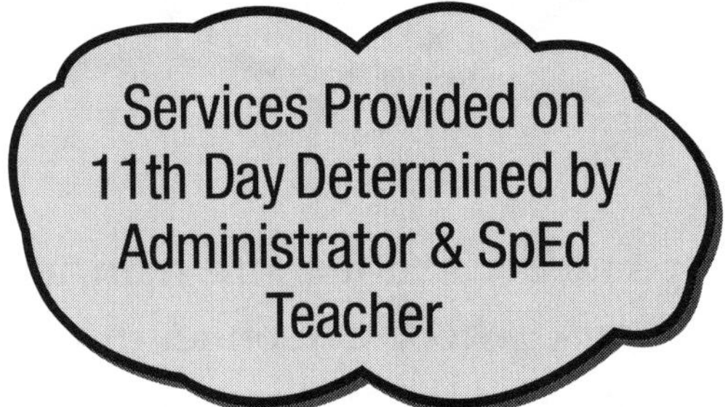

A student who is subject to a proposed removal that constitutes a change of placement may be removed for up to ten consecutive school days while convening the IEP Team. If the student has been previously removed, the day that cumulative removals exceed ten (10) days, services must be provided starting on the 11th day as determined by school personnel, in consultation with the student's special education teacher (§300.530(4).

If the parents agree with the proposed sanction and the proposed provision of FAPE, there is no need to continue with further procedures, except the standard change of placement procedures.

Parental Notification:

- Same Day
- Proposed Sanction
- Procedural Safeguards
- IEP Meeting Date/Time/Place

Not later than the date on which the decision to take disciplinary action that may result in a change of placement is made, the parents shall be notified of that decision and of all procedural safeguards pursuant to IDEA (§300.530).

Best Practice Tip:

Along with this notification, school officials should also send home *Written Prior Notice of IEP Meeting* as required by IDEA prior to convening the IEP Team. The following components of the IDEA discipline procedures must be completed by the IEP Team:

1. Manifestation Determination: Within ten school days of any decision to change the placement of a student with a disability as a disciplinary sanction, the IEP Team (as determined by the parent and the LEA) must complete a Manifestation Determination (§300.530).
2. If the IEP Team determines that the behavior *was* a manifestation of the student's disability, the IEP Team must either review or conduct an FBA (§300.530(f)(1)(i)).
3. The IEP Team must determine the interim alternative educational setting for students: (a) whose behavior has been determined *not* to be a manifestation of their disability (§300.530(c)); and (b) whose behavior has been found to be a manifestation if the student carries or possesses a weapon (§300.530(g)(1)), possesses or uses illegal drugs (§300.530(g)(2)), or has inflicted serious bodily injury (§300.530(g)(3)).

Since the Manifestation Determination must be completed by the IEP Team within ten days, it results in significant time savings to develop or review, as appropriate, the FBA and the determination of IAES services at the same meeting. Be sure to include all of these activities in the *Written Prior Notice of IEP Meeting*.

For disciplinary purposes, the IEP Team consists of the LEA, the parent, and relevant members of the student's IEP Team (as determined by the parent and the LEA (§300.530(e)(1)).

Within ten days of the date the decision is made to change a student's placement as a disciplinary sanction, the IEP Team must be convened to make the following decisions relative to the proposed sanction:

1. Make a manifestation determination (§300.530).
2. Review or conduct a Functional Behavior Assessment (FBA) and a Behavior Intervention Plan (BIP), as needed (§300.530(f)(1)(i)).
3. Determine the services to be provided and the interim alternative setting (§300.530(c)).

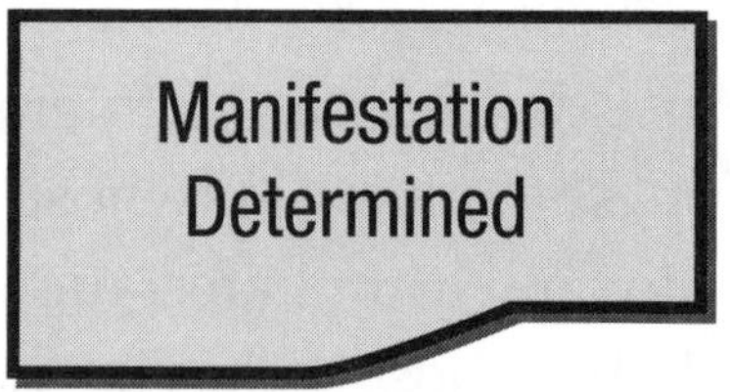

Purpose: The purpose of the Manifestation Determination is to determine *if the conduct in question was caused by, or had a direct and substantial relationship to, the child's disability* (§300.530(e)(i)); *or, if the*

conduct in question was the direct result of the LEA's failure to implement the IEP (§300.530(e)(i)).

Timeline: Within ten school days of any decision to change the placement of a student with a disability as a disciplinary sanction (§300.530).

IEP Team: The appropriate members of the IEP Team are determined by the parent and the LEA (§300.530(e)(i)).

Scope of Review: All relevant information in the student's file, including the IEP and any relevant information provided by the parents.

Best Practice Tip:

The IEP Team should be prepared to defend its manifestation decisions with documentation of the information it considered.

Failure to implement an IEP: At a minimum, in order to determine whether the behavior in question was a direct result of a failure to implement the IEP, the following information should be considered.

- **Classification:** The behavior may be related to behavioral manifestations of the student's disabling condition.
- **Pre-referral information:** Was the behavior noted as a concern that was addressed in the regular classroom?
- **Referral information:** Was the behavior noted as a concern when the student was referred for evaluation?
- **Evaluation:** Is the behavior addressed in the evaluation information in the student's file?
- **IEP:** Are there goals that address the behavior? Is there an FBA? Is there a BIP?
- **Placement:** Is the placement appropriate to meet the special education and related service needs of the student?

If the behavior in question is noted in prereferral, referral, and evaluation documents but is not addressed in the IEP, the behavior may have been managed by the implementation of a BIP. This is an implementation issue that must be addressed in the Manifestation Determination.

In order to defend a finding that the behavior was not a result of failure to implement the IEP, the IEP Team must demonstrate that: (a) it has looked at all required documents in the student's file; (b) the documents are current and in compliance; and (c) the program is appropriate to meet the student's needs.

Conduct in question was caused by, or had a direct and substantial relationship to, the child's disability.

Conduct in question had a direct and substantial relationship to the disability: The IDEA 2004 Conference Committee Report provides guidance that Congress intended that the Manifestation Determination "… analyze the child's behavior as demonstrated across settings and across time when determining whether the conduct in question is the direct result of the disability …" (*Committee Report*, at 224). Presumably, if the behavior has a direct and substantial relationship to the disability, the behavior should have been observed in different settings at different times.

Information available to make this determination may include:

- Anecdotal records of teachers and administrators
- Special education documents such as peripheral data, referral data, evaluation reports, or IEP goals
- Parental observations

Conduct in question caused by the disability: *The Diagnostic and Statistical Manual of Mental Disorders*, Fourth Edition, Test Revision (DSM-IVTR) represents the professional standard for diagnostic criteria for most of the disability categories enumerated in IDEA 2004, along with diagnostic and related features that include behavioral characteristics of these disabilities. Case law suggests that if the behavior prompting disciplinary sanctions is listed as a diagnostic or related feature of the student's disability, there is a high probability that the behavior may be caused by the disability.

(See the end of Section 6 for a sample Manifestation Determination form.)

VIOLATIONS OF THE STUDENT CODE OF CONDUCT

Violations Involving:
Weapons
Drugs
Serious Bodily Injury

School personnel may remove a student to an IAES for not more than 45 school days without regard to whether the behavior is determined to be a manifestation of the disability, if the student (§300.530(g)):

1. Carries a weapon to or possesses a weapon at school, on school premises, or to or at a school function (§300.530(g)(1)).

   Weapon has the meaning given the term "dangerous weapon" under paragraph (2) of the first subsection (g) of section 930 of title 18, United States Code (§300.530(4)), which provides:

   "The term "dangerous weapon" means a weapon, device, instrument, material, or substance, animate or inanimate, that is used for, or is readily capable of, causing death or serious bodily injury, except that such term does not include a pocket knife with a blade of less than 2 1/2 inches in length."

2. Knowingly possesses or uses illegal drugs, or sells or solicits the sale of a controlled substance, while in school, on school premises, or at a school function (§300.530(g)(2)).

   Controlled substance means a drug or other substance identified under schedules I, II, III, IV, or V in section 202(c) of the Controlled Substances Act (21 U.S.C. 812(c)) (§300.530(i)(1)).

   Illegal drug means a controlled substance but does not include a controlled substance that is legally possessed or used under the supervision of a licensed health-care professional or that is legally possessed or used under any other authority under the Controlled Substances Act or under any other provision of federal law (§300.530(i)(2)).

Serious bodily injury is defined as that which involves substantial risk of death, extreme physical pain, protracted and obvious disfigurement, or protracted loss or impairment of the function of a bodily member, organ, or mental faculty (§615(k)(7)(D)); 18 U.S.C.§1365(h)(3).

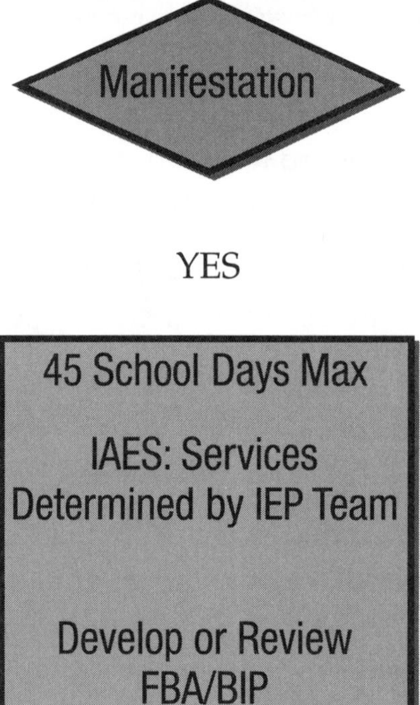

REGARDLESS OF MANIFESTATION, school authorities may remove a student to an IAES for not more than 45 school days (§300.530(g)).

NO

Same # School Days as Nondisabled

IAES: Services Determined by IEP Team

FBA/BIP as Appropriate

No manifestation: Where the IEP team has determined that the behavior in question is not a manifestation of the student's disability, school personnel may remove a student with disabilities for the same duration as students without disabilities (§300.530(c)).

Except:

- Services to enable the student to participate in the general curriculum and to progress toward meeting IEP goals
- FBA/BIP as appropriate: "... receive, as appropriate, functional behavioral assessment and behavior intervention services must be provided" (§300.530(d)(i&ii))

Other Violations of Student Code of Conduct

Removal from school for more than ten school days for other violations of the Code of Student Conduct may be warranted for students with disabilities if the same sanction would be utilized for similarly situation students without disabilities.

NO

Same # School Days as Nondisabled

IAES: Services Determined by IEP Team

FBA/BIP as Appropriate

No manifestation: Where the IEP Team has determined that the behavior in question is *not* a manifestation of the student's disability, school personnel may remove a student with disabilities for the same duration as student without disabilities (§300.530(c)).

Except:

- Services to enable the student to participate in the general curriculum and to progress toward meeting IEP goals
- FBA/BIP as appropriate: "... receive, as appropriate, functional behavioral assessment and behavior intervention services must be provided" (§300.530(d)(i&ii))

YES

Review/Revise IEP

Maintain Current Placement

Develop or Review FBA/BIP

Manifestation: Where the IEP Team has determined that the behavior in question *was* a manifestation of the student's disability, the IEP Team must:

1. Develop or review an FBA and a BIP (§300.530(f)(1)(i&ii)).
2. Maintain the student in his current placement unless his parents agree to a change of placement (§300.530(f)(1)(i&ii)).

Written Prior Notice or Placement Change

Placement in an Interim Alternative Educational Setting (IAES) for more than ten school days is a change in placement. Parents must be given prior written notice before such a change in placement is made.

Parents must be notified of:

1. Final actions to be taken (e.g., length of suspension, dates of suspension)
2. Procedural safeguards
3. The right to challenge the Manifestation Determination

4. The right to challenge the change in placement and the IAES

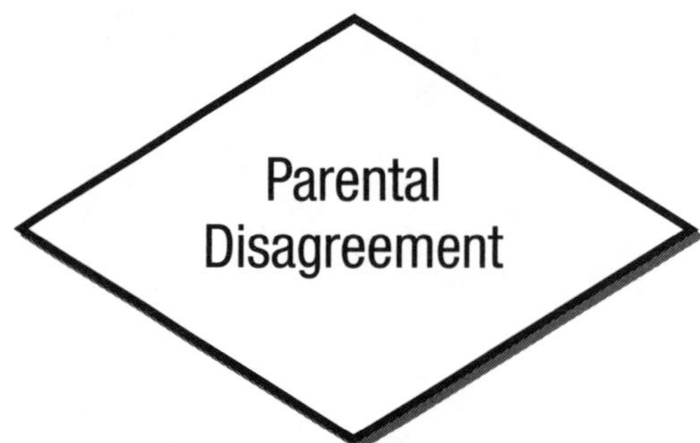

The parent(s) of a student with disabilities who disagrees with a decision regarding IAES or the Manifestation Determination may request an expedited hearing (§300.532).

Expedited Hearing

Resolution Meeting
(Within 7 days)

Hearing
(Within 20 days)

Stay Put: IAES

If an expedited hearing is requested, the following time parameters apply:

- The hearing must be expedited. An expedited hearing must occur within 20 school days of being requested and must result in a decision within 10 school days after the hearing.
- A resolution session meeting must occur within 7 school days of the date the hearing is requested (§300.532(c)(3)(i)).
- The hearing may proceed unless resolution has been reached within 15 school days of the date the hearing is requested (§300.532(c)(3)(ii)).

The hearing officer may do one of the following:

- Return the student to the placement from which he was removed (300.532(b)(2)(i))
- Order a change in placement to an IAES for not more than 45 days

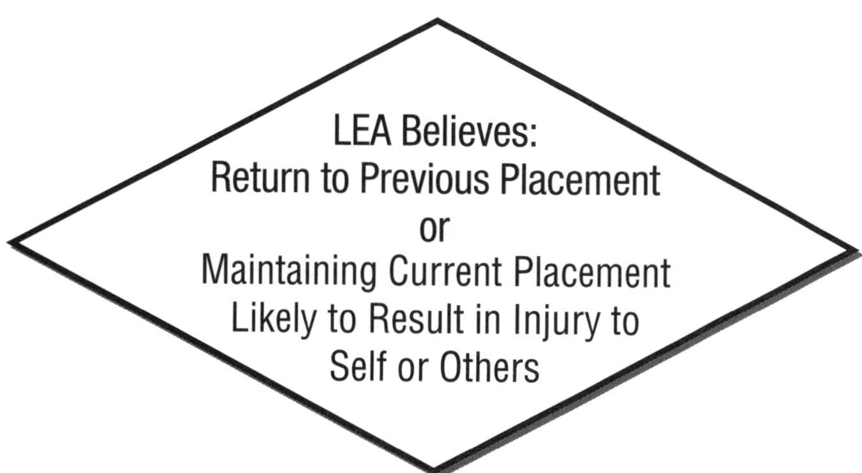

If the LEA believes that maintaining the current placement of the student is substantially likely to result in injury to the student or others, an expedited hearing may be requested (§300.532(a)).

IAES
for
Duration of Removal

An IAES is provided for student with disabilities when:

1. The student has been removed for more than ten school days cumulative within one year.
2. The current removal constitutes a change of placement.

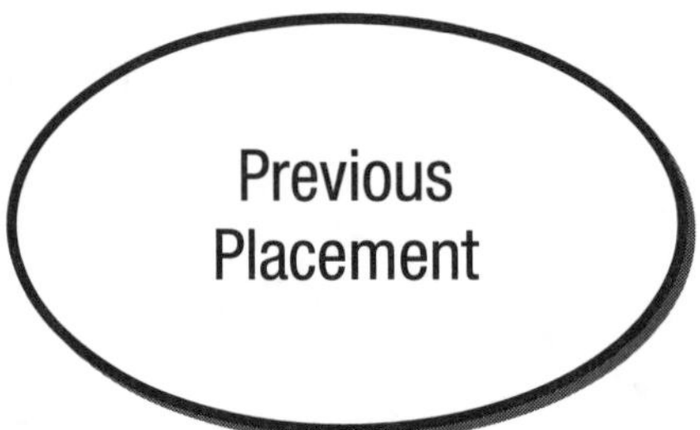

Previous placement is the constellation of services in place before the student was removed to an IAES.

All reference numbers refer to sections of the Federal Register, Vol. 70, No. 118/Tuesday, June 21, 2005/Proposed Rules for 34 CFR Parts 300, 301 and 304, Notice of Proposed Rule Making, U.S. Department of Education.

Section 6

Additional Resources and Information for the Principal

Introduction

You are the principal in your own school. But wait. Was your administrative training program long on theory related to leadership models, policy, and the like? Was it short on the basics for actually running a school and locating needed resources? Basics include such things as organizing a schoolwide Behavior Management Team or Discipline Committee, using students as conflict peer mediators, establishing an effective database for discipline problems, working with chronically truant students, conducting a Functional Behavior Assessment, or even developing a meaningful school Mission Statement. You may also need specific information related to effective interventions for your most problematic, or Seven Percent, students. Using behavioral contracting or a school-to-home note system *appropriately* makes all the difference in whether or not these interventions work!

This section provides practical information on the basics. With a few exceptions, we describe each skill or topic we present in the same format: definition of the skill or topic, a detailed description of it, specific steps needed for implementation, how to troubleshoot it, and things you can do to make it even better. Not every principal needs every skill or technique presented in this section. However, we have included the basics most commonly needed by many principals.

School Mission Statements

Definition

A school Mission Statement is a succinctly written statement that describes the goals and behavioral expectations for the students and school staff.

Description

A school's Mission Statement, a one-paragraph written narrative, is usually posted at the school entry and on walls in other heavy-traffic school areas. A useful, effective Mission Statement is simply stated and easy to understand. Good Mission Statements are short, with key embedded words that represent a school's goals and behavioral expectations. That is, the key words should lead directly to the development of a school's basic All-School Rules. See *Table 6-1* for an example of a school's Mission Statement.

The Mission Statement example in *Table 6-1* is short and emphasizes the key words **safe**, **positive**, **learning**, and **responsible**. Embedded words such as **responsible** may be difficult for many students to understand. Words like responsible must be broken down into their component parts in the All-School Rules. Students must then be helped to understand that, in *this* particular school, being responsible means to engage in the behaviors described in the All-School Rules. For a given school, these rules might state:

- Follow staff directions immediately.
- Keep hands, feet, and objects to yourself.
- Speak kindly, and use good language.
- Take care of the school's and other people's property.

The basic or core All-School Rules for all school environments follow from the Mission Statement.

Taking this concept one step further, additional rules or expectations should flow from the Mission Statement and be clearly defined

Table 6-1

Example of a Mission Statement

It is the mission of Kennedy Junior High School to provide a ***safe*** and ***positive*** educational environment where ***learning*** takes place. It is expected that all students and staff will conduct themselves in a ***responsible*** manner that promotes this safe and positive learning environment.

for each main environment or setting in the school. For example, rules for the lunchroom might state:

- Walk when entering and leaving.
- Talk quietly.
- Stay in your seat until you are ready to leave.
- Put trays and trash where they belong.

Likewise, additional clarification for behavior in halls, during assemblies, in the classroom, during class transitions, or during recess is needed. Developing rules for these settings is discussed more fully in Section 2.

Steps for Implementing a School Mission Statement

Step 1: Decide the key embedded words (no more than three or four) that will represent your school's Mission Statement. Make sure that students understand these words and, if necessary, break them down even further into easily understood components.

Step 2: Write your Mission Statement around the key words you have selected. Make the Mission Statement simple and short. Remember: The overall theme of the Mission Statement should be your school's goals and behavioral expectations (e.g., safe, positive, learning, responsible). You can appoint your school's Behavior Management Committee to write a draft statement, reminding the members to follow the suggestions given here. Once the team has developed a draft statement, you can ask the members to present their work to the entire faculty for input.

Step 3: Once the Mission Statement has been finalized, post it in conspicuous places in the school, such as over the door to the office and on the wall near the entrance to the school. Generally, the Mission Statement is also posted in other key areas of the school building. Some schools even put their Mission Statement on a lighted, programmable moving-text sign to catch students' attention.

Step 4: Use the key embedded words in your school's Mission Statement to develop core All-School Rules. Post these core rules in all of the basic environments of the school such as the lunchroom, the auditorium, the gymnasium, all classrooms, and halls. It is desirable to have faculty come to consensus on the All-School Rules as well as to use and support them in all classrooms and environments. It is confusing for students to have entirely different sets of rules in each of their classrooms and other school environments. Each environment should use the same core All-School Rules and three to four additional, specialized rules unique to those environments.

Step 5: Introduce the Mission Statement to students at an opening school assembly. In this presentation, explain the Mission Statement and describe how the All-School Rules come directly from it. Provide students with concrete examples of the key words from the Mission Statement. You may even want to have faculty help role-play these examples and nonexamples to help clarify them.

Troubleshooting the Mission Statement

Problem: ***Students cannot seem to remember the Mission Statement and its key embedded words.***

Solution: First, check the length of the Mission Statement. Ineffective Mission Statements are wordy and complex. Recheck the key embedded words to make certain they are understandable to students and that the words have been specifically explained to them. Conciseness and simplicity are the keys to a workable Mission Statement. Make sure the Mission Statement is posted in several prominent places in the school. Post one at the main entrance to the school next to the posted All-School Rules or next to the Principal's 200 Club matrix. Other good locations are hallways, the lunchroom, the library, the auditorium, and the gymnasium. You can make a game out of stopping students and asking them to show you where a Mission Statement is posted. If they can, reward them with a 200 Club ticket. It may help to take key words from your Mission Statement and review them along with the school's morning announcements.

Problem: ***Students can recite the Mission Statement and the key embedded words, but they still do not seem to understand what it means.***

Solution: This may be especially applicable with younger students. Again, start by taking a minute or two during morning announcements to give additional, simple explanations. Tell students that you will be stopping some of them to ask them the meaning of the Mission Statement. Then, try stopping two students at a time. Ask if one of them can tell you the key embedded words and if the other can give an example of what each word means. If they are able to, give them each a 200 Club ticket.

Problem: ***The Behavior Management Team is given the task of writing the school's Mission Statement. However, they cannot agree on a simple statement, and the resulting Mission Statement is wordy, complex, and difficult to understand.***

Solution: Give the team a maximum number of words they can use in the Mission Statement. For example, you may tell them that they may not exceed 50 words. Once the Mission Statement is written, ask the team members to test it on a sampling of students. If the students cannot tell the team members its meaning, then it must be rewritten until the students can.

Problem: ***One or two members of the Behavior Management Team insist on including their own philosophies in the Mission Statement, resulting in a statement that is complex and difficult to understand.***

Solution: It is not an uncommon problem for some staff members to insist on including their personal views, irrespective of the need for simplicity and conciseness. However, it can bog down the development of a meaningful Mission Statement. The ultimate test is whether a sampling of students can understand it. If the Behavior Management Team does not seem to get beyond this problem, work with them to guide the process. As a last resort, complete the task yourself if need be.

Problem: ***Students know the Mission Statement and its key embedded words, but staff members do not.***

Solution: This is a problem that can undercut the Mission Statement process. Start each faculty meeting with a review of the Mission Statement and the key embedded words. Emphasize to the whole staff—including aides, the lunchroom staff, and custodians—that all must know and understand the Mission Statement.

Making the Mission Statement Even Better

1. Link the implementation of your Mission Statement with a program like "Mission Possible" and your school's positive discipline program, the Principal's 200 Club. The goal for the Mission Possible program is that in one week's time, all students stopped by school staff can tell them the Mission Statement's embedded words and their meanings. If students can tell staff members these key words and their meanings, they receive a Principal's 200 Club ticket. When all the students stopped in a week can recite the words and their meanings, provide the whole school with special recognition in an assembly or over the intercom, along with a treat.
2. Have the most senior class in the school make a video about the Mission Statement and the core All-School Rules to help teach them to younger students. The students making the video can include examples and nonexamples of the core All-School Rule behaviors. One school with which one of the authors worked even set the video to music from the movie *Mission Impossible*.
3. Adopt a school musical chant that can be sung, using the school's Mission Statement, the All-School Rules, and the school's name. The chant can also be included in the video described in Number 2.
4. Throughout the school year, start each assembly with the Mission Statement musical chant.
5. Throughout the school year, make sure students earn recognition for exemplifying the embedded words in the Mission Statement. Take pictures of students and post them for that week near the Mission Statement with the key words they have exemplified. For example, you might include photos of Cal emphasizing the word **learning** (showing a great spelling test score), Elena depicting the word **positive** (helping a younger student in the lunchroom), Tran representing **responsible** (placing his lunch tray and trash in the proper places), and Bill depicting **safe** (walking in the hall). Teachers can nominate students for the Mission Possible program pictures. Take care that high-achieving students are not the only ones nominated for the program pictures. Quiet, struggling, or problematic students must also be caught displaying appropriate behaviors and be nominated for this recognition.
6. Mission Statements can be designed to include special schoolwide programs such as all-school bully-proofing or social

skills programs. The Mission Statement can include specific references to these behaviors. These references must make a direct connection between student behavior and the skills being taught in these programs.

With these types of programs incorporated into the Mission Statement, the school's Behavior Management Team can select a social skill or anti-bullying behavior of the month. These selected behaviors are then linked to the Principal's 200 Club. Students who, when asked, can tell staff the skill of the month and its meaning—or are caught actually *doing* the behavior itself—earn a Principal's 200 Club ticket.

Box 6-1

Bully-Proofing/ Social Skills Program Resources

Bonds, M., & Stoker, S. (2001). *Bully-proofing your school: A comprehensive approach for middle schools.* Longmont, CO: Sopris West Educational Services.

Bowen, J., Ashcraft, P., Jenson, W.R., & Rhode, G. (under contract) *Tough Kid Bully Blockers Program.* Longmont, CO: Sopris West Educational Services.

Garrity, C., Jens, K., Porter, W., Sager, N., & Short-Camilli, C. (2004). *Bully-proofing your school: A comprehensive approach for elementary schools.* Longmont, CO: Sopris West Educational Services.

Knoff, H. M. (2001). *The stop and think social skills program (pre-K–8).* Longmont, CO: Sopris West Educational Services.

Osher, D., Dwyer, K., & Jackson, S. (2003). *Safe, supportive, and successful schools step by step.* Longmont, CO: Sopris West Educational Services.

Schoolwide Behavior Management Teams

Definition

Behavior Management teams are groups or committees of a school's personnel. Their function is to help design, implement, adapt, and oversee the ongoing disciplinary practices in a school.

Description

Behavior Management teams have different names in many schools. Some of the common names are Discipline Committee, Behavior Team, Student Behavior Committee, and even Schoolwide Assistance Team (SWAT). Behavior Management teams are usually assigned to design a school's discipline procedures. They meet regularly to recommend strategies for working with a school's most difficult students. These teams usually include the principal or assistant principal, teachers, related service personnel such as school psychologists or school counselors, and other staff such as lunchroom or school bus personnel. The most effective Behavior Management teams go beyond designing the basic schoolwide discipline practices. Their functions also include:

- Writing and implementing the school's Mission Statement and All-School Rules
- Taking the lead in designing and implementing a positive schoolwide discipline program such as the Principal's 200 Club
- Suggesting adjustments and changes to the schoolwide behavior management system
- Planning the schoolwide data-collection system and assessing the data on an ongoing basis
- Tracking problem students, recommending individualized interventions for them
- Planning needed in-service training for school staff

Steps for Implementing a Behavior Management Team

Step 1: Present the idea of the Behavior Management Team to the faculty before school starts, at a school retreat or faculty meeting. Ask for nominations of staff members who are looked up to and are known for their effective and positive management of students. These staff members can represent many facets of the school environment, such as teachers, lunchroom workers, counselors, or school psychologists. Also explain that the team always includes the principal.

Step 2: Oversee the election of the Behavior Management Team members from those who have been nominated. Team members are selected by their colleagues' votes based on the colleagues' confidence in their behavior management skills. Reemphasize that the principal is always part of the team.

> **Box 6-2**
> ## Technique Hint
> The principal must always retain membership on the Behavior Management Team. This function cannot be delegated. Having the principal as a team member endorses its importance.

Step 3: Set a schedule for regular and frequent meetings of the Behavior Management Team. It may be necessary to meet more frequently at the beginning of the school year than later in the year. We believe that teams must meet *at least* every two weeks; meeting once a month is not effective.

Step 4: Arrange for regular minutes to be taken at all meetings. If you cannot arrange for a school secretary to do this, ask for a volunteer from the team. The person who takes the minutes should provide you with a copy as soon as possible after the meeting. Make sure that all team members receive a copy of the minutes.

Step 5: Spell out the team's specific functions during the first meeting. The first function is to review or draft the school Mission Statement and the All-School Rules according to the guidelines discussed earlier in this Briefcase.

Step 6: The team's second function is to design and hammer out the details of the school's positive discipline program, such as the Principal's 200 Club. This system is used to reward students who follow the All-School Rules and who know and understand the Mission Statement. The team does not need to use the Principal's 200 Club if there is another effective, positive system in place. Stress to the team that the positive discipline system *must* be directly linked to the All-School Rules and the Mission Statement.

Step 7: The team's third function is to review the school's current data-collection system or to design a new one. The data-collection system must provide information about the most frequently broken All-School Rules, the students sent most often to the office for behavioral problems, the teachers who most frequently send the most students to the office, and the school areas (i.e., classrooms, school yard, rest rooms, lunchroom, hallways, or buses) where the problems occur most commonly. Good school-data systems are designed to be easy to use and produce summary information reports for the types of problems just described. Ensure that the Behavior Management Team regularly receives summary information reports with which to work. If they do not have them, they are operating randomly and blindly.

Step 8: Use the Behavior Management Team to help with chronically misbehaving students. These are the Seven Percent Students we described in Section 2. By regularly reviewing the schoolwide data system printout, the team will know exactly who these students are. Once they are identified, appropriate individualized strategies and interventions can be selected and implemented. Common strategies that are often chosen include:

- Perform a Functional Behavior Assessment of a student's behavioral problems to identify how to approach a solution.
- Assign the student a Tracking Sheet to carry as described in Section 4. In addition to having the sheet initialed by teachers, the student must turn it in at the end of the day to a staff member to go over the student's progress with him. This adult can help the student solve problems in areas needing improvement as well as to recognize and reward improvement. This adult does not need to be a member of the Behavior Management Team.
- Implement a behavioral contract.
- Set up a Home Note system.
- Use a peer mediation process.

Step 9: Use the Behavior Management Team for consultation with teachers who are struggling with discipline in their classrooms. From the school data-collection system printout, it is easy to identify which teachers are making the most discipline referrals for problematic behaviors. It may be that these teachers have been assigned unusually difficult students for the year, or they may be having difficulty with consistently implementing effective behavior management practices in their classrooms. In either case, the team can help to provide needed inservice training, consultation, or assignment of a mentor teacher to help improve their practices in a non-threatening way.

Step 10: The Behavior Management Team also identifies and plans needed inservice training for the school. Again, the school's data-collection system printout will help by identifying the most problematic areas of the school, the most common problematic behaviors, the students who are having the most difficulty, and the teachers who need help.

Step 11: Along with meeting frequently, the Behavior Management Team reports regularly to the rest of the school staff. The team needs to have a standing item on the agenda for regular staff meetings. At these meetings, the team reports on the use of the positive discipline program system, perceived inservice training needs, and efforts to track and manage the most difficult students. A summary of how the school is doing in terms of improvement—or lack of it—based on all major areas of data collected is also shared with the staff. When data are reported, no single staff member should be highlighted as having difficulty with student behavior in the classroom. Encourage questions and feedback from the rest of the staff to the team.

Troubleshooting Behavior Management Teams

Problem: ***The Behavior Management Team does not seem to agree on a Mission Statement or All-School Rules.***

Solution: Reviewing the guidelines in this Briefcase for developing the school's Mission Statement and All-School Rules may help. Providing examples from other schools may also be of use. However, if the team cannot reach consensus, guide the discussion or even complete this task yourself.

Problem: ***The team never seems to get much accomplished.***

Solution: Set up regular meetings for the team. Review the minutes. Determine whether one or two team members are sabotaging the process or impeding progress. If so, speak to each one privately about your concerns, and let them know your expectations of them. If needed, sit in on meetings, model the behavior you expect from them, and guide the discussion yourself for a time. Continue to give private feedback.

Problem: ***The team is not using the data that are collected through the all-school data-collection system, or it is not using the data effectively.***

Solution: Review the data-collection system. It should be designed to collect essential information as previously described. Make sure that one person in the office is in charge of entering data for office and discipline referrals and that discipline reports are being generated when they are requested. If necessary, take the team through the process of reviewing the data several times so that they know how to use the information.

Problem: ***The team has difficulty identifying and monitoring the problematic Seven Percent Students. It also has trouble generating individualized strategies and interventions to support the improvement of these students.***

Solution: Make certain that the team has a pool of staff members who are willing to be assigned to help track difficult students. These staff members do not have to be part of the Behavior Management Team,

Table 6-2
Intervention Resources

Beck, R. (1997). *Responding to individual differences in education (RIDE)*, Version 1.5. Longmont, CO: Sopris West Educational Services.

Sprick, R., & Howard, L. (1995). *The teacher's encyclopedia of behavior management.* Longmont, CO: Sopris West Educational Services.

Sprick, R., Sprick, M., & Garrison, M. (1993). *Interventions: Collaborative planning for students at risk.* Longmont, CO: Sopris West Educational Services.

but they must understand the importance of monitoring how the interventions are working for the students. Also, make sure that the team has access to intervention resources, including experienced master teachers or other staff (e.g., school psychologists or counselors), consultants, and training materials for interventions. *Table 6-2* provides information about intervention resources.

Manifestation Determination

Definition

The Manifestation Determination pertains to students with disabilities who are receiving special education services, and it applies only to their placement. The Manifestation Determination is the conclusion reached as to whether a student's problematic behavior was caused by or had a direct and substantial relationship to his disability. If the behavior is determined to be a manifestation of the student's disability, then a change of placement resulting from the behavioral problem cannot exceed ten school days for general code of conduct violations unless the district calls for a hearing to show that the student is likely to cause injury to himself or others if he is returned to his previous placement. However, the parameters for a change of placement differ for drug, weapons, and violations involving serious bodily injury. Principals may change the placement of a student with a disability to an alternative setting for 45 school days for drug, weapons, and serious bodily injury violations even if the behavior is a manifestation of his disability. Principals may change the placement the same number of days as for students without disabilities if the behavior is not a manifestation of the student's disability.

Description

A Manifestation Determination meeting of the student's IEP Team members is convened by the principal to make the determination as to whether the student's problematic behavior meets the definition. The principal, together with the parents, determine the appropriate IEP Team members to attend the meeting. In order to make the Manifestation Determination, the IEP Team must compare the student's current behavior with *previously* documented information about the student's disability. Manifestation Determination reviews are required only before a student receiving

Table 6.3

Parameters of Manifestation Determination Meetings

Manifestation Determination meetings must:

- Be held immediately, if possible, but in no case later than ten school days after the date on which the decision to take action is made.
- Be conducted by a properly constituted IEP Team with appropriate, written prior notice given to participants.
- Result in decisions that are made on an individual, case-by-case basis, not on generalizations assumed regarding a disability label or diagnosis.
- Result in the IEP Team's considering—in terms of the behavior that is the subject of the disciplinary action—all relevant information, such as evaluation and diagnostic results. This includes such results or other relevant information supplied by the student's parents, observations of the student, and the student's IEP and placement.

special education services is suspended for a cumulative total of more than ten days during an academic school year. Parameters that must be followed regarding Manifestation Determination meetings are described in *Table 6-3*.

Steps for Carrying Out a Manifestation Determination

Step 1: Send out proper written prior notice of the Manifestation Determination meeting to IEP Team members a reasonable amount of time before the meeting is held. Take into account that the meeting must be held as soon as possible and also be within ten school days after the date on which the decision was made to take the planned action.

Step 2: At the meeting, the team must consider all sources of relevant information, including that from the parents and the student, the student's IEP, and the student's current educational placement.

Step 3: Lead the team in a thorough discussion of *whether or not the behavior in question was the direct result of the school district's failure to implement the IEP. Table 6-4* describes the information and questions to review in making this determination.

The IEP Team should be prepared to defend its Manifestation Determination decision with documentation of the information considered by the team.

Step 4: Lead the team in a thorough discussion of *whether the behavior in question was caused by, or had a direct and substantial relationship to, the student's disability. Table 6-5* describes the information and questions to review in making this determination.

Table 6-4

Failure to Implement the IEP

The following information, at a minimum, should be considered in order to determine whether the behavior in question was the direct result of a failure to implement the IEP:

- **Classification**—Is the behavior related to behavioral manifestations of the student's disabling condition?
- **Prereferral documentation**—Was the behavior noted as a concern that was addressed in the regular classroom?
- **Referral documentation**—Was the behavior noted as a concern when the student was referred for evaluation?
- **Evaluation**—Is the behavior addressed in the evaluation information in the student's file?
- **IEP**—Are there goals addressing the behavior? Is a Functional Behavioral Assessment included? Is there a Behavior Intervention Plan included?
- **Placement**—Is the placement appropriate to meet the special education and related service needs of the student?

Should the behavior in question be noted in the prereferral, referral, and evaluation documents but not be addressed in the IEP, the behavior *may* have been managed by the implementation of a Behavior Intervention Plan. This is an implementation issue that must be addressed in the Manifestation Determination.

In order to defend a finding that the behavior was not the result of failure to implement the IEP, IEP Teams must: (a) demonstrate that they have looked at all the required documents in the student's file; (b) verify that the documents are current and in compliance; and (c) validate the appropriateness of the program in meeting the student's needs.

Step 5: If the behavior in question was (1) caused by a failure to implement the IEP, and/or (2) substantially related to the student's disability; and/or (3) caused by the student's disability, the behavior *must be considered a manifestation of the student's disability.* Whatever the outcome of the team's decision, the following components must be documented:

- The behavior that prompted the meeting
- Sources of information that document the behavior.
- Any additional evaluations conducted
- Statements addressing whether the IEP and the placement were appropriate and whether special education services, supplementary aids and services, and behavior intervention strategies were provided that are consistent with the IEP and the placement.

Table 6-5

How Was the Behavior in Question Linked to the Student's Disability?

Behavior was caused by the disability—The *Diagnostic and Statistical Manual of Mental Disorders*, Fourth Edition, Test Revision (DSM-IV TR) represents the professional standard for classification of mental disorders. The DSM-IV TR provides diagnostic criteria for most of the disability categories encompassed in IDEA 2004 along with diagnostic and related features, including behavioral characteristics of these disabilities. Case law suggests that if the behavior prompting disciplinary sanctions is listed as a diagnostic or related feature of the student's disability, there is a high probability that the behavior may be caused by the disability.

Behavior had a direct and substantial relationship to the disability—The IDEA 2004 Conference Committee Report provides guidance that Congress intended that the Manifestation Determination:

> ... analyze the child's behavior as demonstrated across settings and across time when determining whether the conduct in question is the direct result of the disability ...
>
> —*Committee report*, at 224

Presumably, if the behavior has a direct and substantial relationship to the disability, the behavior should have been observed in different settings at different times. Information available to make this determination may include:

- Anecdotal records of teachers and administrators
- Special education documents such as peripheral data, referral data, evaluation reports, and IEP goals
- Parental observations

- Statements addressing whether the behavior in question was caused by, or had a direct and substantial relationship to, the student's disability
- The Manifestation Determination statement (i.e., the behavior was or was not a manifestation of the student's disability)
- Documentation of participation of the IEP Team, along with the provision for dissenting opinions

Figure 6-1 shows a sample of a Manifestation Determination form that has been completed by a student's IEP Team. A blank copy of this form is included at the end of this section.

Table 6-6 gives samples of actual Manifestation Determinations.

Figure 6-1
Sample Manifestation Determination

MANIFESTATION DETERMINATION

Name: Tony Gambino Jr. School: Sunset Jr. High

Date of MD Meeting: 9/15/05 Date of Incident: 9/14/05 Date of Decision to Suspended ≥ Days: 9/14/05

Behavior prompting suspension: fighting in hall with another student

I. APPROPRIATENESS OF PROGRAM:

A. **Current Classification:** Behavior Disordered
Source(s) of information: evaluation, parents, IEP Team

B. **Prereferral:** (Behavior noted as area of concern?) ☑ YES ❑ NO ❑ N/A
If yes, date of Prereferral: 5/03 Concerns noted: physical aggression to peers

C. **Referral:** (Behavior prompting suspension noted as concern at referral?) ☑ YES ❑ NO
If yes, date of Referral: 11/03 Concerns noted: physical aggression toward peers (fighting, hitting, shoving)
Source(s) of information: school records, staff reports

D. **Evaluation:** Date of last evaluation: 2/04 Evaluation (≤ 3 years)?: ❑ YES ☑ NO
1. Does existing evaluation address current areas of educational concern? ☑ YES ❑ NO
2. Additional evaluation needed in the following areas: ❑ Complete Evaluation
❑ Intellectual Development ❑ Academic Achievement ❑ Communication
❑ Adaptive/Social/Behavioral ☑ Other: no additional needed
Date of completion: ________ Person Responsible: ________
Source(s) of information: ________

E. **IEP:** Date of last IEP: 4/05 Is IEP current ☑ YES ❑ NO ❑ N/A
a. Is IEP in compliance? ☑ YES ❑ NO ❑ N/A
b. Have services consisted with the IEP been provided? ❑ YES ☑ NO ❑ N/A
If no, explain: IEP states that Tony is to be escorted by an adult from class to class. This did not occur on 9/14. (substitute teacher)
c. Are behavioral goals included on the IEP? ☑ YES ❑ NO ❑ N/A
If yes, do they address the behavior subject to disciplinary action? ☑ YES ❑ NO ❑ N/A
Source(s) of information: special education file

F. **Placement:** Current permission to place in evidence? ☑ YES ❑ NO ❑ N/A
Current placement appropriate to meet student needs? ☑ YES ❑ NO ❑ N/A
Source(s) of information: IEP Team discussion, school records

G. **Summary:** (a., b., & c. must be marked "YES" to proceed to Finding.)
a. The student was properly evaluated. ☑ YES ❑ NO
b. Parent(s) were included in IEP process. ☑ YES ❑ NO
c. The IEP has been implemented ❑ YES ☑ NO

Finding: Based on consideration of A-G above, it is consensus of this IEP Team that the behavior in question WAS ☑ WAS NOT ❑ a direct result of a failure to implement the IEP.

(front of form)

II. CONDUCT DIRECTLY/SUBSTANTIALLY RELATED TO OR CAUSED BY DISABILITY:

A. **Anecdotal Records:** Is there a record of behavior subject to discipline? ☑ YES ❑ NO ❑ N/A
If YES, not time period and setting where behavior occurred: IEP and other supporting information in Tony's special education file.

B. **Was the behavior in question noted:**
1. When the student was referred for evaluation? ☑ YES ❑ NO
2. In the evaluation summary? ☑ YES ❑ NO
3. Addressed in the IEP? ☑ YES ❑ NO

C. **Has the behavior been exhibited across settings and times?** ☑ YES ❑ NO
Source(s) of information: special education file, school records

D. Is the conduct a recognized associated feature of the student's disability? ☑ YES ❑ NO
Source(s) of information (i.e., DSM-IV-TR): DSM-IV

E. **Finding: Based on consideration of A-C above, it is the consensus of the IEP Team that the behavior in question WAS ☑ WAS NOT ❑ directly/substantially related to or caused by the student's disability.**
Rationale: The IEP Team agrees that the behavior is recognized as a feature of Tony's disability and the IEP was not followed to prevent it.

IV. MANIFESTATION STATEMENT:

In order to make a "No Manifestation" determination the team must find both the following:
1. The behavior in question WAS NOT a direct result of a failure to implement the student's IEP.
2. The behavior in question WAS NOT directly/substantially related to or caused by the student's disability.

It is the consensus of the IEP Team that the conduct WAS ☑ WAS NOT ❑ a manifestation of the student's disability.

Record of participation

LEA Rep.	Craig P.	Date: 9/15
Parent:	Myra G.	Date: 9/15
Special Education Teacher:	Beth U.	Date: 9-15
Regular Education Teacher:	Katie D.	Date: Sept 15
Guidance Specialist:	Jean L.	Date: 9/15
Other: school psychology	Moira K.	Date: 9-15

(back of form)

Table 6-6

Samples of Manifestation Determinations

1. Student with ADHD served as OHI (Other Health Impaired) involved in assault with knife, then suspended with recommendation for expulsion. Two psychologists testified that behavior was related to student's oppositional defiant disorder, not ADHD. Parents were notified of IEP meeting to determine manifestation. At IEP meeting, student was declassified. Principal assigned student to alternative program. Hearing officer determined that the evidence supported the conclusion that the behavior was not manifestation. Since student will receive services commensurate with his IEP in alternative setting, Hearing officer ruled that district had acted appropriately. *Re: Student with a Disability, 27 IDELR 935.*

2. Hearing officer rejected parents' assertion that the district erred when it did not conduct a manifestation review before suspending their child, a student with an unspecified disability. Manifestation reviews are required only before a student is suspended for a cumulative total of ten days during an academic year. Since the student was suspended for only three days and he had no other suspensions during the school year, no manifestation review was required. *Northeast Indep. Sch. Dist., 28 IDELR 1004.*

3. Student with disabilities was not suspended for more than ten days per year; therefore, district was not required to conduct a Manifestation Determination prior to imposing disciplinary sanction since no change of placement occurred. *Board of Education of the Averill Park Central Sch. Dist., 27 IDELR 996.*

4. District found no causal relationship between student's learning disability and cerebral palsy and behavior leading to suspension, even though student had been called names that allegedly aggravated the situation. Hearing officer found no basis for parents' claim that student was disciplined for behavior related to his disability. *Northeast Indep. Sch. Dist., 26 IDELR 939.*

5. Senior high school student with ADHD brought shotgun to school in his pickup truck after hunting the previous day. He considered taking the gun out of the truck on the morning before school but thought he would get in trouble with his father for not cleaning it. School determined that the action was not a manifestation of his disability since the action constituted "poor judgment," which is not part of the diagnostic criteria. The district's determination that the incident was not a manifestation of the student's disability was upheld. Hearing officer determined that students with ADHD usually do not consider the consequences of their actions; thus, a consideration of the consequences is atypical of ADHD and is not consistent with the usual symptoms of the disorder. *Oconee County Sch. Sys., 27 IDELR 629.*

Functional Behavior Assessment (FBA)

Functional Behavior Assessments and Behavior Intervention Plans are typically intertwined. Thus, we will not attempt to separate discussion of one from the other. However, for purposes of this Briefcase, we first discuss FBAs in detail. Then, we focus on the specifics of BIPs.

Definition

FBA is a data collection procedure used to develop an informed guess or "hypothesis" regarding the variables in a student's environment that contribute to his inappropriate behavior. Many different formats exist for documenting the FBA. For example, FBAs for severe, self-destructive behaviors are generally more comprehensive and detailed than those for less severe behaviors such as out-of-seat behavior or general classroom disruption.

Description

There are two basic principles on which the FBA and the BIP are based:

1. Inappropriate behaviors, including rule-breaking behaviors, occur within the context of the student's environment. In other words, the student's behavior does not occur in a vacuum. He and his environment interact with each other. If the inappropriate behavior is to change, the student's environment must be carefully examined to discover what sets off or "triggers" the behavior.
2. The student's inappropriate behavior serves a purpose or a function for him. Another way of saying this is that the student's inappropriate behavior "works" for him in some way, or he would not continue to do it; somehow, the behavior is meeting his needs or wants. Once educators understand that problem behavior serves a purpose for the student, they are better able to manage it. The FBA and the BIP that are developed as a result of problem behavior may be used for a wide range of behaviors—from common classroom issues (e.g., noncompliance, disruption) to more severe behaviors (e.g., self-injury, inflicting injury on others).

A student may be in need of an FBA and a BIP if any of the following situations occur:

- The student engages in behaviors that are substantially likely to cause injury to himself or others.
- The student causes significant or repeated property damage.
- The student's behavior interferes with the education of other students in the classroom.
- The student's behavior interferes with his own education.

- The student's behavior causes an emergency situation.
- The student is suspended as a result of his behavior.

Box 6-3

Technique Hint

When the school's standard behavior management procedures do not work adequately, the reason is frequently that the procedures do not address the purpose or function of the student's problem behavior or the particular way in which the behavior is associated with the student's environment.

Who Conducts an FBA?

Professionals who have knowledge about the student or who become knowledgeable from available data sources and who have been trained in the procedures of FBA conduct an FBA. Ideally, a number of school staff members have information to contribute to the FBA. These individuals might include the student's teacher(s), school counselor, school psychologist, principal or assistant principal, other students, or ancillary staff (e.g., media aide, lunchroom worker, custodian).

Components of an FBA

An FBA may include any or all of the following components, depending on the particular case:

1. **Observation**—Direct observation of the student takes place in the environment or setting where ABC data are collected by an assigned, trained professional. (Refer to Section 4 where ABC data are discussed in detail, relating to the ABC-RISS sheet.) Critical considerations are: (a) time of day; (b) people present; (c) location of the problem behavior; (d) events occurring just prior to the problem; (e) a description of the problem behavior in which the student engaged; (f) positive or negative attention given from peers or adults; (g) tangible items the student might have obtained as a result of his behavior; and (h) the person, situation, or place the student escaped as a result of his problem behavior.
2. **Indirect Assessment**—Information is gathered from all available sources, including people who have knowledge of the student and/or the incident involving the problem behavior. Indirect assessment may include interviews with such individuals or obtaining information they may have in other ways.
3. **Review of Records**—The student's records are reviewed to determine intervention strategies that have been used in the past with the student. Interventions that have been successful, as well as those that have been unsuccessful, can provide useful information.
4. **Hypothesis**—After a careful assessment of the information gathered, an informed guess (or hypothesis) is developed to explain the probable interaction between the student and his environment and how the environment triggers the problematic behavior. *Table 6.7* provides an example of an FBA informed guess or hypothesis.

Table 6-7
Example of an FBA Hypothesis

After reviewing the specific information gathered, the Behavior Management Team—together with the school psychologist as an invited consultant—comes to a conclusion about the reasons behind a student's problematic behavior. They hypothesize that when the math teacher announces a pop quiz, the student displays highly disruptive behaviors (i.e., swearing, throwing papers, overturning his chair) so that he will be sent from the classroom and can avoid the quiz. This gives the team the information they need to alter circumstances and design a Behavior Intervention Plan so that the problematic behavior doesn't occur in the first place. After changing the circumstances and implementing the BIP, the team reviews data on the results of their plan to see if their hypothesis was correct. They will assume that it was correct if the plan worked.

Steps for Conducting an FBA

The steps described below correspond to the information called for to complete the FBA form shown in *Figure 6-2*. This form is also included at the end of this section to be copied for your own use. Following the steps and documenting the responses on the FBA form will result in a completed FBA.

Step 1: Identify and specifically define the problematic or target behavior in which the student is engaging and that prompted the FBA. If multiple behaviors are identified, select one behavior to target initially for intervention. Make certain that the target behavior is *observable* and *measurable*.

Step 2: Collect and document the information. The professional responsible for conducting the FBA meets with and interviews individuals who have knowledge about the student and/or the incident. This professional may call one or more meetings of some or all of these individuals to discuss and collect information. *Antecedents*, or "triggers," that seem to set the stage for the behavior to occur must be identified:

- What is likely to precede or set off the problem behavior? Examples may include the teacher's requesting the class to: "Please take out your math books"; "Clear your desk and get ready for the quiz"; or "Read part of the story out loud to the class."

Figure 6-2
Completed Sample FBA

FUNCTIONAL BEHAVIOR ASSESSMENT (FBA)

FIRST NAME Adam LAST NAME Baum GRADE 5 SCHOOL Crestview DATE 9/18/04
PARTICIPANTS Dr. E. Ville (school psychologist), Les Moore (counselor), M. Genaux (sp. ed. teacher)
This FBA will be utilized for: (Intervention Purposes) IEP Requirements

Describe the problem behavior that prompted this FBA:
Adam is physically aggressive towards other students by pushing, hitting, and kicking them.

Adam is verbally aggressive toward other students by yelling at them, calling them names, and threatening to hurt them.

If more than one behavior is described, do they usually occur together (in a response group)? ☑ YES ☐ NO

If the above statement addresses multiple behaviors, identify **ONE BEHAVIOR** (or response group) to be targeted for intervention:
Physical aggression toward other students in the form of pushing, hitting, or kicking them.

The Target Behavior Is:
OBSERVABLE ✓ **MEASURABLE** ✓

ANTECEDENTS

What is likely to "set-off" or precede the problem behavior?

WHEN is the problem behavior most likely to occur?
During recess or lunch, before school, after school.

Approximate Time: varies

WHERE is the problem behavior most likely to occur?
Outside of the school building usually on the playground.

During what **SUBJECT/ACTIVITY** is the problem behavior most likely to occur? (list subjects)
recess or lunch

The **PEOPLE** that are present when the problem behavior is most likely to occur:
peers (different ones)

OTHER EVENTS or **CONDITIONS** that immediately precede the problem behavior?
Adam is playing with other students.

When is the student most successful? When **DOESN'T** the problem behavior occur?
During art, math, computer time.

CONSEQUENCES

What "PAYOFF" does the student obtain when she/he demonstrates the problem behavior?

The student **GAINS**:
- ☐ Teacher/Adult attention
- ☑ Peer Attention
- ☑ Desired time or activity
- ☑ Control over others or situations
- ☐ Self Stimulation
- ☐ Other

The Student AVOIDS or ESCAPES:
- ☐ Teacher/Adult attention
- ☐ Peer Attention
- ☐ Subjects or Activities
- ☐ Situations
- ☐ Self Stimulation
- ☐ Other

What has been tried so far to change the problem behavior?
- ☐ This is the first occurrence. It will be addressed through this FBA and Behavior Intervention Plan.
- ☐ Consistently implemented rules
- ☐ Posted consequences for behaviors
- ☐ Consistently implemented behavior or academic contract
- ☑ Consistently implemented Home/School Note System
- ☐ Adapted curriculum (HOW?)
- ☐ Modified Instruction (HOW?)
- ☐ Adjusted schedule (HOW?)
  9/7, 9/17
- ☑ Conferences with parents (DATES?)
  9/3, 9/8, 9/13
- ☑ Sent student to office (DATES?)
- ☐ Other

(front of form)

FUNCTIONAL BEHAVIOR ASSESSMENT (FBA)

FUNCTIONAL OR PROBLEM BEHAVIOR

After reviewing the antecedents and consequences, summarize the information below. Consider the following questions:
- Why is the student behaving this way?
- What function or payoff is met by the student's behavior?

WHEN (SUMMARIZE ANTECEDENTS): During less structured times, such as lunch, recess, before and after school—when Adam is playing with other students.

THIS STUDENT (IDENTIFY THE PROBLEM BEHAVIOR): Becomes physically aggressive toward other students by pushing, hitting, and kicking.

IN ORDER TO (SUMMARIZE "PAYOFF"): Gain control over others or situations, obtain desired item or access to an activity, and maintain "status" with peers.

EXAMPLES
1. When in the halls before school, after school, and during transitions, the student pushes other students and verbally threatens to beat them up in order to gain status and attention from peers.
2. When working on independent seatwork during the regular education math class, the student puts his head on his desk in order to escape work that is too difficult/frustrating.

REPLACEMENT BEHAVIOR

Identify the replacement behavior. Remember that replacement behavior is not an absence of the problem behavior (i.e., Do not write: "rather than hitting, I want this student to keep his hands to himself.") Instead, a replacement behavior is a description of the behavior that the student will perform *in place of the problem behavior* which could include socially appropriate alternative behavior, coping skills, anger management skills, techniques to deal with frustrating situations, self advocacy, and others.

RATHER THAN
Becoming physically aggressive towards other students by pushing, hitting, or kicking.

THE STUDENT WILL
1. Use anger control strategies to decrease aggressive behavior responses (i.e., count 1-10).
2. Use negotiation skills with peers.
3. Use conflict resolution skills with peers.

This Definition is:
☑ **Observable** ☑ **Measurable**

EXAMPLES:
1. Rather than pushing students and threatening to beat them up, the student will walk in the halls with his hands at his side and say "HELLO" to those with whom he wishes to interact.
2. Rather than putting his head on his desk, the student will place his red "HELP" card on his desk to let his teacher know he needs assistance.

(back of form)

The authors wish to thank colleague Glenn Dyke for contributing the contents for this sample.

- When (i.e., times of the day) is the behavior most likely to occur?
- Where is the behavior most likely to occur?
- During what subject or activity is the problem behavior most likely to occur?
- Who are the people present when the problem behavior is most likely to occur?

Box 6-4

Technique Hint

Triggers for problem behavior may be environmental (e.g., specific instructions, peer interactions), physiological (e.g., anxiety, hunger, anger, fatigue, illness, pain), or general (e.g., certain classroom activities, curricular expectations, seating arrangements).

- Are there other events or conditions that immediately precede the problem behavior?
- When is the student most successful? When *doesn't* the problem behavior occur?

Box 6-5

Technique Hint

Examples of events that may contribute to the problem behavior may include a missed meal, lack of sleep, medication changes, a fight on the school bus, or an ill family member.

Step 3: Identify the consequences of the problem behavior. In other words, what usually happens *after* the problem behavior is exhibited? Examples may include the teacher's sending the student to the office or to ISS or lecturing the student about lack of follow-through and then backing off from the request. Identifying what happens after the problem behavior requires answering questions such as:

- What payoff does the student get when he demonstrates the behavior? The student may *gain* or *avoid* or *escape* such things as teacher or adult attention, peer attention, a certain activity; obtain a desired item or access to an activity, control over others or a situation, or self-stimulation.
- Is this the first occurrence of the problem behavior? If not, what has been tried so far to change it? Are rules and consequences for behaviors posted and known by students? Has an appropriately written behavioral contract

been implemented? Has a Home Note system been tried? Has the curriculum been adapted or modified? Has the student's schedule been adjusted? Have there been conferences with the student's parents? If so, when? Has the student been sent to the office for the behavior? If so, when?

Step 4: Ask additional questions, including:

- Are there other factors in the environment or setting that appear to influence the behavior?
- Does the student have the desire to change his behavior?
- Does the student have the skills to perform the expected behavior?

Step 5: After reviewing the data collected on antecedents (that set off or precede the problem behavior) and consequences or payoff, develop informed guesses or hypotheses about the potential function(s) of the problem behavior. Consider:

- Events and circumstances associated with the problem behavior
- The purpose or function the behavior may serve for the student

Table 6-8
Additional Examples of FBA Hypotheses

1. When in the halls before school and during transitions, Logan pushes other students and verbally threatens to beat them up in order to gain status and attention from peers.
2. When working on independent seatwork during her regular education math class, Adriana puts her head on her desk in order to escape work that is too difficult or frustrating.

Step 6: Identify *replacement behavior* (i.e., the appropriate behavior that the student should do instead of the problem behavior). The replacement behavior must be *observable* and *measurable*. Keep in mind that this behavior must also address the student's needs or purposes, just as the inappropriate behavior did.

Once these six steps are completed, the information that has been gathered will be used to develop an effective BIP.

Box 6-6

Technique Hint

Select replacement behavior that is not merely an absence of the problem behavior. For example, do not write, "Instead of hitting, Seth will keep his hands to himself." An appropriate alternative behavior in this case may be using newly taught anger management skills, techniques to deal with frustrating situations, or self-advocacy. The replacement behavior might be, "Instead of pushing students and threatening to beat them up, Seth will walk in the halls with his hands at his side and say hello to those with whom he wishes to interact."

Box 6-7

Technique Hint

The *Functional Assessment and Intervention Program* (FAIP) is a commercially available computerized FBA program that generates hypotheses about what is motivating students' problematic behavior. It also suggests strategies and interventions to help develop a Behavior Intervention Plan to respond to the problematic behaviors that have been identified.

Functional Assessment and Intervention Program (FAIP) is available from Sopris West Educational Services at www.sopriswest.com.

Behavior Intervention Plan (BIP)

Definition

A Behavior Intervention Plan is a written document that results from conducting a Functional Behavior Assessment. Information gathered during the FBA process should lead to logical changes in the student's intervention program. The BIP is linked directly to the informed guess or hypothesis that has been formulated regarding the interaction between the student and his environment and how it triggers the problematic behavior. The BIP synthesizes the information that was gathered during the FBA and organizes it into a usable plan of action to help the student.

Description

After the team of professionals collects, analyzes, and develops an informed guess or hypothesis regarding the target or problem behavior in the FBA, the team develops the BIP. The BIP specifies the strategies, modifications, or supports that are needed to address the problem behavior, based on the informed guess. It also addresses the skill or skills the student needs to learn in order to behave more appropriately. In other words, the BIP describes an appropriate alternative behavior that the student will be taught to use in place of his inappropriate problem behavior. This behavior must also serve a purpose or function that is useful for the student just as the problem behavior was. This is the area in which the student is currently said to have a skill deficit.

The BIP also includes a description of reinforcers that will be provided to the student for engaging in the desired behavior, as well as how often and when they will be delivered. Reinforcement that is individually selected for the student and that is expected to be meaningful to him is needed to maintain the new behavior change over time.

What all this adds up to is that a student's problem behavior is a cue for the *educators to alter their responses to the student* and to continue to alter their responses until they get the desired outcome. It is inappropriate for the adults to state or simply assume that "the student is the one with the problem; therefore, he is the one who needs to do all the changing." To do so naively ignores the principles upon which behavior change is based. That is, events and circumstances associated with the problem behavior must be modified—including, at times, the responses and other behavior of the adults. Thus, developing a BIP is a process that requires review and evaluation as well as making needed adaptations and changes in order to achieve success.

Box 6-8

Technique Hint

We become stuck in the same patterns of responding to student misbehavior even when they do not result in the desired outcome.

Steps for Developing a BIP

These steps correspond with the information called for to complete the BIP form depicted in *Figure 6-3*. This form is also included at the end of this section to copy for your use. Following the steps and documenting the responses on the BIP form will result in a completed BIP.

Step 1: Refer to the appropriate replacement behavior identified for the student on the back side of the FBA as well as the "Antecedents" column on the front. Consider needed *preventive strategies* related to this information that must be put in place to reduce the likelihood that the problematic behavior will recur. Identify not only the *needed adjustments* but also how they will be carried out:

- Adjustments as to ***when*** the problem behavior is likely to occur
- Adjustments as to ***where*** the problem behavior is likely to occur
- Adjustments as to the ***subject*** or ***activity*** during which the problem behavior is likely to occur
- Adjustments as to ***people*** in whose presence the problem behavior is likely to occur
- Clarifying and/or reteaching expectations and routines
- Modifying tasks, assignments, and curriculum
- Increasing supervision
- Using special equipment
- Making other needed adjustments

Figure 6-3
Completed Sample BIP

BEHAVIOR INTERVENTION PLAN (BIP)

FIRST NAME Adam LAST NAME Baum GRADE 5 SCHOOL Crestview DATE 9/18/04
PARTICIPANTS Dr. E. Ville (school psychologist), Les Moore (counselor), M. Genaux (sp. ed. teacher)
This FBA will be utilized for: (Intervention Purposes) IEP Requirements

PREVENTIVE STRATEGIES

Preventive measures and adjustments that will be put in place to reduce the occurrence of the problem behavior. (*Refer to the Antecedent column on page 1 of the FBA.*) Mark "YES" and fill in the statement if this is a needed preventive measure. Mark "NOT NEEDED" to indicate that the adjustment has been considered and is not needed.

YES	NOT NEEDED	
✔	☐	Adjustments to be made as to **WHEN** the problem behavior is likely to occur by: increased supervision during lunch, recess, before & after school
✔	☐	Adjustments to be made as to **WHERE** the problem behavior is likely to occur by: assigning a smaller designated play area
☐	✔	Adjustments to be made as to the **SUBJECT/ACTIVITY** during which the problem behavior is likely to occur by:
☐	✔	Adjustments to be made as to **PEOPLE** with whom the problem behavior is likely to occur by:

OTHER ADJUSTMENTS

YES	NOT NEEDED	
✔	☐	Clarifying and/or reteaching expectations/routines. (HOW?) prior to lunch, recess, end of school
☐	✔	Modifying task/assignment/curriculum. (HOW?)
✔	☐	Increasing supervision. (HOW?) playground supervisor in designated play area
☐	✔	Utilizing special equipment. (HOW?)
☐	✔	Other. (HOW?)

INSTRUCTIONAL STRATEGIES

What specific skills will the student need to be taught in order to successfully demonstrate the **REPLACEMENT BEHAVIOR**? (*Refer to the replacement Behavior column on page 2 of the FBA.*)

- ✔ Social Skills: anger control strategies, negotiation skills, conflict resolution skills (See social skills assessment for specific skills)
- ☐ Communication Skills:
- ☐ Study Skills:
- ☐ Academic Skills
- ☐

How will these skills be taught?
- ☐ Individual Instruction
- ✔ Demonstration/Modeling
- ✔ Guided Practice
- ✔ Group Instruction
- ✔ Role Play
- ☐ Independent Practice

Who will provide the instruction? school counselor, sp. ed. teacher
When will the instruction take place? recess, lunch
Where will the instruction take place? counselor's office, sp. ed. classroom
How often will the instruction take place? 3 times per week
How will opportunities for practice/rehearsal be provided? during instruction at recess and lunch times
How will the student be prompted to use the newly acquired skills? Social skills homework assignments (Homework Card) and playground supervisor, sp. ed. teacher tracking form.

(front of form)

Adam Baum

BEHAVIOR INTERVENTION PLAN (BIP)

REINFORCEMENT PROCEDURES

What will be done to strengthen or increase the occurrence of the replacement behavior?

IDENTIFY POTENTIAL REINFORCERS (REWARDS):
What preferred items, activities or people might be used as rewards in an intervention for this student?
class party with peers, mystery motivator reward (to be shared with class)

ESTABLISH SPECIFIC BEHAVIOR CRITERIA:
What exactly must the student do to earn the above reward?
3 recess/lunch periods with no pushing, hitting, or kicking = mystery motivator
12 recess/lunch periods with no pushing, hitting, or kicking = class party

DETERMINE SCHEDULE OF REINFORCEMENT:
How frequently can the student earn the above rewards?
5 points per recess/lunch period
20 points = mystery motivator
80 points = class party

IDENTIFY DELIVERY SYSTEM:
What intervention components will be used to monitor the student's behavior and delivery reinforcement?
- ☐ Self-monitoring
- ☐ Behavioral contract
- ✔ Group contingency
- ☐ Home note system
- ☐ Lottery/raffle tickets
- ☐ Other
- ✔ Point system
- ☐ Token economy
- ☐ Beep tape
- ☐ Chart moves
- ✔ Tracking system

CORRECTION PROCEDURES

What can be done to weaken or decrease the occurrence of the problem behavior?

- ☐ All occurrences of the problem behavior will be ignored, while attending to the appropriate behavior of other students.
- ✔ When the problem behavior occurs the student will be verbally asked to stop and then redirected by…
  - ✔ Using Precision Comments
  - ☐ Completing a Teaching Interaction
  - ✔ Saying the following "That's hurting someone. You need to go sit on the bench."
  - ☐ Other
- ✔ Minimal undesired consequences will be used.
  - ✔ Loss of reward/priviledge. Describe: loss of recess/lunch points
  - ☐ Loss of ____ minutes of ____
  - ☐ Positive practice. Describe:
- ✔ Time away from the opportunity for reinforcement will be used. Describe: contingent observation time out—5 minutes of recess/lunch

IMPLEMENTATION DETAILS

What Tracking System will be used to track the delivery of rewards and/or the use of undesired consequences?
Tracking sheet will have 4 check periods per day:
1. Start of school
2. After AM recess
3. After lunch recess
4. After PM recess

Adam will be rated with an "OK" or "Not OK" rating for each of the 4 check periods by the playground supervisor.

Include any other details/explanations not previously described so that anyone can read this plan and implement the program.

(back of form)

The authors wish to thank colleague Glenn Dyke for contributing the contents for this sample.

Figure 6-3

Completed Sample BIP (continued)

Adam Baum

BEHAVIOR INTERVENTION PLAN (BIP)

TRACKING SYSTEM

Method of data collection

- ❑ Frequency count (tally) across the day.
- ✔ Frequency count from 4 times per day (time of day) to at the end of (time of day) each check period
- ❑ Interval recording every ________
- ❑ second/minutes from: ________ (time of day) to ________ (time of day).
- ❑ Other:

Describe exactly HOW data will be collected/recorded and WHO will do it.

Playground supervisor will record "OK" or "Not OK" rating for each of 4 check periods on Adams tracking sheet.

OK = no instances of pushing, hitting, or kicking peers.

Not OK = 1 or more instances of pushing, hitting, or kicking peers.

Supervisor will keep tally marks on sheet for pushing, hitting, & kicking.

DAILY DATA

incidents of pushing, hitting or kicking peers.

BEHAVIOR BEING MEASURED/UNIT OF MEASURE

9, 8, 7, 6, 5, 4, 3, 2, 1, 0

DATES: 9/20, 9/21, 9/22, 9/23, 9/24, 9/27, 9/28, 9/29, 9/30, 10/1, 10/4, 10/5, 10/6, 10/7, 10/8

DAYS OF WEEK

DATE OF FIRST PROJECTED REVIEW MEETING

Review meeting date: 10/10/04

Participants Mrs. Baum
Mr. Evans, principal
Dr. Ville, psychologist

Evaluation of Data:

- ❑ Desired decrease in problem behavior
- ❑ Desired increase in replacement behavior
- ❑ Undesired increase in problem behavior
- ❑ Undesired decrease in replacement behavior

Action to be taken: ❑ Continue plan ❑ Modify plan ❑ Plan for generalization

Plan of action: ________

(front of form)

________ **BEHAVIOR INTERVENTION PLAN (BIP)**

DAILY DATA

BEHAVIOR BEING MEASURED/UNIT OF MEASURE

DATES

DAYS OF WEEK

DATE OF SUBSEQUENT REVIEW MEETING ________

Review meeting date ________ Participants ________

Evaluation of data: ________

- ❑ Desired decrease in problem behavior
- ❑ Desired increase in replacement behavior
- ❑ Undesired increase in problem behavior
- ❑ Undesired increase in replacement behavior

Plan of action: ________

DATE OF SUBSEQUENT REVIEW MEETING ________

Review meeting date ________ Participants ________

Evaluation of data: ________

- ❑ Desired decrease in problem behavior
- ❑ Desired increase in replacement behavior
- ❑ Undesired increase in problem behavior
- ❑ Undesired increase in replacement behavior

Plan of action: ________

(back of form)

Step 2: Determine the *specific* skills the student needs to be taught in order to successfully demonstrate the appropriate replacement behavior. Consider the following:

- Social skills
- Communication skills
- Study skills
- Academic skills
- Any other applicable skills

Step 3: Decide how the needed skills identified in Step 1 will be taught. Consider:

- Individual instruction
- Demonstration/modeling
- Group instruction
- Role-play
- Guided practice
- Independent practice

Step 4: Determine the following:

- ***Who*** will provide the instruction
- ***When*** the instruction will take place
- ***Where*** the instruction will take place
- ***How often*** the instruction will take place
- How opportunities for ***practice and rehearsal*** will be provided
- How the student will be ***prompted to use*** his newly acquired skills

Step 4: Identify potentially *meaningful reinforcers* that will be provided to the student when he engages in the appropriate replacement behavior. This is a critical part of an effective BIP to increase the occurrence of the replacement behavior. Most commonly, this will include items, activities, or access to preferred people.

Step 5: Establish specific *behavior criteria* for the student to earn the reinforcers. In other words, exactly what must he do to earn them?

Step 6: Determine how often the reinforcers will be provided (schedule of reinforcement).

Step 7: Decide the intervention components that will be used to monitor the student's behavior and to deliver the reinforcers. Common components may include:

- A behavioral contract
- Self-monitoring
- A Home Note system
- Lottery or raffle tickets
- A group contingency
- A point system or token economy
- A beep tape
- Chart moves
- A tracking system

Step 8: Determine what can be done to *decrease* the occurrence of the problem behavior. This may include such things as:

- Ignore all occurrences of the problem behavior while *attending* to the appropriate behavior of other students.
- Tell the student to stop the problem behavior when it occurs and then redirecting him by using a Precision Request, completing a Teaching Interaction, or using other verbalization.
- Inform the student of the loss of privileges or a specific number of minutes of a preferred activity.
- Carry out positive practice.
- Call the parents.
- Enforce a form of time-out (i.e., time away from the opportunity to earn reinforcement).

Step 9: Include on the form any other of the BIP's implementation details and explanations that are needed to ensure that anyone could read the plan and carry out the program. Also decide what kind of tracking system will be used to document the delivery of reinforcers to the student and the use of correction procedures or undesired consequences. Describe exactly how data will be collected and recorded. (The sample BIP form included in this section contains a tracking component with which you may document this information.)

Step 10: Put the decisions made in Steps 1–9 in writing, inform and/or train those who will carry it out, and implement the plan.

Step 11: Set a date for a meeting to review and evaluate the BIP to determine its effectiveness. At the meeting, document who participated in the review meeting on the plan. Items to review include whether or not there was a:

- Desired decrease in the problem behavior
- Desired increase in the replacement behavior

If the plan was unsuccessful, the hypothesis as well as plan implementation must be examined carefully. Decide what adjustments are necessary to proceed. Whether or not the BIP was successful, determine the action to be taken, document it, and select another review date.

Troubleshooting FBAs and BIPs

Problem: ***When the BIP is reviewed, the participants find that the inappropriate behavior is still occurring and the student is not using the selected replacement behavior.***

Solution: Ask and answer the following questions:

- Have reinforcement and undesired consequences been delivered consistently as specified in the plan?
- Have needed skills been taught systematically and reviewed as needed?
- Is selected reinforcement *meaningful* for the student?
- Is the reinforcement sufficient to maintain the replacement behavior?

- Does the student understand how the plan works?
- Do other problem behaviors need to be included?
- Does the student need increased supervision?

One or more of these areas may need to be reexamined or adjusted to achieve success.

Problem: ***The student's problem behavior involved a weapon, and school administrators and other staff are nervous about the student's returning to school. Is there anything else that can be done to ensure everyone's safety?***

Solution: Consider adding specific pocket checks, locker checks, and/or the use of a metal detector to beef up the BIP where the particular situation calls for it.

Problem: ***The student's problem behavior (in this case, swearing or out-of-control behavior) has increased, even though the staff says the BIP is being carefully followed.***

Solution: If the questions in the first problem in this section have been satisfactorily answered, consider another possibility. Could the student be gaining inadvertent reinforcement for the bad behavior through adult attention, peer attention, or other available means?

If staff argue with or give a lot of attention to the student when the problem behavior occurs, these actions may be reinforcing the student sufficiently to keep the behavior going. Likewise, if peers give the student a lot of attention when he engages in the problem behavior, he may like the notoriety. Attention may be more reinforcing to the student than any reinforcers he can earn as specified in the BIP. Staff may need to be carefully coached about responding to the student in a calm, matter-of-fact manner, without arguing. (Review the section on explosive crises in Section 4 for further help with this situation.) Concerning managing peers, you may have to quickly remove the problem student from the situation or disperse or remove the peers themselves to avoid or prevent their reinforcement. Another alternative for managing peers is to set up a group contingency, whereby the peers earn group reinforcement for ignoring the bad behavior of the student and encouraging his appropriate behavior. Or, the problem student can earn reinforcement for the whole group of peers by engaging in the appropriate replacement behavior.

Box 6-9

Technique Hint

Glenn swears at the teacher every time he is asked to complete a classroom task. As a consequence, the teacher sends him out into the hall. When Glenn returns, the next time he is asked to complete a task, he swears again. It is obvious that the consequence is maintaining, or reinforcing, the behavior. The more the teacher sends Glenn out into the hall, the more he swears at the teacher. This is an example of *negative reinforcement*; the behavior may be different in different classrooms (throwing books or spitwads or being out of one's seat), but the purpose or function is the same—avoiding academic demands.

Problem: ***It has been hard for the school to come up with* meaningful *reinforcers for which the problem student is interested in working. Any ideas?***

Solution: If the student's parents are supportive and have not already been actively participating in the plan's solutions, consider involving them. Interested parents have control over meaningful reinforcers, particularly if the student is in secondary school. Access to car keys, money, and desired activities can often be controlled by parents. If the parents are capable of following through and are interested in doing so, ongoing communication with parents can reap huge dividends. A Home Note system may be one way of communicating effectively.

Problem: ***There are no clear consequences that seem to motivate or drive the problem behavior.***

Solution: There are only a few motivators that drive problem behaviors. These include: (a) positive reinforcement (i.e., the student gets *something he wants* by engaging in the problem behavior); (b) negative reinforcement (i.e., the student avoids or escapes something he does not like by engaging in the problem behavior); or (c) punishment (i.e., the student reduces or stops engaging in the behavior because he receives an undesired consequence). It sometimes takes good detective work to figure out what is motivating the student. First, understand that peer attention is a powerful motivator for many problem behaviors. Second, students may work to escape many school situations or adult requests by engaging in the problem behavior. Third, sometimes a student's environment is so negative (i.e., he receives attention only when he behaves inappropriately) or frustrating (i.e., he is not able to do the required academic work) that he engages in the problem behavior. Those involved in developing a student's BIP should review the student's current FBA information and select what they consider the *most likely* scenario to be. Their hypothesis or best guess will then be ultimately proven either correct or incorrect. If it is incorrect, the group should reexamine the information and formulate another hypothesis or best guess to prove or disprove through the implementation of the BIP.

Problem: ***There are no clear triggers or antecedents that seem to set off the student.***

Solution: The triggers for the antecedents or "A" in the ABC Functional Behavior Assessment format can be subtle; common triggers include transition times or downtime that is unsupervised. Another trigger for some students is an inappropriate request or command from an adult. For example, using a question format (i.e., "Wouldn't you like to ... ?"; "Would you ... ?"; or "Don't you think it's time to ... ?") when a "no" response from the student is not acceptable can cause a problem. Having a certain set of peers present when the problem behavior occurs can suggest that the problem behaviors are motivated by peer attention. Do not forget that some triggers occur in environments other than school and can act as the "setting events" for problem behavior in school. For example, students may have stayed up late on the weekend and may be overly tired on Monday morning as a result. Divorcing or battling parents who fight in front of their child before he comes to school can also provide setting events for the problem behavior.

Problem: ***The FBA data clearly show which events trigger the problem behavior and which consequences motivate the behavior, but no one seems to be able to decide which interventions should be implemented.***

Solution: It is advisable to determine whether simple alteration of the problem behavior triggers can change the behavior. For example, if supervision is increased for transition times, certain peers are steered away from the student, or a call is made to the student's parent to make sure he gets to bed at a reasonable time, the problem behavior may improve. However, if an intervention program is designed to implement a consequence for the problem behavior, it is important to make certain the consequences are primarily positive rather than negative. Sometimes, selecting an appropriate replacement behavior and then teaching it may be the only intervention needed.

Problem: ***The BIP that has been developed for the student has been filed away and was never implemented.***

Solution: Maintain a separate data file for each student. Include FBAs as well as BIPs in these files. Require that staff make regular (daily is desirable) data entries for students. Have an assigned staff member keep track of projected review dates for students' BIPs and the actions that were taken. Review these periodically and follow up on those that do not take place or that seem to have chronic, ongoing problems. Impress on staff the particular importance and legal obligation for students receiving special education services to follow through with the intervention and educational steps of the BIP. The plan is a form of school contact for service with potential legal ramifications if it is not followed and if proper documentation is not maintained.

Box 6-10
Technique Hint

The *Project Ride* program is a useful, commercially available computerized software program with helpful videotapes to assist school staff in designing effective interventions for problematic behavior.

The *Functional Assessment and Intervention Program* (FAIP) mentioned in Box 6-8 also generates suggested interventions based on the triggers, or antecedents, and consequences assessed through the FBA process. Both programs are available through Sopris West Educational Services at www.sopriswest.com.

Behavioral Contracting

Definition

Behavioral Contracting involves placing contingencies for rewards or reinforcement into a written document that is agreed to and signed by the student, the teacher and/or the principal, and any other individuals who are appropriately involved with the contract. Contracts can be effectively used with students of all ages to increase appropriate behaviors and decrease inappropriate ones.

Description

When adults see the word "contract," they generally think of corporate mergers or sports stars signing agreements for millions of dollars. Contracts also have everyday meaning for most adults in terms of buying or renting cars, getting married, as well as business and employment agreements. Contracts are used in conjunction with many adult behaviors because they are explicit and set expectations. For similar reasons, contracts can also be used effectively when working with the Tough Kids in your school.

Steps for Implementing a Behavioral Contract

Step 1: Define specifically the exact behavior for which the contract is being drawn up. Poor examples include "Improve responsibility" or "Show respect for authority" because they are vague and/or judgmental. Better examples include "Hand in work by the end of the period without being asked," "Talk in a calm voice to classmates without arguing," or "Follow directions the first time you are asked."

Box 6-12

Technique Hint

Break the initial Behavioral Contract into smaller steps, if necessary, so that the student will be successful. It is important for the student to be successful in earning the contract reward so that she will be motivated to continue.

Box 6-13

Technique Hint

Rewards should not take a lot of time to deliver, nor should they be expensive.

Step 2: Select the contract reward or reinforcer with the help of the student. An effective reward as part of a Behavioral Contract is absolutely critical! Too many schools draw up what they call "contracts" and include only *penalties* for nonperformance of the desired behavior. These are truly not Behavioral Contracts; they are written threats that students are coerced into signing and, most importantly, *they are not effective!*

Step 3: Define the contract criteria, including the *amount of the behavior* required, the *amount of reward* or reinforcement to be provided, and the *time limits* for performance.

Box 6-14

Technique Hint

Cumulative criteria are usually preferable to consecutive criteria. Cumulative criteria allow the student to make mistakes or to have some periods of not meeting the criteria without having to start over from the beginning.

Step 4: If necessary, include a "bonus clause" for exceptional performance or behavior completed before the contract time limits. Consider adding a "penalty clause" for nonperformance if the initial contract does not work, even though the rewards are valued and the payoff time is short.

Step 5: Negotiate the contract with the student:

- Indicate why a contract is necessary and that you want to help.
- Discuss the contract behavior, rewards, and performance criteria.
- Indicate that the behavior contract, rewards, and criteria are negotiable. Emphasize, however, that a contract is needed and its implementation is *not* negotiable.
- Tell the student what you suggest in these areas. Ask for the student's input.

- Do not allow the student to set unrealistically high standards for himself. Encourage the student to begin slowly, and then expand the expectations for him gradually.
- Indicate that a "penalty clause" may be necessary, if applicable.
- Indicate that the contract may need to be renegotiated in the future.

Step 6: Put the terms of the contract in writing.

> **Box 6-15**
>
> **Technique Hint**
>
> Writing and signing a contract prevent misunderstandings and indicate agreement with the terms at the time that all the participating parties sign the contract.

Step 7: Set a date for reviewing and possibly renegotiating the contract.

Step 8: Have all participating parties sign the contract. Keep a copy, and make a copy for each participant.

Troubleshooting Behavioral Contracting

Problem: ***The student begins by working hard and then loses motivation.***

Solution: The reward payoff may be delayed too long; cut the time period in half. Delaying the reward too long is one of the most frequent problems with contracting.

Problem: ***The student appears confused and never really gets started.***

Solution: The required behavior may not be defined or explained clearly enough, or too much of the required behavior may be expected initially. Discuss and explain the expectations thoroughly with the student. If necessary, model and role-play the target behavior. If the student understands the requirement but is still not performing, then the requirement may be too great. Try reducing the behavior requirement for one week (e.g., half the problems, half the points). After the student has received the contract reward at least once, gradually begin to increase the contract requirements again.

Problem: ***The student is still unmotivated and disinterested even after the delay in earning the reward has been shortened, the expectations have been clarified, and he has earned a contract reward at least once.***

Solution: A penalty clause may be needed to prompt the student to actively participate.

Problem: ***When the contract started, the student was excited about it but now appears frustrated and anxious.***

Solution: Check the performance criteria. Student frustration can result from expectations that are too difficult. Be sure to use cumulative criteria rather than consecutive criteria.

Problem: ***The student is openly defiant and will not participate in the contracting.***

Solution: Indicate to the student that you want to negotiate the terms of the contract and value his input. If possible, invite an adult who is important to the student to participate in the negotiations, especially if a penalty clause is set. The person may be a parent, a coach, a favorite teacher, or a counselor. Make certain beforehand, however, that the invited person supports the idea of a contract.

Making Behavioral Contracting Even Better

The following points are helpful in ensuring that the Behavioral Contract effects change in a student's behavior:

- **Agreement:** You must negotiate the consequences and rewards for specific behaviors with the student.

Box 6-16

Technique Hint

Negotiations should not be one-sided in the sense that adults dictate the terms to the student and the student then agrees to them.

- **Formal exchange:** The reward is always given *after* the contract behavior is produced. Once the contract is in effect, you must not relax the behavior requirements at any point in the contract period.
- **Behavior:** The contract behavior must be specifically and objectively defined, including an expected standard (e.g., by 3:30 P.M. next Friday) for performance.
- **Goal Setting:** Contracting and goal setting can be combined to assist the student in setting his own goals. A penalty clause and a bonus clause may also be useful with goal setting.
- **Advertising for Success:** Contracting for performance improvement can be developed and then the improvements publicly posted.
- **Group Contingencies:** Contracts can be developed for whole classrooms or student teams (or groups) of your choosing. The procedures are basically the same as for contracting with individual students.

Box 6-17

Technique Hint

Adults must be certain that each student included in a *group contingency contract* is capable of meeting the contract's expectations.

- **Home Notes:** Contracting can be used in combination with Home Notes (included in this section). When a student has accumulated a certain number of acceptable Home Notes, the agreed-upon contracted reward is delivered.

Cautions With Behavioral Contracting

It must be remembered that most contracts in life operate with a delayed reward or payoff system. However, when working with particularly Tough Kids, delays frequently destroy the initial steps that are required to get them started. Contracts used with Tough Kids are most effective when:

1. They are used as a way of phasing out more frequent rewards, or they are used after the student has begun to perform appropriately.
2. They are used with older or more motivated students. Contracts with long delays will be ineffective for younger or very unmotivated students. In these cases, it is better to start with an hourly, twice-daily, or daily reward system.

Home Notes

Definition

A Home Note, or Home-to-School Note, is an informational note that goes from school to home and then back to school. It shares information between the parents and the teacher or other school professional about a student's school behavior and/or academic performance.

Description

The Home Note is generally filled out at school with global ratings for specific behavior and/or academic progress. The note is then signed or initialed by the professional who is overseeing its use and then sent to the student's home. The professional may be a school counselor, vice-principal, teacher, or

other designated adult. The note is reviewed by the student's parents, signed or initialed by one of them, and then sent back to the adult at school. Good Home Note programs also have the parent apply some type of reward for good school behavior and performance and mild undesired consequences for poor behavior and performance. There are typically two types of notes: a daily Home Note and a weekly Home Note.

Steps for Implementing a Home Note Program

Step 1: Decide what type of Home Note is necessary. Daily home notes are helpful when the program begins because they keep parents well informed and allow daily consequences for behavior. Weekly notes are helpful when a student's performance has improved or when the parents need to be informed less frequently. Both types of forms are provided at the end of this section.

Step 2: Set up a conference with the student's parent. Solicit the parent's cooperation and help her decide on the rewards and undesired consequences at home for the behavior and/or performance described in the note.

Box 6-18
Technique Hint

Rewards in the home for a **younger student** include extra television time, an extended bedtime, more computer time, or one-on-one time with a parent. *Undesired consequences* include an earlier bedtime, grounding on the weekend, temporary loss of or time-out from a favorite toy, no television time, or loss of part of an allowance.

Rewards for an **older student** include access to driving privileges, gas money, use of the phone (including cell phone), music, or extended curfews. *Undesired consequences* include loss of part of an allowance, loss of phone privileges, missing a desired activity, or completing extra chores at home.

Step 3: During the parental conference, decide on which behaviors should be included on the Home Note. The behaviors can be a mix of school behavior (such as tardiness) and academic behavior (such as homework completion). The note should include no more than five behaviors to rate at one time.

Box 6-19
Technique Hint

Good school behaviors to target include following the school rules, being on time, and having good attendance. Good academic behaviors to target are homework completion and good ratings in performance in one or more of the student's subjects.

Step 4: During the conference, decide how the behaviors should be rated. Some Home Notes provided in this Briefcase have built-in rating scales. The ratings should be simple and global.

Box 6-20
Technique Hint

Illustrations of faces (smiley, neutral, or frowny) or plus signs and zero signs are good visuals to use for rating the selected behaviors of **younger students**.

Caution!

A minus sign is not a good choice of a rating symbol because it can be easily changed into a plus sign by the student.

For **older students**, a numerical rating from 1 to 3 (1 = Unsatisfactory, 2 = Average, 3 = Great) may be used. Another option is to list the ratings and then circle the student's rating in ink.

Step 5: During the conference, decide what type of rewards and undesired consequences should correspond to each rating. Remember, the note should be mostly positive, not negative.

Box 6-21

Technique Hint

For each smiley face that a **younger student** earns, he could receive 10 minutes of extra television time or have his bedtime delayed for 10 minutes (5 smiles = 50 minutes' extra time). For each frowny face, the student could have his television timed reduced by 10 minutes or his bedtime moved up 10 minutes (3 frowny faces = to bed 30 minutes early).

The ratings can provide an **older student** time driving the family car, a specific number of gallons of gas for its use, extra time on the phone (or cell phone), or more opportunities to listen to music on the family sound system.

Step 6: During the conference, suggest that *no* excuse from the student be accepted for not taking the note home or returning it to school. Common student excuses include:

- "I forgot."
- "Mr. Rodriguez wasn't at school today."
- "There was a special activity scheduled at school, and I didn't see Mrs. Ross today."

Box 6-22

Technique Hint

For **younger students**, a good undesired consequence for neglecting to take the note home is going to bed one hour early with loss of television privileges. For not returning the note to school, loss of recess or free-time privileges and calling the parent are appropriate.

For **older students**, a good undesired consequence for neglecting to take the note home is loss of driving or telephone privileges. If the student continues not to take the note home, then grounding can be used (e.g., one day for each day the note is not taken home).

Step 7: Explain the procedure to the student after meeting with the parent. Indicate:

- How the Home Note will be rated and used
- Which rewards and undesired consequences will be included
- That no excuses will be accepted for not taking the note home or returning it to school

Box 6-23

Technique Hint

Explain to the student the steps to follow to be rated if the counselor, vice-principal, or other adult is unavailable (e.g., an office secretary or other designated adult could help the student) or if special situations arise, such as an assembly or movie (e.g., go to the adult before the activity or ask for a rating during it).

Step 8: Begin the Home Note program on a Monday. Rate the student's behavior or performance and, if at all possible, give the student positive ratings for the first several days. After the student has been rated, initial the note, and give it to the student. Remind the student that no excuses will be accepted for loss of the note.

Box 6-24

Technique Hint

Inform the student that you may call his parent to let him know that the note is coming home. It helps to call the first day and at least one other day during the first week of the Home Note program to answer any questions and encourage the parent to carry out his part of the program.

Troubleshooting Home Notes

Problem: *A student loses the Home Note.*

Solution: Ensure that the student loses an important privilege either at school or at home. For example, the student could lose a school privilege such as all recess time for the day. Or, at home the student could lose his television privilege and have to go to bed an hour earlier. Remember: Do not accept excuses for a lost note.

Problem: *A student forges or changes a parental signature on the note or changes a note rating from "bad" to "good."*

Solution: The school staff member and the parent should exchange telephone numbers and/or e-mail addresses in order to verify the ratings. If a student forges a rating, the consequence should be the loss of a privilege as just described.

Problem: *The adult who is supposed to rate the student is not there, and the student is unsure of how to get a rating.*

Solution: Leave written instructions in a special folder for one or two "back-ups" (i.e., designated adults) in the event of such a case. Make arrangements with these adults ahead of time. Explain to the student who these adults are and how to obtain a rating from them.

> **Box 6-25**
> ## Technique Hint
> In this situation, write the instructions for the student to follow on the note in the Comments section.

Problem: *A student refuses to take the note altogether.*

Solution: This rarely happens; but if the student rejects taking the note or destroys it, apply the same consequence as for a lost note. These consequences can be enforced both at home and at school until the student complies.

Problem: *A student argues with the school staff member about a rating.*

Solution: Tell the student that if he continues to argue, you will give him an even lower rating or will write a note to his parents in the Comments section about the inappropriate arguing.

> **Box 6-26**
> ## Technique Hint
> It helps to call the student's parent after an episode of arguing to make sure that the note made it home.

Problem: *A parent offers an extremely large reward in a time period that is too long before the reward can be delivered (e.g., a bicycle, a four-wheeler, a trip, a remote control, a large sum of money).*

Solution: Express your concern to the parent about the promised large reward. Help the parent compile a list of smaller rewards to be given within a much shorter time period, and suggest the large reward as an additional *bonus*.

Problem: *A parent is incapable of administering rewards and undesired consequences at home.*

Solution: Put together a reward kit that contains simple rewards (e.g., candy, stickers, school supplies) and deliver it to the student's home so the parents can use it when their child brings home good notes. If the parent agrees to review the notes but still doesn't use rewards from the prepared kit, give them in the classroom when the student returns the note the following day. If the parents are incapable of applying undesired consequences at home, discuss dropping the undesired consequences at home and instead apply them at school.

Problem: *A student's parents refuse to participate in the Home Note program and will not even sign the note.*

Solution: Ask the parents for a face-to-face meeting in which you discuss the problem with them. Make the meeting positive, and respond to their concerns. It helps to appeal to the parent who seems more willing to participate and work with you. Explain that the note is not designed to punish the student but rather to give the student feedback about his behavior and performance. Emphasize the idea of cooperation between the home and school and how this will benefit the student. Ask the parents if they are willing to try the program for as little as two weeks. If the parents still refuse, indicate that you would like to give the student the note anyway and hope they will look at it. In this case, you will need to apply the rewards and undesired consequences at school.

Box 6-27

Technique Hint

Make sure that the note is mostly positive during this trial period.

Problem: ***You suspect that a parent may emotionally or physically abuse the student if he receives a poor rating on the note.***

Solution: Invite the parent to come in for a meeting and ask for his cooperation in making the Home Note program positive. Indicate that you want to downplay the undesired consequences. Tell the parent that if he punishes too much and rewards too little, the student will learn to dislike both the program and the school. If you suspect that abuse is continuing, stop the program. Always follow your school district's policy for reporting suspected abuse. This is a serious problem, but fortunately, it rarely occurs.

Problem: ***The student insists he is responsible, does not need a Home Note, and does not want to be in the program.***

Solution: Indicate to the student that he may, in fact, be responsible. However, one way to show responsibility is to do well while in the Home Note program. Develop a contract with the student. For example, when the student has good daily notes for four weeks, switch him to a weekly note that is rated only on Fridays. When the student has four good weekly notes in a row, take him off the note program for a trial period. However, let the student know that if his behavior or performance slips, the weekly note system will be resumed.

Making Home Notes Even Better

1. For secondary students, use the Home Information Note depicted in *Figure 6-4*. This note has seven areas for seven periods in a junior high or high school. The subjects and teachers' names should be written in each space in the order that the student attends classes. The Home Information Note can be either a daily or weekly note. For a weekly note, write "Weekly" in the blank space in the upper left-hand corner. For a daily note, staple five notes together and write "MON" in this space for the first note, "TUE" for the next note, and so on for the whole week. The Home Information Note can also be used with elementary students. It is particularly useful because it includes spaces for assigned homework, upcoming tests, and missing work. The spaces can also be used for different behaviors or performance by applying correction fluid on the printed headings and writing in different ones as needed. Additional Home Information Note forms in several formats are included at the end of this section. Use the one that best meets your students' needs.

Figure 6-4
Home Information Note

Home Information Note

Name: Duke Jenson Date/Week of: 9/11 Phone: 363-9548

Periods	Teacher Initials	Class Performance (circle one)	Assigned Homework	Upcoming Tests?	Missing Work?
Math (Mr. Evans)		G Great (A) Average U Unsatisfactory	p. 195 all problems	Friday - fractions	
English (Ms. Genaux)		G Great (A) Average U Unsatisfactory	Read story, p. 63		Book report
Shop (Mr. Dyke)		G Great A Average (U) Unsatisfactory	Bridge project		
Resource (Dr. Rhode)		(G) Great A Average U Unsatisfactory	None		
Health (Mrs. Ruedas)		G Great A Average (U) Unsatisfactory	read pgs. 92-108	Open book on effects of sun (W)	
P.E. (Mr. Erlacher)		G Great (A) Average U Unsatisfactory	none		
Art (Mrs. Barkdull)		(G) Great A Average U Unsatisfactory	Free drawing		

Comments: Was prepared in English.

Tardy to Health twice this week.

School Staff Signature: *Mrs. Garcia, counselor*

Parent's Signature *Billy Joe D. Jenson*

Box 6-28
Technique Hint

Caution!

Remember to allow the student to collect notes cumulatively (e.g., he may have two good weeks, a poor week, and then a good week) for the contract. A consecutive contract (e.g., three weeks in a row of good home notes) is too punishing.

Peer Mediation

Definition

Peer mediation is a conflict resolution process in which student problem behaviors or conflicts are resolved by peers. The approach we suggest in this Briefcase involves the use of student body or class officers to serve as the school's peer mediators. Student body or class officers work well as mediators because:

- They are respected by other students.
- They are actively involved with their peers.
- They generally experience less conflict and display fewer problem behaviors than the average student.

Peer mediation is also an important learning experience for student body or class officers. They learn that being elected to a school office involves important responsibilities to their peers and the school that go beyond an election campaign, making posters, and a popular vote. By participating in peer mediation, they experience listening, synthesizing information, deliberating, and making important decisions. They learn that these decisions affect their peers and the overall behavioral climate of the school.

Description

The peer mediation approach in this Briefcase focuses on two types of school conflict in which:

1. Students break school rules and are referred by school staff for some type of consequence or action.
2. Two or more students are having a conflict, and one of the students makes a formal written request to involve peer mediators to help solve the problem.

This approach involves the elected student body or class officers to serve as the peer mediators. Typically, the student body officers include the school president, vice-president, and secretary or similar officers. Another effective approach is to have the most senior class officers serve as the mediators. For example, in a high school, the senior (twelfth-grade) class officers may serve as the peer mediators. In an elementary school, if the highest grade level is 5, then the fifth-grade class officers may serve as the peer mediators.

The mediators meet when needed—that is, when there are staff referrals or student requests for mediation. Typically, mediators meet once or twice per week, often at lunchtime or before or after school. Holding meetings is usually best on Fridays or Mondays.

During peer mediation meetings, referred students present their cases. Peer mediators then ask them questions. Next, there is a closed-door deliberation period where peer mediators discuss the case and decide on the actions to be taken. The mediators' decisions are subject to the principal's approval and are binding on the referred students. After the principal's approval has been obtained, peer mediators write up the actions or consequences on a Peer Mediation Contract. The actions or consequences are delivered to the referred students verbally, who are then asked to sign the contract. Referred students are also given a written copy of the contract.

Box 6-29

Technique Hint

It is best if there are two adults present in peer mediation meetings. One adult (e.g., a school psychologist, a teacher, or a counselor) can advocate the case of the referred student if necessary, and one adult—usually the principal—can represent the school's interests.

It is important that peer mediators be trained in their role before implementing the program. Arrange for and conduct training for the selected student officers during the first weeks of the school year, or even prior to the start of school, if possible. This training must include these activities:

- Discuss proper behavior for peer mediators during meetings.
- Establish peer mediation rules.
- Learn how to conduct the meetings.
- Decide on appropriate actions or consequences.
- Write Peer Mediation Contracts.

The end result of the training is a peer mediation system that reduces school conflict and teaches responsibility to both the peer mediators and the students who participate in the mediation process.

Steps for Implementing Peer Mediation Training

Step 1: Establish a time and place for the training. It is ideal is to conduct the training in the actual room where peer mediation meetings will be held.

Step 2: Provide to peer mediators a written summary of what you will be covering in the training. Include the steps and all other informational items related to peer mediation meetings.

Step 3: During the training, establish rules for the peer mediation meetings. Typically, the rules should include:

- Allow others to talk without interruption.
- Stay calm, and talk quietly.
- Do not allow name-calling or threatening of others.
- Do not joke about or make fun of others.

Decide with your peer mediators if additional rules are needed. Once rules have been finalized, assign a peer mediator to print them on a poster and post them in the meeting room. The rules must be posted before the first peer mediation meeting. Explain that when students who come to peer mediation break the rules, adults will handle the problem.

Step 4: Establish rules for the peer mediators. These rules usually include:

- Avoid talking to other students about meeting information or decisions.
- Allow referred students or other peer mediators to talk without interruption.
- Listen attentively when others are speaking.
- Avoid jokes, smart remarks, or accusations.
- Avoid whispering or talking to others during proceedings.
- Be polite to others at all times.

Rules for peer mediators need not be posted. However, they must be thoroughly discussed and explained. Have the mediators role-play examples and nonexamples of the rules to ensure that they are understood and that all questions have been answered.

Step 5: Assign one of the peer mediators to review the rules for referred students at the initial presentation of each new problem. It is this mediator's job to make certain that participants understand the ground rules.

Step 6: Tell the peer mediators that after the rules have been explained, the Peer Request for Mediation is read out loud next. Decide who will do this. Assign one of the peer mediators to make copies of this referral form for all the mediators to share at each meeting. The form can be from a school staff member who is referring a student, or it can be from a student who is having a conflict with another student or students. (*Figure 6-5* depicts an example of the Peer Request for Mediation, which is also included for copying at the end of this section.) Typically, the peer mediator who reads the referral form is the one in charge of conducting the meeting. In most schools, this job is rotated among peer mediators on a monthly basis.

Step 7: Indicate that after the referral form has been read, the peer mediator conducting the meeting asks the referred student to present his side of the problem. If two or more students

Figure 6-5

Peer Request for Mediation

Peer Request for Mediation

Referring Student: ________________ Today's Date ________

Student(s) You are Referring: ________________

____

Description of Problem: ________________

____

____

How would you like to see this problem resolved? ________________

____

____

____

Additional Comments: ________________

____

Student Signatures: ________________

Peer Mediator Signatures: ________________

School Staff Member(s) Signatures: ________________

are referred, each one is given a turn to present his side of the story.

Step 8: Explain that after referred students have a chance to explain their respective views of the problem, mediators are allowed to ask questions for clarification. Remind mediators that this is not a time to make accusations, joke with, or interrupt each other.

Step 9: Let the peer mediators know that after questioning referred students, they deliberate the consequences or actions to be taken to address the problem. The referred student or students are asked to leave the room during this time. Select a specific nearby location in which referred students can wait. Once mediators agree on a consequence or action, they present it to the principal for approval.

Step 10: Indicate that the approved consequences from the deliberation are then written on the Peer Mediation Contract. (*Figure 6-6* is an example of this form, which is included at the end of this section.) The mediators schedule a review date and document it on the form. The peer mediators and the principal sign the contract. The referred students will return to a mediation meeting on that date to review their progress related to the problem.

Figure 6-6

Peer Mediation Contract

Peer Mediation Contract

Student Name(s): ____________________

Date: ____________________

Who Referred the Problem?: ____________________

Description of Problem: ____________________

____

What Needs to be Done/Decision: ____________________

____

Is a Follow-up Meeting Needed ❑ YES ❑ NO If "YES," the meeting date is: ____________________

Additional Comments: ____________________

____

Student Signatures: ____________________

Peer Mediator Signatures: ____________________

____

School Staff Member(s) Signatures: ____________________

Step 11: Let the mediators know that after the contract has been signed, they should invite the referred student or students back into the meeting room. The mediator conducting the meeting reads the Peer Mediation Contract with the consequences that have been determined. He should ask the referred students if they have any questions. If they do, he answers the questions so that the students know exactly what to do. Their attention is also called to the review date on which they are to report back to the peer mediators. They are then asked to sign the contract and told that the consequences are binding and not negotiable. The students are given their own copies of the contract.

Step 12: After teaching, explaining, and reviewing all of the components for carrying out a mediation meeting, have the peer mediators practice the steps. Using real problems that have actually occurred in the school as examples, also provide the mediators with "mock" mediation referrals. Role-play several mediation meetings, assigning the referred student roles to one of the adults or peer mediators for the training. Provide feedback, suggestions, and coaching as needed.

Step 13: After training has been completed, introduce the concept of student body or class officer peer mediation to the entire student body near the beginning of the school year. Typically, this is best done in a student orientation assembly. Explain which officers will be serving as the school's peer mediators. Inform the students that serving as a peer mediator is not a choice but an important duty that goes along with holding an elected office in the school.

Troubleshooting Peer Mediation

Problem: ***Students who have been referred to peer mediation behave inappropriately, make threatening remarks during the meeting, or even become uncontrollable.***

Answer: Rules must be established ahead of time for the peer mediation meetings. These rules must be posted and reviewed with all referred students at the start of the meeting. Once the meeting has begun, warnings for breaking the rules should be given by the adults attending the meeting. If the inappropriate behavior continues after two warnings, the adults should stop the meeting and develop a Peer Mediation Contract with the student individually outside the peer mediation meeting. Any time a student becomes uncontrollable (i.e., refuses to follow the rules or becomes verbally or physically aggressive), the meeting must stop immediately. Parental notification or perhaps even a conference may be needed.

Problem: The peer mediators behave inappropriately during the meeting.

Answer: Again, rules must be taught ahead of time during the mediator orientation training. However, should inappropriate behavior occur in an actual meeting, one of the adults should quietly slip the offender a note, if possible, specifying what the mediator said or did that was inappropriate and suggesting an alternative. If the mediator appears confused, or additional inappropriate behavior takes place, one of the adults should call for a short recess. The adult should then discuss the problem in private with the mediator. Periodically, the adults who work with the peer mediation program should review the rules for expected behavior with the peer mediators.

Problem: ***The referred student does not adequately represent himself because he appears intimidated, is inarticulate, or refuses to participate.***

Answer: The adults in the peer mediation meeting should assist or actively represent referred students whenever they appear unable to adequately represent themselves.

Problem: ***The peer mediators set inappropriate consequences or actions.***

Answer: There is a general tendency, especially when peer mediators are new to the process, to set consequences that are too harsh or too strict. If the consequences suggested by the peer mediators are too stringent, the principal or other adult should amend them during the peer mediation deliberation phase. Under no circumstances should consequences be humiliating or degrading to referred students.

Problem: ***A peer mediator is referred for mediation.***

Answer: When a peer mediator is referred by school staff or mediation is requested by another student, the referred mediator works only with the principal. The principal develops the Peer Mediation Contract for the peer mediator. The peer mediator should not participate in a mediation meeting conducted by his peer mediator colleagues.

Making Peer Mediation Even Better

1. After your first year of implementing peer mediation, use copies (with names blocked out) of previous Peer Requests for Mediation and Peer Mediation Contracts as training materials for new peer mediators. Going over both of these forms helps to instruct peer mediators about past problem behaviors that have caused student referrals as well as appropriate, reasonable consequences set by past mediators.

2. Include one extra peer mediator on the team who is not a student body or class officer. After one month, rotate this position to another member of the student body, for example, to a younger student body officer or a student recommended by teachers or other staff. Rotating this peer mediator role gives additional students a chance to participate in the process. It also helps to disseminate information about the peer mediation process to other members of the student body.

3. Assist current peer mediators in making a training video for new members. The video can cover all required aspects of training for new peer mediators. It may be helpful to include a mock peer mediation meeting from start to finish so that new mediators have an idea of what one looks like. The video might include a short interview in which current peer mediators each state one important thing they learned from

their experiences and would like to pass on to new mediators.

4. Peer mediation can be combined with other school programs such as an all-school social skills program or a bully-proofing program. For example, if students are bullying or teasing others or calling them names, they can be referred for peer mediation. The peer mediators can develop a contract for referred students in which they are required to practice appropriate social skills and return at a later date to review their progress.

Truancy

Definition

Some school districts regard truancy as an absence for all or part of a school day that is unexcused by the school alone. Others view truancy as an absence from school that is unexcused by both the parents and the school. In the case of the first definition of truancy, parents are sometimes viewed by the school as actual accomplices to the problem or, at the very least, not part of the solution. While parental collaboration should be sought in dealing with truancy, lack of parental interest or willingness should never be used as an excuse for not intervening. Schools can still make great improvements when they deal effectively with truancy problems.

Description

Truancy involves a student's missing an entire school day or selective parts of the day. Research shows that truancy typically starts to becomes a significant problem at about age ten, or the fifth grade (Achenbach & Edelbrock, 1983). When a student misses a *whole* day of school:

1. The student is usually truant with a select group of peers.
2. The decision to be truant is often made just before school starts in the morning when the student meets up with his peers.
3. The truant student and his peers usually go to a specific location such as one of their homes or apartments where the parents are not present. The location may also be a car in which they go riding.
4. The morning or the first part of the student's school day is viewed as negative by him or it is academically or socially frustrating for him.

Sometimes a student misses only part of a school day when he is truant; in this case, he may repeatedly miss a specific class or subject. The *partial*-day truant student usually:

- Is truant with peers.

- Is truant near the school campus in a location such as a store, gas station, or restaurant.
- Misses the class or portion of the school day that he perceives as negative or frustrating.

Students who are truant for part of a school day often return to school after missing select classes.

There are also special truancy cases in which the truancy is related to emotional problems of the student. An example of this type of truancy case is a student with school phobia. However, this type of truancy case is beyond the scope of this Briefcase.

> Box 6-30
> **Technique Hint**
>
> An excellent resource for truancy cases that are beyond the scope of this Briefcase is the book *School Refusal Behavior in Youth: A Functional Approach to Assessment and Treatment* (Kearney, 2001).

Steps for Stopping Truant Behavior

Step 1: Assess who the truant students are in your school through attendance rolls or referrals by teachers. Determine whether truant students are *whole*-day or *partial*-day truant. To pinpoint this for each student, we suggest conducting an FBA of the student's truancy behavior, using the procedure outlined earlier in this section of the Briefcase.

Step 2: If the student is whole-day truant, interview him and his teacher(s) to determine:

- Peers with whom the student is truant.
- Where the student and his friends are when they make their decision to be truant (e.g., on the bus going to school, riding in a car to school, at the convenience store where they meet before school).
- Where they go when they are truant (e.g., ride around in a car, go to an apartment or the mall).
- What the student's first classes and subjects are in the morning or during the time he is truant.

Step 3: If the student is a partial-day truant, interview him and his teacher(s) and assess the same information as described in Step 2. In this case, focus on determining the class periods or subjects the student misses the most. The location of the truancy for the partial-day truant student is usually closer to the school campus than for the full-day truant student.

Step 4: Call the parents of the truant student and those of his peers who are also truant. We suggest inviting all of the parents to the school for a collaborative meeting to help stop the truancy. In this meeting, make no assertions about which student is the most problematic or "the ringleader." Also, refrain from making comments about who is to blame for the problem. Emphasize the need for a cooperative effort to stop the truancy. If the peers involve the opposite sex, stress to the parents the need for monitoring the students' behaviors and the possible implications of the truancy, should it continue. Truancy in conjunction with peers often involves illegal substances and drugs. Stress to the parents the school's obligation to make legal referrals for truancies when illegal substances and drugs are involved. Have the parents exchange telephone numbers to help monitor their children.

Step 5: Determine where the student and his peers go when they are truant. If a car is involved, work with the parents of the student with the car to revoke his driving privileges for a period of time whenever a partial- or whole-day truancy occurs. If an unsupervised home or apartment is used by students, try to stop the students' access to it. Parents may need to enlist the use of neighbors or friends to help monitor the home or apartment and inform the school and parents when students are there during school hours. It is important to eliminate the opportunity to use the place students go when they are truant.

Step 6: Try to assess at what point before school the student decides with his peers to become truant. Limit or supervise this environment. For example, ask your school's police or resource officer or an office staff member to make regular stops by the convenience store or restaurant near the school where students go when they are truant to help supervise students on their way to school. Ask the proprietors of the business where students are truant to call when students are there during school hours. Give the proprietors a specific phone number and name to contact at the school.

> **Box 6-31**
>
> **Technique Hint**
>
> Many businesses do *not like* to have students loitering around their places when they should be in school. Some report increased shoplifting during these times. Others say that their nonstudent patrons do not like the atmosphere created by truant students.

If a student is making a decision to be truant on the school bus, have the bus driver escort the truant student and his peers into the school to ensure class attendance. If the bus driver is unable to do this, assign a specific staff member (e.g., the assistant principal or a counselor) to meet the bus in the morning to escort the students into the building. If the decision to be truant is being made in a student-driven car on the way to school, arrange with the parents for the driving or carpool privilege to be withdrawn for a period of time. The main focus of this step is to supervise the environment in which students frequently make the decision to be truant and to eliminate as many opportunities as possible for truancy or planning a truancy.

Step 7: Review the student's class schedule to determine his first class in the morning. (This is often the class or period in which the student is having academic or social difficulties.) You may want to "load" the student's early morning schedule with favored classes or a favored activity (e.g., helping in the office) to at least get him in the building.

Step 8: If the student engages in partial-day truancy, assess which classes or periods he misses most often. Frequently, changing his class schedule or teacher can help. Also determine where the partial-day truant student goes when absent. If it is a public place such as a restaurant or convenience store, ask the owners to notify the school. Again, if possible, have the school police or resource officer or a school staff member visit these locations during times when truancy is high. If the student is sitting in or driving a car during truant times, assign him a special parking space close to the school where the car can be easily observed during high-risk times of the day. If this does not work, discuss with the student's parents whether his driving privileges can be revoked temporarily.

Troubleshooting a Truancy Program

Problem: ***Are there any special tips to use when students are truant for the whole day?***

Solution: If a student is truant for the whole day, we suggest a Home-to-School Note program. The Home Note procedure was described earlier in this section of the Briefcase. Home Notes require the cooperation of parents who not only sign the note but also base privileges on the note's being initialed by teachers as to school attendance. Home Notes build a link between the school and the home and make it more difficult for students to be truant.

Making a Truancy Program Even Better

1. Do not use Out-of-School Suspension as a consequence for truancy. This amounts to delivering a punishment that is the same thing as the "crime" and only makes the situation worse. Trust us on this one!
2. If the student comes to school the day after being truant, do not immediately place him in In-School Suspension. This amounts to punishing the student for coming to school. Look for other interventions such as parental notification, Home Notes, Tracking Sheets, or even Prime Time In-School Suspension, where the student makes up his missed time on his time.
3. Realize that some parents may have only limited control over their child. A single parent who works may have difficulty monitoring his child to the degree that is needed. Enlist this parent's help to cooperatively solve the problem by limiting driving privileges; monitoring

the home or apartment while the parent works; or basing home privileges such as phone use, allowance, or access to friends on the student's school attendance. We do not recommend threatening a parent with legal actions, truancy schools, or fines to gain his cooperation with the school.

4. Develop a truancy Behavioral Contract with the student for coming to school and checking in the first thing in the morning. (See Behavioral Contracting in this section for details.) Select a privilege or reward for the student who checks in with a designated adult before school starts. The contract should state that if the student does not check in, his parents will be notified immediately as well as all of the parents of his peers who engage in truancy with him.

5. If a student is a partial-day truant, try using a student Tracking Sheet as described in Section 4 of this Briefcase. The student must carry the sheet to each teacher to initial it. Then, the student returns the sheet to a designated adult at the end of the school day.

Schoolwide Data Collection Systems

Definition

Schoolwide data collection, by our definition, is a computerized system in which the school's data relating to discipline are routinely entered. These data include the discipline problems themselves, referred students' names and identifying information, referring teachers, areas of the school where the problems occurred, and several other important pieces of information. The system then allows school administrators to generate reports on demand that give specific snapshots of discipline problems in the school and complete statistics related to those problems.

Description

Running a school without a computerized schoolwide discipline data collection system is like sailing a giant tanker without radar. Sooner or later, you will make mistakes because you are sailing blind. Schoolwide data collection systems generally run on free-standing PC or Macintosh computers. The systems do not require an expensive computer network or being linked with central office computers. Every time office referrals for discipline problems occur, staff should enter data that include the student's name, grade, teacher, problematic behavior, date on which the behavior occurred, and the actions taken or consequences administered.

Generally, an assistant principal, a counselor, or a combination of the two are responsible for entering the data. Then the principal can generate complete reports concerning school discipline problems on demand. These summary reports include:

- The names of the students presenting the most chronic problems
- The types of discipline problems that occur most frequently
- The most problematic areas of the school
- Which teachers are referring the highest number of discipline problems
- What time of day the problems are occurring most often

Box 6-32

Technique Hint

One low-cost schoolwide data collection system is called Discipline Tracker (available at www.edusoftware.com). This program is easy to use and invaluable in evaluating a school's discipline problems. It includes the following information in the form of discipline reports:

- Most common infractions
- Referrals by teachers
- School areas with the most infractions
- Students with the most infractions
- Actions taken by the school for students
- Individual discipline summary by student
- Group disciplinary summaries
- Infractions by grade, sex, and ethnicity
- Pending In-School Suspensions
- General notices to parents
- Custom letters to parents
- Teacher feedback summaries

The principal or the School Behavior Management Team can use these reports to plan programs that manage these problem behaviors and students.

Steps for Implementing a Schoolwide Data Collection System

Step 1: Load the program onto a secure, password-protected PC or Macintosh computer in the school's central office or in the office of a school administrator. The computer must be in an area of the school that does not have student access.

Step 2: Develop a standard Discipline Record Form that includes all the basic information you want entered into the data fields of your computerized data collection system. *Figure 6-7* contains a sample form you may wish to use or adjust.

Step 3: Require that any student who is referred to the office by a staff member or who has committed a major discipline incident in the school to have a Discipline Record form filled out by the referring staff. The Discipline Record form contains the information that will be entered into the computer system.

Step 4: Introduce the computerized discipline program to the faculty, and demonstrate its various capabilities—from generating reports and customized parent letters to pinpointing problem areas of the school.

Step 5: Assign one staff member—usually someone who works in the school office—to enter the data from the Discipline Record forms into the computerized program daily or several times each week.

Figure 6-7
Discipline Record

Discipline Record Form

Student Name ____________ Grade ________
Referring Staff ____________
Witnesses ____________
Problem Behavior ____________
____
Where Problem Occurred ________ Date ________
Action Taken ____________
Parent Contacted?
❑ Yes
❑ No
If yes, indicate:
❑ Letter
❑ Phone
❑ Other ________
Comments ____________
____
____
____
Form Filled out by ____________

Step 6: Generate reports at least once each week to summarize discipline data in the school. These reports should pinpoint students who present chronic problems (i.e., the Seven Percent Students), along with other critical information.

Step 7: Generate special customized forms and letters as needed for the most problematic students. These can include individualized ISS and After-School Detention notices for students and customized letters to their parents explaining their children's discipline difficulties at school.

Box 6-33
Technique Hint

Caution!

Never assign a student to enter discipline data into the school's data collection system.

Troubleshooting a Schoolwide Data Collection System

Problem: ***All relevant data are not entered into the schoolwide data collection system.***

Solution: This is one of the biggest problems with a schoolwide data collection system. The solution is to make certain that one person is in charge of data input, that he knows which data are to be entered—and, if necessary, tracked down—and that he has a specific time each week by which all data must be entered into the system.

Problem: ***Data from the schoolwide data collection system are not used.***

Solution: The principal's leadership is critical to see that this happens. If it is important to the principal, it will be important to other school staff! Designate the school's Behavior Management Team to oversee this task and receive report summaries, but continue to communicate regularly with the team. The team can be responsible for identifying the Seven Percent Tough Kids with chronic problems, designing individual interventions for them, helping the teachers who refer the most discipline problems, and selecting and designing inservice training for school staff that addresses the most common behavior problems identified in the reports.

Problem: ***The data in the schoolwide data collection system are accessed by unauthorized staff or students.***

Solution: Always require that a specific password be used to access information in the schoolwide data collection system. Make certain that only authorized staff know the password.

Problem: ***All of the data in the computerized schoolwide data collection system have been lost.***

Solution: At the end of each day, instruct the system's authorized staff to save the data onto some other format (e.g., a zip drive or the computer's hard drive). That way, you will never lose more than one day's data. Authorized staff will then need to reenter only one day's Discipline Record forms. In the case of a major mishap, past summary reports can be used to re-create some of the lost information.

Making a Discipline Data Collection System Even Better

1. It is important to share the summary reports regularly with the school's Behavior Management Team so that they can identify students with chronic discipline problems and design individual intervention programs for them earlier rather than later. As these students are identified, the Behavior Management Team may require them to check in with a specific staff member each day to pick up their Tracking Sheets. During the school day, the students' teachers rate them on how appropriate their behavior was and sign their sheets. At the end of the day, the students return them to the designated staff member, and together they review the progress for the day as recorded on the Tracking Sheet. Students who earn their way off the Tracking Sheet program by behaving appropriately can make significant progress over time.
2. The Behavior Management Team can use the information from schoolwide data collection system to identify teachers who are experiencing the most discipline problems in their classrooms. This information would indicate which teachers have made the most discipline referrals over a specific time period (e.g., one month). These teachers may need additional help in their classrooms, more training in effective behavior management, or consultation from a more experienced teacher.
3. The summary reports from the schoolwide data collection system can provide valuable information on needed inservice training for the entire school staff. The summary reports identify the most common problem behaviors, the time of day they occur, and where they occur. For example, the school staff may need additional training in how to reduce tardiness, problems in the halls between classes, loudness and sloppiness in the lunchroom, fighting on the playground or in the schoolyard, or noncompliance in the classroom.

4. Information gathered from the use of Other Class Time-Out, Prime Time In-School Suspension, and Restrictive In-School Suspension can be used in conjunction with the schoolwide data collection system. Even if students are not sent to the office with OCT, this information can be entered into the system, which can be tailored to provide specific reports for all of these undesired consequences. The program can be particularly useful in generating daily master lists of students who are required to report to Prime Time ISS and RISS as well as those who showed up for them and those who did not.
5. The schoolwide data collection system can also identify students who are behaving *appropriately* in school. It can keep track of students who have earned Principal's 200 Club slips and those who have actually won the Principal's Mystery Motivator rewards. The system can generate customized positive letters to parents, indicating that their child earned these positive recognition awards.
6. It is helpful to use the previous year's report from the schoolwide data collection system to set goals for the next year. Goals can be set for reducing office referrals, supervision can be stepped up for dealing with problematic areas of the school, and the Seven Percent Tough Kid students can be identified and interventions planned for them from the first day of school.

Summary

In this section, we presented essential tools for principals that are often missing from their college preparation courses. We began with the school's basic Mission Statement, which is the "signature" statement for the school and its goals. It is important to keep the Mission Statement simple, understandable (especially to students), and linked directly to the All-School Rules. The Mission Statement and All-School Rules are the behavior backbone by which the school establishes its basic expectations for students and the goals for the school. A well-constituted Behavior Management Team made up of some of the school's best staff can be indispensable in helping the principal design and implement the school's Mission Statement and All-School Rules. We also discussed the essential steps in setting up an effective Behavior Management Team.

We described other essential tools for the principal, such as how to complete a Manifestation Determination, a Functional Behavior Assessment, and a Behavior Improvement Plan. These processes are key to providing appropriate interventions for many of the special education students in the required instances as well as for many of the Seven Percent Students. Suspensions, safe schools violations, and violations of students' rights can all be tied to these processes. A principal who does not understand these processes invites litigation and problems with parents.

We offered some of the best research-based solutions for stopping truancy, a common headache for principals. These techniques include identifying the truant student and his truant peers, reducing the number of places that students go to be truant, supervising settings where students impulsively decide to be truant, and making the first part of the school day enjoyable for these students. We covered contracting to improve behavior and the Home Note system along with peer mediation to solve common student problems; we also provided forms for their use.

Finally, we covered schoolwide data collection systems. Without a systematic way to collect data on the school's most difficult behavioral issues, principals are condemned to make the same mistakes over and over. Schoolwide data collection systems provide a road map that shows which students are having the most behavioral problems, which teachers are struggling the most with behavior management issues, and which behavior problems are occurring most frequently and where. Without a practical, easy-to-operate schoolwide data collection system, a school is blindly sailing the sea of behavioral problems without a rudder!

We commend you for working to improve your skills in and knowledge of effective schoolwide behavior management. We believe that working hard to keep all students in school and to keep them learning—even the Seven Percent Students—is one of the most important jobs there is. Best of luck to you as you continue with this critical undertaking!

MANIFESTATION DETERMINATION

Name: ______________________________ School: ______________________________

Date of MD Meeting: __________ Date of Incident: __________ Date of Decision to Suspended ≥ Days: __________

Behavior prompting suspension: ______________________________

I. APPROPRIATENESS OF PROGRAM:

A. Current Classification: ______________________________

Source(s) of information: ______________________________

B. Prereferral: (Behavior noted as area of concern?) ❑ YES ❑ NO ❑ N/A

If yes, date of Prereferral: _______ Concerns noted: ______________________________

C. **Referral:** (Behavior prompting suspension noted as concern at referral?) ❑ YES ❑ NO

If yes, date of Referral: _______ Concerns noted: ______________________________

____

Source(s) of information: ______________________________

D. Evaluation: Date of last evaluation: ________ Evaluation (≤ 3 years)?: ❑ YES ❑ NO

1. Does existing evaluation address current areas of educational concern? ❑ YES ❑ NO
2. Additional evaluation needed in the following areas: ❑ Complete Evaluation
   - ❑ Intellectual Development ❑ Academic Achievement ❑ Communication
   - ❑ Adaptive/Social/Behavioral ❑ Other: ______________________________

Date of completion: _________ Person Responsible: ______________________________

Source(s) of information: ______________________________

E. IEP: Date of last IEP: __________ Is IEP current ❑ YES ❑ NO ❑ N/A

a. Is IEP in compliance? ❑ YES ❑ NO ❑ N/A

b. Have services consisted with the IEP been provided? ❑ YES ❑ NO ❑ N/A

If no, explain: ______________________________

____

c. Are behavioral goals included on the IEP? ❑ YES ❑ NO ❑ N/A

If yes, do they address the behavior subject to disciplinary action? ❑ YES ❑ NO ❑ N/A

Source(s) of information: ______________________________

F. **Placement:** Current permission to place in evidence? ❑ YES ❑ NO ❑ N/A

Current placement appropriate to meet student needs? ❑ YES ❑ NO ❑ N/A

Source(s) of information: ______________________________

G. Summary: (a., b., & c. must be marked "YES" to proceed to Finding.)

a. The student was properly evaluated. ❑ YES ❑ NO

b. Parent(s) were included in IEP process. ❑ YES ❑ NO

c. The IEP has been implemented ❑ YES ❑ NO

Finding: Based on consideration of A-G above, it is consensus of this IEP Team that the behavior in question WAS ❑ WAS NOT ❑ a direct result of a failure to implement the IEP.

II. CONDUCT DIRECTLY/SUBSTANTIALLY RELATED TO OR CAUSED BY DISABILITY:

A. **Anecdotal Records:** Is there a record of behavior subject to discipline? ❑ YES ❑ NO ❑ N/A

If YES, not time period and setting where behavior occurred: ______________________

____

B. **Was the behavior in question noted:**

1. When the student was referred for evaluation? ❑ YES ❑ NO
2. In the evaluation summary? ❑ YES ❑ NO
3. Addressed in the IEP? ❑ YES ❑ NO

C. **Has the behavior been exhibited across settings and times?** ❑ YES ❑ NO

Source(s) of information: ______________________

D. Is the conduct a recognized associated feature of the student's disability? ❑ YES ❑ NO

Source(s) of information (i.e., DSM-IV-TR): ______________________

E. **Finding: Based on consideration of A-D above, it is the consensus of the IEP Team that the behavior in question WAS ❑ WAS NOT ❑ directly/substantially related to or caused by the student's disability.**

Rationale: ______________________

____

IV. **MANIFESTATION STATEMENT:**

In order to make a "No Manifestation" determination the team must find both the following:

1. The behavior in question WAS NOT a direct result of a failure to implement the student's IEP.
2. The behavior in question WAS NOT directly/substantially related to or caused by the student's disability.

It is the consensus of the IEP Team that the conduct
WAS ❑ WAS NOT ❑
a manifestation of the student's disability.

Record of participation

LEA Rep.	______________	Date: ________
Parent:	______________	Date: ________
Special Education Teacher:	______________	Date: ________
Regular Education Teacher:	______________	Date: ________
Guidance Specialist:	______________	Date: ________
Other:	______________	Date: ________

FUNCTIONAL BEHAVIOR ASSESSMENT (FBA)

FIRST NAME ________ LAST NAME ________ GRADE ______ SCHOOL ________ DATE ________

PARTICIPANTS ________________________________

This FBA will be utilized for: Intervention Purposes IEP Requirements

Describe the problem behavior that prompted this FBA:

____

If more than one behavior is described, do they usually occur together (in a response group)? ❑ YES ❑ NO

If the above statement addresses multiple behaviors, identify **ONE BEHAVIOR** (or response group) to be targeted for intervention:

____

The Target Behavior Is:

OBSERVABLE _____ **MEASURABLE** _____

ANTECEDENTS

What is likely to "set-off" or precede the problem behavior?

WHEN is the problem behavior most likely to occur?

____

Approximate Time: ________

WHERE is the problem behavior most likely to occur?

____

During what **SUBJECT/ACTIVITY** is the problem behavior most likely to occur? (list subjects)

____

The **PEOPLE** that are present when the problem behavior is most likely to occur:

____

OTHER EVENTS or **CONDITIONS** that immediately precede the problem behavior?

____

When is the student most successful? When **DOESN'T** the problem behavior occur?

____

CONSEQUENCES

What "PAYOFF" does the student obtain when she/he demonstrates the problem behavior?

The student **GAINS**:

- ❑ Teacher/Adult attention
- ❑ Peer Attention
- ❑ Desired time or activity
- ❑ Control over others or situations
- ❑ Self Stimulation
- ❑ Other

The Student AVOIDS or ESCAPES:

- ❑ Teacher/Adult attention
- ❑ Peer Attention
- ❑ Subjects or Activities
- ❑ Situations
- ❑ Self Stimulation
- ❑ Other

What has been tried so far to change the problem behavior?

- ❑ This is the first occurrence. It will be addressed through this FBA and Behavior Intervention Plan.
- ❑ Consistently implemented rules
- ❑ Posted consequences for behaviors
- ❑ Consistently implemented behavior or academic contract
- ❑ Consistently implemented Home/School Note System
- ❑ Adapted curriculum (HOW?) ________
- ❑ Modified Instruction (HOW?) ________
- ❑ Adjusted schedule (HOW?) ________
- ❑ Conferences with parents (DATES?) ________
- ❑ Sent student to office (DATES?) ________
- ❑ Other

FUNCTIONAL BEHAVIOR ASSESSMENT (FBA)

PROBLEM BEHAVIOR

After reviewing the antecedents and consequences, summarize the information below. Consider the following questions:

- Why is the student behaving this way?
- What function or payoff is met by the student's behavior?

WHEN ______________________

SUMMARIZE ANTECEDENTS ______________________

THIS STUDENT ______________________

IDENTIFY THE PROBLEM BEHAVIOR ______________________

IN ORDER TO ______________________

SUMMARIZE "PAYOFF" ______________________

EXAMPLES
1. When in the halls before school, after school, and during transitions, the student pushes other students and verbally threatens to beat them up in order to gain status and attention from peers.
2. When working on independent seatwork during the regular education math class, the student puts his head on his desk in order to escape work that is too difficult/frustrating.

REPLACEMENT BEHAVIOR

Identify the replacement behavior. Remember that replacement behavior is not an absence of the problem behavior (i.e., Do not write: "rather than hitting, I want this student to keep his hands to himself.") Instead, a replacement behavior is a description of the behavior that the student will perform *in place of the problem behavior* which could include socially appropriate alternative behavior, coping skills, anger management skills, techniques to deal with frustrating situations, self advocacy, and others.

RATHER THAN ______________________

THE STUDENT WILL ______________________

This Definition is:

❑ **Observable** ❑ **Measurable**

EXAMPLES:
1. Rather than pushing students and threatening to beat them up, the student will walk in the halls with his hands at his side and say "HELLO" to those with whom he wishes to interact.
2. Rather than putting his head on his desk, the student will place his red "HELP" card on his desk to let his teacher know he needs assistance.

BEHAVIOR INTERVENTION PLAN (BIP)

FIRST NAME ________ LAST NAME ________ GRADE ______ SCHOOL ________ DATE ________

PARTICIPANTS ____

This BIP will be utilized for: Intervention Purposes IEP Requirements

PREVENTIVE STRATEGIES

Preventive measures and adjustments that will be put in place to reduce the occurrence of the problem behavior. (*Refer to the Antecedent column on page 1 of the FBA.*) Mark "YES" and fill in the statement if this is a needed preventive measure. Mark "NOT NEEDED" to indicate that the adjustment has been considered and is not needed.

YES	NOT NEEDED	
❑	❑	Adjustments to be made as to **WHEN** the problem behavior is likely to occur by: ________
❑	❑	Adjustments to be made as to **WHERE** the problem behavior is likely to occur by: ________
❑	❑	Adjustments to be made as to the **SUBJECT/ACTIVITY** during which the problem behavior is likely to occur by: ________
❑	❑	Adjustments to be made as to **PEOPLE** with whom the problem behavior is likely to occur by: ________

OTHER ADJUSTMENTS

❑	❑	Clarifying and/or reteaching expectations/routines. (HOW?) ________
❑	❑	Modifying task/assignment/curriculum. (HOW?) ________
❑	❑	Increasing supervision. (HOW?) ________
❑	❑	Utilizing special equipment. (HOW?) ________
❑	❑	Other. (HOW?) ________

INSTRUCTIONAL STRATEGIES

What specific skills will the student need to be taught in order to successfully demonstrate the **REPLACEMENT BEHAVIOR**? (*Refer to the replacement Behavior column on page 2 of the FBA.*)

- ❑ Social Skills: ________
- ❑ Communication Skills: ________
- ❑ Study Skills: ________
- ❑ Academic Skills ________
- ❑ ________

How will these skills be taught?

- ❑ **Individual Instruction**
- ❑ **Demonstration/Modeling**
- ❑ **Guided Practice**
- ❑ **Group Instruction**
- ❑ **Role Play**
- ❑ **Independent Practice**

Who will provide the instruction? ________

When will the instruction take place? ________

Where will the instruction take place? ________

How often will the instruction take place? ________

How will opportunities for practice/rehearsal be provided? ________

How will the student be prompted to use the newly acquired skills? ________

_______________ # BEHAVIOR INTERVENTION PLAN (BIP)

REINFORCEMENT PROCEDURES

What will be done to strengthen or increase the occurrence of the replacement behavior?

IDENTIFY POTENTIAL REINFORCERS (REWARDS):
What preferred items, activities or people might be used as rewards in an intervention for this student?

____
____
____
____

ESTABLISH SPECIFIC BEHAVIOR CRITERIA:
What exactly must the student do to earn the above reward?

____
____
____
____

DETERMINE SCHEDULE OF REINFORCEMENT:
How frequently can the student earn the above rewards?

____
____
____
____

IDENTIFY DELIVERY SYSTEM:
What intervention components will be used to monitor the student's behavior and delivery reinforcement?

- ❑ Self-monitoring
- ❑ Behavioral contract
- ❑ Group contingency
- ❑ Home note system
- ❑ Lottery/raffle tickets
- ❑ Other ______________
- ❑ Point system
- ❑ Token economy
- ❑ Beep tape
- ❑ Chart moves
- ❑ Tracking system

____
____
____

CORRECTION PROCEDURES

What can be done to weaken or decrease the occurrence of the problem behavior?

❑ All occurrences of the problem behavior will be ignored, while attending to the appropriate behavior of other students.

❑ When the problem behavior occurs the student will be verbally asked to stop and then redirected by…

- ❑ Using Precision Comments
- ❑ Completing a Teaching Interaction
- ❑ Saying the following

____
____
____

- ❑ Other

____
____

❑ Minimal undesired consequences will be used.

- ❑ Loss of reward/priviledge. Describe:

____
____

- ❑ Loss of ______ minutes of ______________
- ❑ Positive practice. Describe:

____
____
____

❑ Time away from the opportunity for reinforcement will be used. Describe:

____
____
____

IMPLEMENTATION DETAILS

What Tracking System will be used to track the delivery of rewards and/or the use of undesired consequences?

____
____
____
____
____
____
____
____
____
____
____
____

Include any other details/explanations not previously described so that anyone can read this plan and implement the program.

____
____
____
____
____
____
____
____
____
____
____
____
____
____
____
____

BEHAVIOR INTERVENTION PLAN (BIP)

TRACKING SYSTEM
Method of data collection

- ❑ Frequency count (tally) across the day.
- ❑ Frequency count from ________ (time of day) to ________ (time of day).
- ❑ Interval recording every ________
- ❑ second/minutes from: ________ (time of day) to ________ (time of day).
- ❑ Other:

Describe exactly HOW data will be collected/recorded and WHO will do it.

DAILY DATA

BEHAVIOR BEING MEASURED/UNIT OF MEASURE

DATES

DAYS OF WEEK

DATE OF FIRST PROJECTED REVIEW MEETING

Review meeting date:________ Participants ________

Evaluation of Data:

- ❑ Desired decrease in problem behavior
- ❑ Undesired increase in problem behavior
- ❑ Desired increase in replacement behavior
- ❑ Undesired decrease in replacement behavior

Action to be taken: ❑ Continue plan ❑ Modify plan ❑ Plan for generalization

Plan of action:

BEHAVIOR INTERVENTION PLAN (BIP)

DAILY DATA

BEHAVIOR BEING MEASURED/UNIT OF MEASURE

DATES

DAYS OF WEEK

DATE OF SUBSEQUENT REVIEW MEETING ______

Review meeting date ______ Participants ______

Evaluation of data: ______

- ❑ Desired decrease in problem behavior
- ❑ Desired increase in replacement behavior
- ❑ Undesired increase in problem behavior
- ❑ Undesired increase in replacement behavior

Plan of action: ______

DATE OF SUBSEQUENT REVIEW MEETING ______

Review meeting date ______ Participants ______

Evaluation of data: ______

- ❑ Desired decrease in problem behavior
- ❑ Desired increase in replacement behavior
- ❑ Undesired increase in problem behavior
- ❑ Undesired increase in replacement behavior

Plan of action: ______

Contract

I, ________________________________, agree to do the following behaviors:

1. ______________________________
2. ______________________________
3. ______________________________

When: ______________________________

How Well: ___________________________

If I am successful, I will receive ________________________________,

given by ________________________, on ____________________.

Bonus Clause ____

____

Penalty Clause ____

____

____
(Student Signature) Date

____
(Teacher Signature) Date

Homework Contract

I, ______________________________, agree to complete the homework assignment(s) for the following subjects:

1. ______________________ 4. ______________________

2. ______________________ 5. ______________________

3. ______________________ 6. ______________________

with at least ____________________% accuracy in __________(#) out of ____________(#) subjects, over a time period of ______________ to ____________________.

For meeting criteria on __________(#) out of __________(#) days, I can earn ____________________________to be delivered______________ (when) by ________________________ (person).

____
(Student Signature) Date

____
(Teacher Signature) Date

Lunchroom Contract

Behavior

Who ______________________________

What 1. ______________________________

2. ______________________________

3. ______________________________

When ______________________________

How Well______________________________

Sign here. ______________________________
(Student) Date

____
(Teacher) Date

Lunchroom Record: "+" = Criteria Met, "0" = Criteria Not Met				
Monday	Tuesday	Wednesday	Thursday	Friday

Reward

Given by ______________________________

What______________________________

When ______________________________

How Much ______________________________

Class Lunchroom Contract

We, the undersigned, agree to perform the following behaviors in the lunchroom:

1. ____________________ 3. ____________________ 5. ____________________
2. ____________________ 4. ____________________ 6. ____________________

We will perform these behaviors for the contract period from ______________ to ________________. As a reward, we will receive ____________________ on ______________________________.

Student Signatures:

____________________ ____________________ ____________________
____________________ ____________________ ____________________
____________________ ____________________ ____________________
____________________ ____________________ ____________________
____________________ ____________________ ____________________
____________________ ____________________ ____________________
____________________ ____________________ ____________________
____________________ ____________________ ____________________
____________________ ____________________ ____________________
____________________ ____________________ ____________________

The teacher agrees to see that the reward is carried out.

____
(Teacher Signature) Date

Recess Contract

Who ______________________________ Date ________________________

What to Do:

1. ____________________________
2. ____________________________
3. ____________________________

What **Not** to Do:

1. ____________________________
2. ____________________________
3. ____________________________

If I earn ____ (#/name of rating) or better ratings during ______________________________________ time, I will receive ____ to be provided by ____________________ , on ________________________ .

____
(Student Signature) Date

____
(Teacher Signature) Date

Morning Recess:

❏ Excellent ❏ Good ❏ OK ❏ Poor

Lunch Recess:

❏ Excellent ❏ Good ❏ OK ❏ Poor

Afternoon Recess:

❏ Excellent ❏ Good ❏ OK ❏ Poor

Home Information Note

Name: Date/Week of: Phone:

Periods	Teacher Initials	Class Performance (circle one)	Assigned Homework	Upcoming Tests?	Missing Work?
		G Great A Average U Unsatisfactory			
		G Great A Average U Unsatisfactory			
		G Great A Average U Unsatisfactory			
		G Great A Average U Unsatisfactory			
		G Great A Average U Unsatisfactory			
		G Great A Average U Unsatisfactory			
		G Great A Average U Unsatisfactory			

Comments:

School Staff Signature:

Parent's Signature

Home Information Note

Name: Date/Week of: Phone:

Periods	Teacher Initials	Class Performance	Assigned Homework	Upcoming Tests?	Missing Work?

Rating Scale Unsatisfactory = ________ Average = ________ Great = ________

Comments:

Daily Home Note

Name: Date:

Parent's Initials						
Behavior(s)	Teacher(s) Initials	MON	TUE	WED	THUR	FRI

Rating Scale Unsatisfactory = 1 Average = 2 Great = 3

Comments:

Teacher's Phone Parent's Phone:

Weekly Home Note

Name: Week of:

Subject(s) or Behavior(s)	Teacher(s) Initials	MON	TUE	WED	THUR	FRI	Comments

Rating Scale G = Great A = Average U = Unsatisfactory

Parent's Initials:	MON	TUE	WED	THUR	FRI

Any homework?

Any upcoming tests?

Any missing work?

Peer Request for Mediation

Referring Student: ______________________________ Today's Date ______________

Student(s) You are Referring: ______________________________

____

Description of Problem: ______________________________

____

____

How would you like to see this problem resolved? ______________________________

____

____

____

Additional Comments: ______________________________

____

Student(s) Signatures: ______________________________

Peer Mediator Signatures: ______________________________

School Staff Member(s) Signatures: ______________________________

Peer Request for Mediation

Referring Student: ______________________________ Today's Date ______________

Student(s) You are Referring: ______________________________

____

Description of Problem: ______________________________

____

____

How would you like to see this problem resolved? ______________________________

____

____

____

Additional Comments: ______________________________

____

Student(s) Signatures: ______________________________

Peer Mediator Signatures: ______________________________

School Staff Member(s) Signatures: ______________________________

Peer Mediation Contract

Student Name(s): ______________________________

Date: ______________________

Who Referred the Problem? ______________________________

Description of Problem: ______________________________

____

What Needs to be Done/Decision: ______________________________

____

Is a Follow-up Meeting Needed? ❑ YES ❑ NO If "YES," the meeting date is: ______________

Additional Comments: ______________________________

____

Student(s) Signatures: ______________________________

Peer Mediator Signatures: ______________________________

____

School Staff Member(s) Signatures: ______________________________

Peer Mediation Contract

Student Name(s): ______________________________

Date: ______________________

Who Referred the Problem? ______________________________

Description of Problem: ______________________________

____

What Needs to be Done/Decision: ______________________________

____

Is a Follow-up Meeting Needed? ❑ YES ❑ NO If "YES," the meeting date is: ______________

Additional Comments: ______________________________

____

Student(s) Signatures: ______________________________

Peer Mediator Signatures: ______________________________

____

School Staff Member(s) Signatures: ______________________________

Discipline Record Form

Student Name ______________________ Grade ____________

Referring Staff ______________________________________

Witnesses ____

Problem Behavior _____________________________________

____

Where Problem Occurred ______________ Date ____________

Action Taken ____

Parent Contacted?

- ❑ Yes
- ❑ No

If yes, indicate:

- ❑ Letter
- ❑ Phone
- ❑ Other ______________________

Comments ____

____

____

____

Form Filled out by ____________________________________

References

Achenbach, T. M., & Edelbrock, C. (1983). *Manual for the child behavior checklist and revised child behavior profile.* Burlington: University of Vermont, Department of Psychiatry.

Age Discrimination in Employment Act of 1967 (Pub. L. No. 90-202) (ADEA), *as amended as it appears* in Volume 29 of the U.S.C., beginning at § 621.

Americans with Disabilities Act of 1990, Pub. L. No. 101-336, enacted July 26, 1990.

Bethel School District v. Fraser, 478 U.S. 675 (1986).

Black, D. D., & Downs, J. C. (1993). *Administrative intervention: A school administrator's guide to working with aggressive and disruptive students.* Longmont, CO: Sopris West Educational Services.

Board of Education of the Averill Park Central Sch. Dist., 27 IDELR 996.

Board of Education of the Hendrick Hudson Central School District v. Rowley, 458 U.S. 176 (1982).

Board of Education of Independent School District No. 92 of Pottawatomie County et al. v. Earls, Docket No. 01-332, Reversed: 10th Cir. (2002).

Bowen, J., Jenson, W. R., & Clark, E. (2004). *School-based interventions for students with behavior problems.* New York: Kluwer Academic, Plenum.

Caledonian-Record Publishing Co. Inc. v. Vermont State Colleges, 6 FAB 36 (Vt. 2003).

Cornfield v. Consolidated High School District, 991 F.2d 1316 (7th Cir. 1993).

Education for All Handicapped Children Act, Pub. L. No. 94-142 (1975).

Edward v. Rees, 883 F.2d 882 (10th Cir. 1989).

Elementary and Secondary Education Act (1965). No Child Left Behind Act of 2001, Pub. L. No. 107-110.

Equal Access Act, 20 U.S.C. 4071, Title 20, Chapter 52, Subchapter VIII, § 4071-74 (1984).

Evans, C. (1999). *Navigating the dual system of discipline: A guide for school site administrators.* Bloomington, IN: The Forum on Education.

Falvo v. Owasso Indep. School District, 534 U.S. 426 (2002).

Family Educational Rights and Privacy Act. 20 U.S.C., § 1232(g) (1974).

G.D. v. Westmoreland, 930 F.2d 942 (1st Cir. 1991).

Gladwell, M. (2000). *The tipping point.* Boston: Little, Brown and Company.

Goss v. Lopez, 419 U.S. 565 (1975).

Government Records Access and Management Act (GRAMA), UCA 63-2(2) (1992).

Gun-Free Schools Act, 20 U.S.C. 1751, 115 Statute 762, Pub. L. No. 107-110, § 4141 (1994).

Hamrick by Hamrick v. Affton School District Board of Education, 135.W. 3d 678 (Mo. App. 2000).

Hardin County Schools v. Foster, No. 1999-SC-000333-DG (Ky. 2001).

Hawken, L. S. (2002). *Evaluation of a targeted group intervention within a school-wide system of behavior support.* Digital Dissertations (AAT3055691).

In the Interest of Isaiah B., 500 N.W. 2d 637 (Wis. 1993).

Individuals with Disabilities Education Improvement Act of 2004, Pub. L. No. 108-446.

Jeffrey S. v. School Board of Riverdale School District, 21 IDELR 1164 (1995).

Jensen v. Reeves, 45 F. Supp. 2d 1265 (D. Utah 1999).

Jensen et al. v. Reeves et al., No. 99-4142, 2001 WL 113829 (10th Cir. 2001).

Jenson, W. R., Sloane, H. N., & Young, R. (1988). *Behavior analysis in education: A structured teaching approach.* Englewood Cliffs, NJ: Prentice Hall.

Kearney, C.A. (2001). *School refusal behavior in youth: A functional approach to assessment and treatment.* Washington, DC: American Psychological Association.

Kennedy v. Dexter Consolidated Schools, 955 P.2d 693 (N.M. App. 1998).

Knop v. Northwestern School District, 26 F. Supp. 2d 1189 (D. South Dakota 1998).

Leconte, 211 EHLR 146 (OSEP 1998).

Letter to Anonymous, 30 IDELR 705 (OSEP 1998).

Letter to Pasadena Unified School District, (FPCO 1999).

Letter to Schaffer, 34 IDELR, ¶ 151 (OSERS 10/26/00).

Letter to Watkins, 7 FAB21 (FPCO 2003).

Lewis, T. J., & Sugai, G. (1999). Effective behavior support: A systems approach to proactive school-wide management. *Focus on Exceptional Children, 31*, 1–24.

Lovell v. Poway Unified School District, 90 F.3d 367 (9th Cir. 1996).

M.K. v. School Board of Brevard County, 708 So. 2d 340 (Fla. 5th Dist. Ct. App. 1998).

McLaughlin v. United States, 476 U.S. 16 (1986).

Myles S. v. Montgomery County Board of Education, 20 IDELR 237 (M.D. Ala. 1993).

Nelson, J. R., & Carr, B. A. (1996). *The think time strategy for schools: Bringing order to the classroom.* Longmont, CO: Sopris West Educational Services.

New Jersey v. T.L.O., 469 U.S. 325 (1985).

No Child Left Behind Amendments (2000) of the Elementary and Secondary Education Act (1965). Safe and Drug Free Schools Act of 2001: Title IV (20 U.S.C. 71 OC) Part A, Safe and Drug Free Schools and Communities.

Northeast Indep. Sch. Dist., 26 IDELR 939.

Northeast Indep. Sch. Dist., 28 IDELR 1004.

Northwest Regional Educational Laboratory (2004). *School Improvement Research Series* (SIRS). Portland, OR.

Occupational Safety and Health Administration (OSHA), Part 1924. Safety Standards Applicable to Workshops and Rehabilitation Facilities Assisted by Grants. Authority: § 12, 18, Vocational Rehabilitation Act Amendments of 1965 (29 U.S.C. 419, 41b).

Oconee County Sch. Sys., 27 IDELR 629.

People in the Interest of P.E.A., 754 P. 2d 382 (Colo. 1988).

Ratner v. Loudon County Public Schools, No. 00-2157, 2001 WL 855606 (4th Dist. 2001).

Re: Student with a Disability, 27 IDELR 935.

Reavis, K. H. K., Kukic, S. J., Jenson, W. R., Morgan, D. P., Andrews, D. J., & Fister, S. (1996). *Best practices: Behavioral and educational strategies for teachers.* Longmont, CO: Sopris West Educational Services.

Rehabilitation Act of 1973. Section 504.

Rhode, G., Jenson, W. R., & Morgan, D. P. (2003). *The tough kid new teacher kit: Practical classroom management survival strategies for the new teacher.* Longmont, CO: Sopris West Educational Services.

Rhode, G. Jenson, W. R., & Reavis, K. H. (1992). *The tough kid book: Practical behavior management strategies.* Longmont, CO: Sopris West Educational Services.

Rim of the World Unified School Dist. v. Superior Court of the County of San Bernardino, 6 FAB 8 (Cal. Ct. App. 2002).

Singleton v. Board of Education, U.S.D. 500, 894 F. Supp. 386 (D. Kansas, 1995).

Sprague, J., & Nishiolia, V. (2003). *Linking whole school PBIS and delinquency prevention: Skills for success.* Second Annual Teton Summer Institute, Jackson Hole, WY.

Sprick, R., Sprick, M., & Garrison, M. (1992). *Foundations: Developing positive school-wide discipline policies.* Longmont, CO: Sopris West Educational Services.

State v. Twayne, 933 P. 2d 251 (N.M. App. 1997).

Stern v. New Haven Community Schools, 529 F. Supp. 31 (E.D. Mich. 1981).

Tinker v. Des Moines Independent School District, 393 U.S. 503 (1969).

Title VII of the Civil Rights Act of 1964. (Pub. L. No. 90-202) (ADEA), *as amended as it appears* in Volume 42 of the U.S.C., beginning at § 2000(e).

Todd v. Rush County Schools, 133 F. 3d 984 (7th Cir. 1998).

Trinidad School District No. 1 v. Lopez, 963 P.2d 1095 (Colo. 1998).

United States v. Katz, 389 U.S. 347 (1967).

U.S. Department of Education Office for Civil Rights. *A Resource Guide for Educators and Policy Makers* (2000).

Vernonia School District v. Acton, 515 U.S. 646 (1995).

Ward v. State of Florida, 636 So. 2d 68, 71 (Fla. Dist. Ct. App. 1994).

White, R., Algozzine, B., Audette, R., Marr, M. B., & Ellis, E. D. (2001). Unified discipline: A school-wide approach for managing problem behavior. *Intervention in School and Clinic*, *37*, 3–8.

Zamora v. Pomeroy, 639 F. 2d 662 (10th Cir. 1980).